To

Jesus Shall Reign

Any Luck

Rev 22:20

He is coming!

Jesus Shall Reign

A GUIDE TO THE BOOK OF REVELATION

Gary Tuck

RESOURCE *Publications* · Eugene, Oregon

JESUS SHALL REIGN
A Guide to the Book of Revelation

Resource Publications
An Imprint of Wipf and Stock Publishers
199 W. 8th Ave., Suite 3
Eugene, OR 97401

www.wipfandstock.com

PAPERBACK ISBN: 978-1-6667-0817-2
HARDCOVER ISBN: 978-1-6667-0818-9
EBOOK ISBN: 978-1-6667-0819-6

I wish I could dedicate this to everybody who has supported me in this project. So I will. Thanks, everybody. You and I know who you are. But I must single out my lovely and amazing wife, Lynne. In you, God has given me treasure and blessing beyond words. Thank you for your unwavering faith in God and in me.

Jesus shall reign where'er the sun
Does his successive journeys run;
His kingdom stretch from shore to shore,
Till moons shall wax and wane no more.

—ISAAC WATTS

Table of Contents

Introduction

> Knowledge of Revelation is not correlated to knowledge of God, worshiping God. That is, it is possible—and undoubtedly actual—that we can become experts on the meaning of Revelation and not grow closer to God. It is my prayer that readers of this work will be aided and challenged to pursue the Creator and Lord of all, to join in the worship of the martyrs in Rev 15:4: "Who will not fear, O Lord, and glorify your name?"

IF YOU ARE INTERESTED in looking at this book, you must at least be curious about the amazing book of Revelation, the last book of the Christian Bible.

For some, this is not your first attempt to find help in making sense of it. Many of you have hoped again and again to stumble across a satisfying approach that cracks its code and opens it up with clarity. Surely John meant for the book to be understood. You have probably found at least a modicum of help in most of the resources you have checked. But I suspect that very few of you have arrived at a place where you feel confidently satisfied.

Many readers throughout the book's history have regarded it as the most exhilarating, baffling, encouraging, mystifying, fascinating, awe-inspiring literary work ever. It predicts the worst of times and the best of times.[1]

Its features include beasts, coded numbers, coded colors, and obvious Old Testament allusions whose sense in Revelation is far from obvious.

Many think of Armageddon and 666 and blood baths, then go either eschato-manic or eschato-phobic.

---

1. Dickens's worst and best can't begin to compare with these. Charles Dickens wrote that classic line, "It was the best of times, it was the worst of times," at the beginning of *A Tale of Two Cities*.

There is the beast with seven heads, ten horns, ten crowns; the great red dragon, who also has multiple heads and horns and crowns; scorpion-locusts that attack not vegetation but people; cavalry of 200 million mounted on lion-headed, snake-tailed, fire-breathing horses; frog-like spirits pouring/emerging from the mouths of the unholy trinity of Satan, antichrist, and false prophet; a prostitute city; plagues on land, sea, fresh water sources, and heavenly bodies. How are we ever to make sense of such? Not to mention a glorious Lord of all whose feet resemble gleaming bronze, eyes fire, hair snow, tongue a double-edged sword; and a city that comes down from heaven with streets of gold, gates of pearl, and precious stones for foundation.

But Revelation is not intended to be opaque. On the contrary, it is intended to be clarifying about the future of God's program for Earth. It is for the faithful to understand.[2] So the first law for insight is not brilliance but devotion to the hero of the book, the King: blessed are those who hear *and obey* (i.e., bow willingly to the great King, Rev 1:3). We are bidden to see through John's eyes, or rather, through John's verbal descriptions of what he saw. That is how the ultimate divine author intended we should read this. We *must* see, as John saw first, the glorious Lord. And we must respond as he did. The faithful reader cannot do otherwise.

The title the author provided is "The Revelation of Jesus Christ." All revelation (generically speaking) is always God revealing *himself*, not just revealing truth or even Truth. And he has ways of and reasons for revealing himself to some, while at the same time hiding himself from others. That's what he does.[3]

As you read this and the book on which it is based, humble your heart at his throne and invite him to reveal himself to you.

---

2. Though it will certainly be much more discernible in the days of fulfillment, much like Daniel's prophecies of Alexander and Antiochus.

3. See for instance John 14:22–24: "'Lord,' Judas (not Judas Iscariot) said, 'what has happened that you are going to reveal yourself to us and not to the world?' Jesus replied, 'If anyone loves me, he will obey my word, and my Father will love him, and we will come to him and take up residence with him. The person who does not love me does not obey my words. And the word you hear is not mine, but the Father's who sent me'" (NET).

What This Book Is and What It Is Not

This book is about keys to unlocking and understanding the book of Revelation. It is not a comprehensive commentary. It is not going to attempt to answer every question that can be asked about Revelation and the end times. It is not a comprehensive review of all views that have been promoted.

Part 1 is intended to present the grand scheme of the book by providing crucial points of orientation to guide you in your reading of Revelation, especially macro themes and macro structure. It will offer corrections to longstanding but mistaken and misleading interpretations—corrections that steer you in a direction I believe will help you track with the author's thought and tacitly urge you to disregard distracting rabbit trails, or at least to defer attention to them until the main ideas have been recognized and reorganized. I am trying to help you think like the author. In this part, I will offer novel interpretations of several features, at several points challenging some widely held positions.

Parts 2 and 3 are two outlines (one skeletal, one complete) and an argument respectively, providing in different summary forms convenient presentations of the coherent flow of the book. Part 4 is a verse-by-verse commentary.

I begin from the assumption that this is heavenly truth in normal human literary garb. Like all the Bible, it is the pure Word of God, hence infallible and inerrant. Hence also it is critically important, need-to-know material. The explicit original readership, seven first-century churches of western Asia Minor, needed to know the author's point and points. Every church of every generation since then has also needed to know the message of this book. So the main ideas must be knowable to us, as to all the generations before us. But I believe some issues will not be known in detail until the day of their fulfillment.

One of the challenges a book like this must face is the quantity and variety of baggage that contemporary readers of Revelation bring with them. If you are dissatisfied with your sense of the message of the book, I urge you to attempt to suspend your assumptions and opinions and open your mind to the possibility of rejecting some of those and viewing the book from a fresh perspective. At several points, this will probably be rather surprising to those who have become acquainted with standard views.[4] That is, through my own study, at several points I have come to reject standard views.

This book is written with my students in mind. Since my students include prospective and now veteran pastors, I hope many pastors will find benefit in it. It is especially for the serious student of Revelation. So I urge you to reread Revelation, to read it multiple times from various translations (and in the original Greek, if you can), and to keep your Bible close at hand while you are reading this book.

In the interest of full disclosure, I am comfortable with being labeled a progressive dispensationalist and a moderate Calvinist.

Interpretive Principles

This book is especially about the big picture. Of course, we must also zoom in to consider fine details. After all, any big picture must be composed of numerous fine details. As in the interpretation of anything complex, both macro and micro features are important. But macro is always first. Always! The micro gets its meaning from the macro. This is another way of saying that details get their meaning from context, especially literary context. The big picture is the picture.[5]

At the level of details, often a critical factor is to pay primary attention to one feature rather than another. For instance, in the sixth trumpet judgment (Rev 9:13–21[6]), it is certainly easy to get caught up in the horrifying bloodbath of loss of human life (v. 15) and the descriptions of the horses and their riders (vv. 17–19), and in the process lose sight of the main point of that judgment scene—the stubborn refusal of the survivors to repent (vv. 20–21).

Implied in the word exegesis is the assumption that the goal of interpretation is the sender's/author's intended meaning. This is essential for

---

4. For instance, the widely assumed identification of the four horsemen of the apocalypse as being conquest, war, famine, death.

5. This is in response to the unexpressed assumption of traditional exegesis, which is that exegesis refers to the study of details, progressively finer. But if exegesis is leading out the author's meaning, then we must account for the macro. And if microexegesis requires strategies and skills, so also does macroexegesis.

The other crucial corollary is that micro before macro—the unexpressed traditional approach to exegesis—is upside down. True understanding must proceed from the macro to the micro. See Adler and Van Doren, *How to Read*, 75–76, rules 2 and 3.

6. I will argue later for the sixth trumpet extending all the way to Rev 11:14, where the author indicates that the second woe finally ends.

any successful communication. Before a receiver can agree or disagree with a sender, he must accurately understand what that sender has intended to say. The understanding side of the communication transaction thus requires sublimating one's own views. Agreeing or disagreeing is a subsequent operation. Honest interpretation begins with just that: honesty.

Orientation to the Book of Revelation

The book of Revelation is about the end of the world as we know it, the end times, the theological category known as eschatology, the study of last things. This book seeks to bridge biblical literature and Christian theology. I start with literary analysis in an attempt to build theology that is exegetical, not eisegetical.

Revelation is "The Revelation of Jesus Christ." That is, Jesus Christ is the main subject; it is Christocentric. The book reveals Christ, displaying him in dazzling glory that seems to have nearly killed John (see Rev 1:17), in awesome power, love and grace, eternal justice and dominion. The revelation of Jesus Christ is about more than just the second person of the Trinity and the Incarnation, inasmuch as those do not clearly say King. Nor is the Christ merely about his first coming; the Christ is about more than the redemption of the cross and victory of the resurrection. Biblical Christology includes all that the Old Testament says about the Savior of Israel and the seed of the woman. The preeminent point the OT makes about this One is that he is a King, and he must be the King supreme to whom all other kings must and shall certainly bow. The paramount issue of life and the universe is that he shall reign forever; hence all creation must bow and obey.[7] That is the big deal about the second coming. So the second coming is essential to Christology and must not be relegated merely to eschatology. Jesus is the Christ, the Messiah, the Davidic King of Israel, destined to extend his dominion over all nations. So Revelation is not just eschatology; it is Christology.[8]

Revelation is not a (coded) timeline, though we cannot miss the obviously logical way it ends: eternal new creation. So it is not utterly apart from or counter to linear temporal sequence either. But we need to

---

7. Refusal to do so is the essence of sin. That he shall reign is the essence of the gospel. (The atonement, important as it is, is not the essence of the gospel.)

8. In fact, eschatology is so Christocentric as to be a subsidiary of Christology.

restrain any impulse to impose an expectation of pure or mere linearity. We must let the author tell his story. We must seek to be honest listeners. We must be humble so as to admit that the understanding we bring to our reading may in fact be misleading and disserving us. We must with discipline keep asking, how would this have sounded to first-century Christians (in those west Asian churches)?

The entire book is for all seven churches and hence for all churches in every generation. "He who has an ear, let him hear what the Spirit says to [*all*] the churches." We need this book today: we need to read it, study it, meditate on it, teach what we understand of it, and, most importantly, constantly renew our loyal devotion to the King of heaven and his Son, the Messiah, King of Israel and of Earth.

Revelation is also *Jerusalem-centric*. Daniel expresses God's priorities as he prays about the well-being of "your people and your city" (Dan 9:16, 19, 24, 26). Ps 132:11–14 speaks of God's choice of Jerusalem directly connected to his choice of Messiah to sit on David's throne. In Zech 1:16–17, God declares his resolution to redeem Jerusalem, even if no one volunteers to help. We should not be surprised that God would direct our attention to that city and that region when revealing how he intends to bring history in this first creation to its consummation.

My Approach to Revelation in a Nutshell

Structure:

The great structural challenge of the book is chapters 6–19.

Chapters 6–19 are framed by the white horse rider, the same in both places.

Chapters 6–11 are the seven-sealed scroll, the seventh seal being the seven trumpets, the seventh trumpet being the second coming.

Chapters 12–19 focus on those who would overthrow God's rule—Satan, beast one (antichrist), beast two (false prophet), Babylon—their followers, their demise.

Primary Themes: Second Coming and King/Kingdom

The book is about Jesus coming to claim the kingdom of Earth, of which he is the rightful King. That kingdom is and has been abused under wrongful misrule by the serpent of Eden. But God is going to bring history to an ultimate climax. So the great conflict of the book is the clash of kings and kingdoms.

Jesus is now waiting for the moment described in chapter 5, when the Father, the Supreme King, the High King of heaven will hand him the title deed of Earth, the seven-sealed scroll.

The bulk of the book (chs. 6–19) is about the seven years (Daniel's seventieth week) of clashing, which has multiple purposes:

- to wrest control of Earth's throne (though that is something Jesus could do in an instant);

- to punish the rivals and those who choose to align with them;

- to afford last chances to repent;

- to avenge the deaths of faithful martyrs.

The climax is the end of that seven years, which are ended by Jesus's second coming.

Secondary Themes

Two more themes are repentance and martyrs. Still more themes are judgment, victory (overcoming), worship. But these are all subsidiary to kingship.

While not a literary theme per se, one more important issue of the author's work is the element of urgency, seen especially in the language of soonness, concentrated at the beginning and ending.

My Working Hypothesis

This is the last book written by the last living apostle. John, the disciple Jesus loved, is an old man who has outlived all of his brother apostles. He is familiar with all the rest of our canon, OT and NT,[9] having himself written four books by this time. Banished to the island Patmos, he receives this one final inspiration to write what is the capstone to the

9. It seems highly likely that all twenty-two books not written by him had been composed as much as two or more decades before. Having the stature he did, every one of those books would have been delivered to him within a relatively short time once they had been copied, individually and, at some point, in collections.

corpus of normative inscripturated revelation. Of course it must be about the grand climax of history and the inauguration of the glorious, eternal kingdom of God as he envisioned it from eternity past.

God gives John yet one more extravagant privilege to receive and describe visions finishing ancient themes and information about the program of God in bringing creation history to its climax and conclusion. John's design is much greater than merely informing Christians from his day about the end of the events to come; it was that we the faithful should continually grow in fixing our longing and adoring gaze on our glorious Creator and Lord.

Acknowledgments

Great respect is due the authors of many fine commentaries, some of whom are referenced here and there in this study. One of my concerns is not to duplicate much that can be easily accessed in standard resources.

"Many have undertaken to draw up an account of the things " (Luke 1:1 NIV). I certainly am not presuming to write with similar infallible authority. Still I hope that what I have written is worthy of being added to the body of approaches to reading and explaining Revelation and advances the discussion concerning the book of Revelation and the larger revelation concerning the end of history.

PART 1: THE GRAND SCHEME OF THE BOOK (Themes and Structure)

Jesus

Let's just get it out there on the table: the book of Revelation is about Jesus. It's not about end times, it's not about battles and beasts and plagues. Sure, it includes those. But the book is not about those.

The opening statement of the book is: "The Revelation of Jesus Christ . . ." The opening vision (Rev 1:12–16) is of him in such dazzling splendor that John, "the disciple whom Jesus loved," falls at his feet as a dead man (1:17). Out of that vision flow the letters to the churches, and upon that vision the rest of the book is built. The climax of the book (19:11—20:6) is his coming—that is, his second coming. In the closing statements, the author quotes him reminding the reader not once, not twice, but three times that he is coming (i.e., coming again; 22:7, 12, 20).

He is the main event, not only in history past but history future as well. It makes all the sense in the world that the last book of divine revelation should be about the main person in history and eternity.

From and About (1:1–2)

"The Revelation of Jesus Christ . . ." Question: does that mean this revelation is from Jesus? Or does it mean this revelation is about him, that he is the content of the revelation? The expression itself is ambiguous, isn't it? Apart from context, the phrase could be used to express either of those senses.

The interpretation rule that should guide us on this question is to ask, where in the near context did the author rule out sense A or sense B?

Some might ask, did ancient authors have any consciousness of ambiguity or double entendre?[1] For us to ask such a question suggests doubt about their intelligence. How ignorant do we think they were? Of course they understood. English cannot be the first language to have quirks that allow double meaning. Clever speakers and authors have always been able to marshal the accidents of their language to communicate humorously and powerfully. Ambiguities can be a speaker's friend. When a careful communicator wants to avoid ambiguity, there will always be ways to disambiguate.

So the conclusion must be, our author was fully conscious of the ambiguity of the title "The Revelation of Jesus Christ." So where in the context did he rule out either sense? The best answer is that he is saying that Jesus is the source and the content of the revelation: it is both from him and about him.

This is an eternally important point. Life is about Jesus, salvation is about him, eternity is about him.

That it should also be delivered from or through him fits with the biblical pattern. Heb 1:1–2[2] is about the idea that Jesus is the great prophet of the new revelation, the new covenant. Other NT passages suggest the correspondence between Jesus and Moses as the respective prophets of the new covenant and the old.[3]

John's Great Vision (1:12–16)

For three years, it was as though John and Jesus had been camping buddies. Of course, there was something uniquely different. But they did spend a lot of time together, along with several other friends, in both special and ordinary life experiences. This present vision was special. If John had occasionally lost sight of the disparity of stature between himself and

---

1. One renowned NT scholar, arguing against the double sense of the word *telos* in Rom 10:4, snarkily asserted, "The most dubious of all is the popular interpretation that Paul had both aspects simultaneously in his mind. Even if we cannot make up our mind between two linguistically possible options, it is suspect methodology to conclude that Paul could not either" (Räisänen, *Paul*, 53).

2. "Long ago, at many times and in many ways, God spoke to our fathers by the prophets, but in these last days he has spoken to us by his Son" (ESV).

3. John 1:17; Heb 3:2–6; 2 Cor 3:6–16. One should also remember Moses's prediction of a surpassing successor prophet in Deut 18:15, 18, which we rightly take as referring to Jesus (John 6:14; Acts 3:22; 7:37).

his Lord, in this vision it was brought to his consciousness in stunning, unforgettable vividness.

The first eight verses of the book are introductory. Verses 7 and 8 are transitional, a hinge preparing the reader for that which follows immediately, as well as for the larger body of the work. At verse 9, John begins to tell his story. His story begins with the vision he shares, which in turn is an essential foundation for what follows. Jesus appeared to him, but this experience was unlike any that he had before, with the one exception of the Mount of Transfiguration.[4]

The first point that must guide our interpretation of the verbal description of the vision, since these features are so extremely foreign to us, is to grant that the author meant for us to be as impressed as he was (v. 17) that this was a supremely glorious personage and that unqualified worship is the only proper response. So even if we never appreciate fully the importance of each feature—such as the feet being like burnished bronze[5]—we cannot fail to recognize that John was overwhelmed and fully expected the faithful reader to be similarly impressed, to respond in the only faithful way as he did: spontaneously, reflexively to cast himself—*ourselves!*—at Jesus's feet. If that has not happened, we have not yet grasped the author's intended meaning, because the author/Author certainly intended that.

We must acknowledge apparent Old Testament allusions, and we must study those OT contexts to acquire as complete an understanding of the symbolism as possible.[6] Even still, we will surely come up short. Some knowledge is forever lost to history. We can never time travel back

---

4. See Luke 9:28–36 and parallels in Matt 17:1–8; Mark 9:2–8; as well as Peter's recollection and comment in 2 Pet 1:16–18.

5. "The Greek . . . is very difficult to interpret" (Osborne, *Revelation*, 90). A survey of several commentaries yields the following catalog of symbolic interpretations: the Lord's moral purity (Beale, Swete, Thomas); the glory of God (Johnson, Kistemaker), triumphant, divine, righteous judgment (Johnson, Kistemaker, Moffatt, Walvoord); chastening authority (MacArthur); strength and stability (Ford, Mounce). Osborne concludes, "It signifies not only glory and strength but warns of potential judgment" (*Revelation*, 91).

So again, if we are not able to settle conclusively the meaning of the image, we surely cannot be far from the author's sense if we opt for any of these. One more factor is the association of this feature with all the others. In that sense, we can make a pretty good guess, much as we do with an unfamiliar word in a sentence that is otherwise easy to understand.

6. See the verse-by-verse commentary for a table of the features with the closest OT parallels, which I find mostly in Dan 7 and 10.

to first-century Israel and live for decades in the milieu of those temple worshiping people. That is not to suggest, however, that we cannot come to a high degree of recognition and appreciation of the author's idea. Nevertheless it is to suggest that the author/Author's meaning consists of both cognitive and rhetorical elements. Until we are persuaded as he intended his readers to be persuaded, we have not fully grasped his meaning. This book is about the Lord, the supreme and eternal Sovereign of earth and the entire created universe. "Who will not fear you, O Lord, and glorify your name?"[7]

This great vision of the exalted Lord is not freestanding, inert. It is surrounded by a setting of the seven branched golden menorah (Rev 1:12–13, 20) which represents the seven churches. To these the Lord dictates separate letters of commendation and warning. The number seven, while literal, is also undoubtedly symbolic, and surely the symbolic value is what is most significant to the author. Seven must be interpreted, generally, as indicating completeness, if not perfection.[8] The greater point seems then to be that the churches—all churches in that day and ours, and all generations from then to today—must fear this one above all, for we will answer to him.

A paramount component of the main message of the book is that this one is coming in final judgment. He will deal decisively and finally with all opposition; for opposition is wickedness, deserving eternal capital punishment in the court of the High King of heaven. If that judgment is threatened against his own churches first (chs. 2–3), how much more certain and terrible and right will be his judgment against those who never even feigned loyalty to him. If his most loyal servant, John, could not refrain from falling at his feet as a dead man, so must all true followers.

---

7. Rev 15:4. Of course the specific reference of this verse is the heavenly King, God the Father. But the point applies equally to the Son, the earthly King. After all, they are not ontologically two but one. To fear the Father is to fear the Son, and vice versa. See 1 John 2:23.

8. There is no consensus among scholars as to the precise symbolic meaning of seven in the Bible and in the ancient world of the biblical authors. That is because they were not all working from some style guide or glossary of symbols; it was more a matter of feel than an articulate plan. The greatest consensus is first that there surely is something symbolic about the use of numbers, especially seven in Revelation. The next level of consensus is that this number most likely derives from the days of creation week. Thus the connotation of divine completeness seems to be justified. See White, "Number"; Osborne, *Revelation*, 75.

Faith is submission and absolute loyalty. For he in whom we believe is the supreme King.

The centrality of Jesus is evident in many other passages throughout the book in both explicit and subtle terms.[9] But those can be folded into discussions below.

Primary Themes: Coming and King/Kingdom

First Theme: Coming

The main thing the OT taught the faithful to look forward to was the coming of a Savior, Messiah. The key word in that is not coming, but Messiah.[10] The NT scriptures similarly teach the church to look forward to the coming of Messiah (Christ). All our hopes, all the world's hopes, are wrapped up in this. Apart from him, there is no real, ultimate hope. The great twin messages of the NT are that that one came and is coming again. He is what the NT and OT are about; he is what eternity is about.

Unfortunately, for many the term second coming has come to have strange baggage and connotations too many and varied to attempt to itemize. I urge you to unburden yourself as much as you can of any such baggage you might be able to bring to your consciousness and suspend your commitments to it, so that you might be better able to look at the book of Revelation with fresh wonder and curiosity.

It is eminently appropriate that canonical revelation would conclude with a final information dump, a revealing, about the most important event in history since creation and the first coming, the most consequential event in the determined future of humanity and planet Earth. That

---

9. Especially chs. 2–3, 5. Thirty-one Lamb references in twelve chapters; Christ seven times in four chapters; Lamb or Christ in fifteen chapters (absent from chs. 2–3, 4, 9–10, 16, 18).

10. The early church, including those churches most directly related to Paul and those others more associated with the original twelve, quickly gravitated to the terms Christ and Lord as the preferred titles for Jesus, as in the Lord Jesus Christ. The thrust of both of these is kingship. Thus Christ effectively means King. The church acquired that term from Ps 2:2 and Dan 9:26–27, but also from its frequent use in 1–2 Sam.

Other important Old Testament terms are son of man, son of David, the prophet, priest-king, and branch. But because Israel was taught to look forward to such a one, it is natural that he also came to be known as the coming one (Matt 11:3; John 11:27; cf. Deut 18:15, 18; Ps 118:26; Hab 2:3; Mal 3:1–2; Isa 40:10; Zech 9:9; Heb 10:37).

the book of Revelation is centrally about the Lord's second coming[11] is prominently indicated by the author at the beginning and ending, is developed throughout all the major sections, and is itself the book's climax (Rev 19:11). Without naming names, I want to register my deep dismay at published studies of Revelation that downplay the second coming, some failing even to mention it at all.

The reader is supposed to not miss some very obvious clues. Three in particular are most telling: statements of the Lord's coming in the prologue (Rev 1:7), at the book's climax (Rev 19:11–21) and three times in the epilogue (Rev 22:7, 12, 20). Discussion of the first one must be extended considerably longer than those of the latter two. Discussion of the last one can be quite brief.

Coming in Rev 1:7

> Behold, he is coming with the clouds, and every eye will see him, even those who pierced him, and all tribes of the earth will wail on account of him. Even so. Amen. (ESV)

The first six verses of the book are a two-part introduction to the book, consisting of a statement of the central topic and its source with a statement of the value of the book (vv. 1–3)[12] and a stereotypical epistolary greeting, including doxology (vv. 4–6). At verse 9, John launches into a description of his initial vision, which then rolls into the next and the next and so on. But in verses 7–8 he issues an announcement: "Behold, he is coming with the clouds . . ."[13] The source of that announcement is

---

11. There are three synonymous Greek verbs the author of Revelation uses that would normally be translated by the English *come*: *erchomai*, which occurs a total of thirty-six times; *hēkō*, six times; and *deurō*, twice. Of these forty-four occurrences, about seven (7:13, 14; 8:3; 17:1 [2x]; 21:9 [2x]) are thematically insignificant. That is, our author has chosen a word that is very common for discussions of ordinary life experiences.

12. Osborne calls the first eight verses a prologue and the opening paragraph (vv. 1–3) a forward (*Revelation*, 51).

13. I disagree with the NET Bible, which places v. 7 in parentheses and supplies a note explaining their decision thus: "These lines are placed in parentheses because they form an aside to the main argument." We will demonstrate that this announcement is the furthest thing from an aside. It focuses the reader directly to the main idea, as several commentaries note. See for instance Thomas, who says this verse speaks of "the personal return of Christ": "The current verse obviously is the theme verse for the whole book" (Thomas, *Revelation 1–7*, 76–77). Johnson too insists, "This is a clear

identified as "the Alpha and Omega . . . he who is and who was and who is coming, the Almighty."

The reader must notice that the very first thing the author writes, following some basic introductory matters, is a pair of lines so similar in key wording and thought to primary OT prophecies of Israel's Savior-Messiah as to be unquestionably direct references. First he takes the reader to the great son of man prophecy of Dan 7:13–14.[14]

Daniel 7 is comprised of a vision (vv. 1–14) and its interpretation (vv. 15–28). The vision then is comprised of four scenes: four beasts (with special emphasis on the fourth, vv. 2–8), the Ancient of Days (vv. 9–10), the judgment of the four beasts (with special emphasis on the fourth, vv. 11–12), and the son of man (vv. 13–14).[15] The idea is that there would be a succession of four empires to rule over Israel from the time of Daniel to the inauguration of the glorious, eternal kingdom of God: Babylon, Medo-Persia, Greece, Rome (scene 1, vv. 2–8, matching the four metals of the statue in Dan 2:31–45). God, the ultimate Judge, the Ancient of Days, would sit for judgment (scene 2, vv. 9–10). The four beasts/kingdoms would be tried, convicted, sentenced, executed (scene 3, vv. 11–12). Then the approved one, the one "like a son of man," would step forward, also before the Ancient of Days, to be crowned King of all, filling the vacuum of power created by the removal of the four, charged to reign forever (scene 4, vv. 13–14).

He is man in contrast to the four who are beast, alluding back to Gen 1, suggesting that the earth has been topsy-turvy, with beasts instead of *adam*, man, ruling the vassal kingdom of earth. The entire book of Daniel is devoted to the question of the course of earth history from Daniel's day to the final resolution of the problem of Gen 3: the ultimate

---

reference to the return of Christ (22:7, 12, 20)" ("Revelation," 422).

14. Johnson says, "There are [in Revelation] no fewer than thirty-one allusions to" Dan 7 ("Revelation," 422).

John substitutes the pronoun he for "one like a son of man."

The second half of v. 7 comes from Zech 12:10, a prophecy of Israel's humble repentance and national conversion: "I will pour out on the house of David and on the inhabitants of Jerusalem, the Spirit of grace and of supplication, so that *they will look on me whom they have pierced; and they will mourn for him,* as one mourns for an only son, and they will weep bitterly over him like the bitter weeping over a firstborn" (NASB; italics added).

15. Actually, the Aramaic original is best translated "one like *a* son of man." That is how the LXX represents it. So when John says the same thing in Rev 1:13 and 14:14, it is best to understand these not as possible allusions to Dan 7 but as absolutely certain direct quotes in word for word translation and specific references to that character.

establishment of the kingdom of God (Dan 2:44). So the original son of man prophecy describes emphatically a supreme royal being, a King of kings. He cannot be any other than the promised Son of David, the heir to the throne of Israel.[16] As King of Israel, his gracious rule would overflow to bless all other nations of earth as well.

A key word in John's announcement is coming (*erchetai*). It may not look especially noteworthy to casual readers, but John can be subtle that way. Another of his subtle assumptions is that the reader will recognize his reference as coming from Dan 7, such that he does not feel it necessary in this place to use the expression Son of Man. It seems John is asking, "To whom else could this refer? This is so obvious, I will just leave it to the reader to recognize that referent."

The statement at the beginning of Rev 1:7, "coming with the clouds," also dovetails with the description of the Lord's ascension in Acts 1:9–11:

> And after he had said these things, he was lifted up while they were looking on, and a cloud received him out of their sight. And as they were gazing intently into the sky while he was going, behold, two men in white clothing stood beside them. They also said, Men of Galilee, why do you stand looking into the sky? This Jesus, who has been taken up from you into heaven, will come in just the same way as you have watched him go into heaven. (NASB)

The author of Acts seems to be saying that the Lord Jesus will return to earth in his resurrected (glorified) physical body, accompanied by a cloud. Surely John was aware of that teaching tradition; surely John cherished his undimmed, vivid, eyewitness memory of that event! Surely he assumed his readers would readily pick up on that.

Here at the beginning of the body of the book John states his thesis in bold, unmistakable terms: this book is about Jesus the Son of Man in his triumphant coming, the second coming.

16. It is telling that Stephen's first statement after the lethal stones began to rain down on his body connected Son of Man with "standing at the right hand of God" ("I see the heavens opened and the Son of Man standing at the right hand of God," Acts 7:56 ESV). That is, Luke connects Daniel's Son of Man with the Ps 110:1 Lord of David. Son of Man is Son of David, King of Israel. See also Matt 26:64; Mark 14:62; Luke 22:69.

Coming in Rev 19:11–21

The climax of the dramatic conflict of the book is described in Rev 19:11–21 in the account of the Lord riding on his white horse. The section begins with him in heaven—"I saw heaven opened, and behold, a white horse, and he who sat on it is called faithful and true"—and concludes with him engaging and destroying his earthly enemies. It has strong indicators of ultimacy. That is, his enemies, especially the beast and false prophet, meet their ultimate demise. (The final judgment of the dragon and kings of the earth is delayed only by the one thousand years of 20:1–6.[17])

So while the word "come" is absent from this section, it seems John certainly expected his readers to supply that idea, to see that this is the fulfillment of the great expectation of the book and of Christian preaching. All the great promises and hopes are wrapped up in the Lord's coming, as it sets in motion a sequence of events, the rollout of all as yet unfulfilled prophecies, both of judgment and redemption (with ruling), both temporal and eternal. Up to this moment, the triumph of good over evil has been only words, unrealized prophetic promises, not effectual actions. Up to this moment, the appearances were bleak, the bleakest ever in human history, for the deliverance and vindication of the righteous, the triumph of God's Champion, and the defeat of the archvillains. This is the fulfillment, the realization: his coming.

Coming in Rev 22

Finally, in the epilogue to the book (Rev 22:6–21) the one John has been listening to throughout says three different times, "I am coming quickly" (vv. 7, 12, 20). The importance of this cannot be overstated. There is no excuse for the reader not to get the message. His second coming is certain to be the most important event in all history. We must believe his words, and we must prepare now for eternity by bowing in submissive faith.

Additionally, there are three cries of the faithful supplicating the Lord to do precisely that. First, "the Spirit and the bride say, 'Come'" (Rev 22:17). Immediately after that, the author urges the hearer (of the oral reading of the book), "Let the one who hears say, 'Come'" (v. 17). Following the final statement of the Lord's announcement, the author himself

---

17. Premillennialism has a much easier time with these verses than amillennialism or postmillennialism.

responds, "Amen. Come, Lord Jesus" (v. 20). It is hard to miss the prominence of the theme in the closing words of the book.

Secondary References to the Lord's Coming

Beyond these three most telling instances of the theme of coming are numerous lesser clues, especially in the word come in one form or another.
If the importance of the theme is established by the references discussed
above, several other references seem at least likely to speak of it also.

To five of the churches in chapters 2 and 3, the Lord announced he is
coming. Some of these are threatening warnings of judgment in the event
the church does not comply with his demand of repentance; others are
comforting words of deliverance to faithful churches.

> To Ephesus: Remember therefore from where you have fallen;
> repent, and do the works you did at first. If not, I will come to
> you and remove your lampstand from its place, unless you re-
> pent. (2:5 ESV)

> To Pergamum: Therefore repent. If not, I will come to you soon
> and war against them with the sword of my mouth. (2:16 ESV)

> To Thyatira: Hold fast what you have until I come. (2:25 ESV)

> To Sardis: Remember, then, what you received and heard. Keep
> it, and repent. If you will not wake up, I will come like a thief,
> and you will not know at what hour I will come against you.
> (3:3 ESV)

> To Philadelphia: I am coming soon. Hold on to what you have,
> so that no one will take your crown. (3:11 NIV)

The impending judgment day is said about six times to be coming or even
to have come.

> The sixth seal: Then the kings of the earth and the great men and
> the commanders and the rich and the strong and every slave and
> free man hid themselves in the caves and among the rocks of
> the mountains; and they said to the mountains and to the rocks,
> "Fall on us and hide us from the presence of him who sits on
> the throne, and from the wrath of the Lamb; for the great day
> of their wrath has come, and who is able to stand?" (6:15–17
> NASB)

The seventh trumpet: Then the seventh angel sounded; and there were loud voices in heaven, saying, "The kingdom of the world has become the kingdom of our Lord and of his Christ; and he will reign forever and ever." And the twenty-four elders, who sit on their thrones before God, fell on their faces and worshiped God, saying, "We give you thanks, O Lord God, the Almighty, who are and who were, because you have taken your great power and have begun to reign. And the nations were enraged, and your wrath came, and the time for the dead to be judged, and the time to reward your servants the prophets and the saints and those who fear your name, the small and the great, and to destroy those who destroy the earth." (11:15–18 NASB)

An angelic announcement to all earth: He said with a loud voice, "Fear God, and give him glory, because the hour of his judgment has come." (14:7 NASB)

An angel: Another angel came out of the temple, crying out with a loud voice to him who sat on the cloud, "Put in your sickle and reap, for the hour to reap has come, because the harvest of the earth is ripe." (14:15 NASB)

The sixth bowl: Behold, I am coming like a thief. Blessed is the one who continues watchful and clothed so that he will not walk unclothed and men see his shame. (16:15)

Mourners wailing over their loss when Babylon falls: Woe, woe, the great city, Babylon, the strong city! For in one hour your judgment has come. (18:10 NASB)

Do not all of these also refer to the Lord's second coming or events that closely accompany that? Additionally, the climax of the book, Rev 19:11, indicates that it is when the Lord comes that judgment is finally poured out.

In answer to all these is the celebratory announcement of the imminent wedding of the Lamb:

Let us rejoice and be glad and give the glory to him, for the marriage of the Lamb has come and his bride has made herself ready. (19:7 NASB)

Only a few words later, we read of the climactic coming of the Lord:

I saw heaven opened, and behold, a white horse, and he who sat on it is called faithful and true, and in righteousness he judges and wages war. (19:11 NASB)

With all of these taking on special significance, two more groups of coming statements might be considered as possibly also reinforcing the theme.

Is it going too far to suggest that the unique formula "the one who is and was and is to come" (Rev 1:4, 8; 4:8) takes on a shade of coming? One could ask why the author shifted from forms of the verb be in the past and present ("who is and was") to a form of the verb come ("is to come" or "is coming") for the future tense. Strict grammarians might suggest he should have phrased it, "who is and was and shall be."[18] Admittedly, there is commonly something futuristic about the verb come in both English and Greek (and presumably many other languages). Nevertheless, it is tantalizing to entertain the notion that our author welcomed a kind of double entendre in this expression, speaking of course primarily of God's eternality, yet perhaps also subtly hinting at the certain and decisive divine visitation yet to come upon earth.

Additionally, one might wonder whether we are meant to hear a reference to the Lord's second coming in the commands issued to the four horsemen of the first four seal judgments—"Come!"—(Rev 6:1, 3, 5, 7), especially if, as I will argue below, the rider of this white horse is the Lord Messiah himself.

The evidence is strong, if not overwhelming, that the author meant for us to have the hope of the Lord Jesus's coming very present in our reading of the entire book, that the book is actually about that: he is coming.

Second Theme: King-Kingdom

The second primary theme of the book of Revelation is king-kingdom. Monarchy seems a relic of the unenlightened and primitive world of our ancestors. The American Revolution and Constitution led the modern world into a new era of democratic self-rule and separation of powers, replacing monarchy and dictatorship. Monarchy is to us such a queer and quaint mode of government that we can often be blinded against

---

18. Note Rev 17:8. Of the beast it is said, "he was and is not and is to come" (ESV). The third verb in this expression is not however a form of the word come (*erchomai*), but is actually a form of a verb of being, *pareimi*. Perhaps the author was concerned that this one not be seen as a coming one.

appreciating its place in the Scriptures, especially in God preferring to reveal himself to mankind for all of history—indeed, for eternity—as King.[19]

The most obvious clues to its importance include the repetition of the words king and kingdom and correlative terminology such as reign, throne, crown, rule, etc.; the emphasis on the kingship of God and his eternal reign in the new creation; and the rival king figures, including kings of the earth, the beast, and Satan.[20]

It is reasonable to assume this author fully expected astute readers to anticipate the issue of kingship, given its emphasis, especially in the OT but also in the NT.

The reader must not miss the prominence of kingship as early as Rev 1:4–6:

> John to the seven churches that are in Asia: Grace to you and peace, from him who is and who was and who is to come, and from the seven spirits who are before his throne, and from Jesus Christ, the faithful witness, the firstborn of the dead, and the ruler of the kings of the earth. To him who loves us and released us from our sins by his blood—and he has made us to be a kingdom, priests to his God and Father—to him be the glory and the dominion forever and ever. Amen. (NASB)

There God the Father and God the Son are both introduced as Kings, and the saints are said to have been made a kingdom. To the Father is ascribed glorious eternal kingship, and the Son's kingly rule is exerted over "the kings of the earth."

The very next statement (v. 7) alludes to the royal Son of Man: "Behold, he is coming with the clouds of heaven." In verse 9, John speaks of belonging to the kingdom. In verse 13, he indicates that the one he saw and described in verses 13–16 was none other than the royal son of man from Dan 7:13–14.

When John is summoned to heaven, the first thing he says he saw is the throne of heaven and him who sits on it (Rev 4:2). He refers to

---

19. I am impressed with the great divine revelations of Isa 6, Ezek 1, and Rev 4, in all of which God reveals himself to his prophets as King. As well, Paul's spontaneous eruptions into doxology in 1 Tim 1:17 and 6:15 depict God as King.

20. The twenty-four elders (Rev 4:4, 10), the locusts (Rev 9:7) and the woman (Rev 12:1) also wear crowns (*stephanos*). The elders also have thrones.

this throne another twenty-six times,[21] including most significantly its preeminent place in the new creation (22:1, 3).

The Lamb will be opposed by the kings of the earth under the command of the beast. The Lamb will of course triumph "because he is King of kings and Lord of lords" (Rev 17:12–14). In the scene of his glorious triumph over his enemies, the Son is crowned with many diadems (19:12) and is again named "King of kings and Lord of lords" (19:19). He announced to Laodicea that the Father has granted him the privilege of sharing his throne (3:21), which is eventually described as fulfilled in the new creation (22:3).

Also in Rev 3:21, the Lord promises overcomers the privilege of reigning with him on his eternal throne. The redeemed are promised that they will reign on earth with the Lamb (5:10). They are then seen reigning with him throughout the millennium in 20:4–6 and again eternally in the new creation in 22:5.

Though described in the middle of the book (Rev 11:15, seventh trumpet), the preview of the outcome of the great conflict reassures the reader that "the kingdom of the world shall have become the kingdom of our Lord and of his Messiah,[22] and he shall reign forever and ever."

There is an anti-kingdom with anti-kings. Satan has crowns (Rev 12:3), as does the beast (13:1); Satan also has a throne (13:2), and so does the beast (16:10). There are "the kings from the east" and "the kings of the whole world" who join with Satan and both beasts in the Armageddon event (16:12, 14). There are also "kings of the earth" who side with the anti-kingdom (6:15; 17:2, 18; 18:3, 9; 19:19), though some of them (perhaps) ultimately come to enjoy eternal heavenly blessing (21:24). But they all must bow to King Jesus (1:5). The whore Babylon smugly boasts that she sits—is enthroned—as queen (18:7).

The situation is that both heaven and earth are domains. As depicted in Ps 2, heaven is spiritual and is the domain of the Suzerain God the Father, the King of heaven (who is spirit); earth is material and is the vassal domain of humankind (cf. Gen 1:26, 28; Ps 115:16). Our first parents forfeited their and our rule by failing to comply with the edict of their Overlord, the Creator King of heaven. That earthly throne seems then to have been usurped by Satan, as Jesus (Luke 4:6–8; John 12:31; 14:30; 16:11), Paul (2 Cor 4:4), and John (1 John 5:19) concede that he does in

---

21. Rev 3:21; 4:2, 9, 10; 5:1, 7, 9, 11, 13, 15, 17; 6:16; 7:10, 15; 8:3; 12:5; 14:3; 16:17; 19:4, 5; 20:11, 12; 21:3, 5; 22:1, 3.

22. In fulfillment of Ps 2.

fact in some way rule earth today. Jesus, enthroned at God's right hand, is shown to be heaven's favorite son, as it were (Ps 110:1). But as honored as that place is, that is not his ultimate place of rule: he is to be eternally the King of the new earth in fulfillment of Ps 2:7–9.

As I understand the concept, when Jesus was rejected as King of Israel, the determined station from which he should rule not only his nation but the whole earth, he fled, as it were, into exile, to heaven's second throne. (Remember, there are twenty-four more thrones and thus twenty-four more kings in the throne room; Rev 4:4. Cf. 2 Kings 25:28.) There he waits for the Father's word, according to the Father's timing, for him to come to challenge Satan for the throne of earth, to destroy, along with Satan, all those who preferred that one rather than himself, the rightful King, and then to install himself (with the heavenly King's pre-authorization, of course) as earth's King forever.

The great story line of the book of Revelation is the contest for the throne of earth. When heaven's King gives the signal, the Lamb receives the scroll and initiates the actions to claim what is rightly his, the throne of earth; to punish, judge, and destroy those who had opposed his rule, thus avenging his martyred followers; and to repair the damage caused by Satan's malevolent, maleficent misrule; and to set up his eternal, glorious kingdom for his faithful followers.[23]

The Coming of the King

These two—coming and kingship—are the most dominant themes of the book.[24] Together they form the core of the message of the book. The main idea of Revelation is that Jesus is coming to claim the throne and crown which are rightly his: he is coming to become the King of earth.

---

23. I take it our Lord's current session, as it is sometimes called, is an honorary enthronement. He is reigning but not ruling there. Heaven already has its King, God the Father, who, by seating Jesus on a throne at his right hand, has confirmed to all angels, good and evil, that the throne of earth will certainly be handed to him in the Father's time, fulfilling the announcement of Ps 2:6. Rev 5 is about him receiving heaven's authorization, and Rev 6 is him leaving that honorary throne to take the throne of earth, to fulfill the eternal grand plan by ruling earth.

24. As noted earlier, other crucial themes of the book include repentance, martyrs, judgment, victory, and worship, the last three of which are in fact subsidiary to or an aspect of kingship.

Literary Structure

Also crucial to tracking with the thought of the author is this matter of literary structure, or the author's intrinsic outline, the other primary strategy of macroexegesis. That is, we must attempt to discover or reverse engineer the outline plan of the author. Toward that end, we must be careful not to impose an alien plan. We seek, after all, to discover the author's intended meaning.

This project has proven quite elusive to interpreters of Revelation, as evidenced by the variety of proposals and lack of consensus. I will propose a plan and defend it. While those other plans deserve comment elsewhere, I will not give them thorough responses or even mention all of them in this book. I believe this presentation will be sufficiently compelling to render many of those plans unacceptable.

First, I agree with the many who see in Rev 1:19 what amounts to an authorial statement of the outline: "Write therefore the things you have seen and the things which are and the things which shall come to pass after these things." There is a past-present-future format to John's writing assignment, hence, the format of the book of Revelation.

The last expression, "the things which shall come to pass after these things," is almost exactly repeated in Rev 4:1,[25] and so I conclude, along with the reasonability of a futuristic meaning of all, that the author intended that we regard chapters 4 to 22 as that section. That leaves chapters 1 to 3 for the past and present. It then makes good sense to connect "the things you have seen" with the vision of the glorious Lord as he described it in 1:12–18. Then it also makes sense that the letters to the churches contemporary to John's writing (chs. 2–3) amount to "the things which are."

Beyond that larger structural plan, we are still left with the task of recognizing the internal structure of chapters 4–22. A quick overview summary of the content of those chapters is as follows:

---

25. "The things which shall come to pass after these things" is almost word for word identical to the ending of Rev 4:1, the setting for that heavenly throne room scene (*ha dei/mellei genesthai meta tauta*); there is no meaningful difference between *mellei* and *dei* in these statements. Nowhere else does the author use this phrasing.

4–5	Heavenly throne room scene
6–8	Seal judgments
8–11	trumpet judgments
12–13	introduction to the archvillains (Satan-dragon and two beasts)
14	three scenes (to be developed later)
15–16	bowl judgments
17–18	judgment of Babylon the Great, the mother of whores
19	heaven's celebrations, Messiah's conquest
20	millennium, final judgment of Satan and all the wicked
21–22	new creation, new Jerusalem

That's actually fairly simple, fairly easy to commit to memory. But making sense of an internal organization plan has been the elusive challenge.

Simply stated, my proposal is that chapters 6–20 are comprised of two subsections: 6–11 (the scroll: seals and trumpets) and 12–20 (archvillains).

The larger section (6–20) begins and ends with the rider on the white horse, who of course is the Coming One, the King of kings.[26] The seventh seal is the seven trumpets, and the seventh trumpet is the second coming of Messiah.

The seven-sealed scroll is supremely consequential. John's despair over the prospect that none might ever be able to claim it (Rev 5:4) is the author's dramatic way of indicating that. The second coming, with the announcements of the kingdom and final judgment (11:15–18), is the culmination of the scroll, the great hope of the saints, the turning point, the historical event so critical that it sets in motion the fulfillment of all the remaining elements necessary to the completion of God's perfect plans.

The breathtaking[27] finality of the scroll is also indicated by the suspenseful delays between the sixth and seventh seals and the sixth and seventh trumpets.[28]

---

26. See appendix 1, where I defend the interpretation that the first white horse rider is the same as the second.

27. "When the Lamb broke the seventh seal, there was silence in heaven for about half an hour" (Rev 8:1).

28. Though I will argue that actually the sixth trumpet includes not only the second half of Rev 9 but all of 10 and the first part of 11, continuing to the announcement of the end of the second woe in the middle of ch. 11.

The last verse of chapter 11 is a buffer[29] separating the seventh trumpet from the utterly new images and message of chapter 12, confirming
that there is a major break following the trumpets.[30] It is not properly
part of the seventh trumpet, nor is it the beginning of the two signs of the
woman in labor and the dragon (12:1–3).

That twelfth chapter is not about the woman or her child, though
it begins with that great sign (Rev 12:1–2). Instead, the chapter is the
formal literary introduction of the dragon, Satan. His identity is defined
by the three scenes of the chapter: his disposition toward the woman and
her child, the Messiah (vv. 1–6); his expulsion from heaven (vv. 7–12);
and his end-time murderous rage against the woman and her other
children (vv. 13–17). Immediately following that and connected to the
dragon chapter is the formal introduction to the two beasts, the antimessiah[31] and his false prophet (ch. 13). Discussion of the fourteenth chapter
must wait.

The fifteenth chapter is introductory to the seven bowls; the sixteenth chapter is the seven bowls.[32] In two of those bowl statements—the
first and fifth (vv. 2, 10)—the object of the wrath of all seven is identified
as the followers of the beast and his kingdom. The beast is also a key
character in the sixth bowl (v. 13). The seventh bowl serves in part to
introduce the next two chapters, in which the main character is new to
the story,[33] the last major character of the book—Babylon (Rev 16:19),

29. Which is not to say that it does not have meaning of its own. It also echoes
language in Rev 8:5 at the beginning of the seven trumpets about thunder, lightning,
earthquake.

30. This is one of several reasons to reject the position that the seventh trumpet *is*
the seven bowls (Thomas, *Revelation 1–7*). Another is that Rev 11:15–18 bears strong
marks of ultimacy. Also, the case for the thread tying chs. 12–19 together is very
strong. The bowls are about judgment on the beast and his followers; his introduction
begins with the dragon, ch. 12.

31. For a discussion of the humanity of these, see appendix 1, "The Rider of the
First White Horse."

32. I must take issue with Beale in his argument that the first four verses of ch. 15
belong structurally not with what follows but with chs. 12 to 14 (Beale, *Revelation*,
621). This he does because he sees the unit defined by signs indicated by the word sign
(*sēmeion*) itself in Rev 12:1, 3; 15:1. The simple answer is that this flies in the face of the
very obvious connection of 15:1 with all of chs. 15 and 16, which are from beginning
to end about the seven bowls, as virtually all other commentators recognize.

33. That is, she is here for the first time in the spotlight, and for the first time she is
named Babylon. We will see however that she is one and the same with the great city
of Rev 11:8.

the great whore. But she is introduced as one intimately associated with the beast. The nineteenth chapter begins with the heavenly celebration of the demise of that whore (19:1–5). Then without any pause or transition, the heavenly celebration shifts to the even more joyous occasion of the Lamb's impending wedding (19:7–9). As Babylon, a city, was the whore, faux-bride to the beast, the counterfeit messiah (17:3), so now (the new) Jerusalem, a city, is the pure virgin bride and wife of the Lamb, the true Messiah (cf. 21:2, 9–10). The paragraph introduced by the second white horse (19:11) is the climax of the great conflict of the book. It is by all accounts the second coming.

So the case for the section from white horse to white horse being comprised of the two blocks, chapters 6–11 and 12–20, has passed the first test of the broadest strokes. Finer details must now be examined.

Chapters 6–11: The Seven-Sealed Scroll

The Seventh Seal = Seven Trumpets

There can be no serious challenge to the notion that the author intended all seven seals to comprise a block, as also the seven trumpets. The crucial assertion I am making here is that the seals and trumpets go together, the content of the seventh seal being the seven trumpets. Thus the scroll extends through chapter 11, culminating with the seventh trumpet.

There are several clues supporting the assertion that the seventh seal is the trumpets.

The expectation factor is strong. The author elevates that in chapter 5 when he opens the chapter with attention to the scroll in the right hand of the King of heaven (Rev 5:1).[34] That by itself indicates its supreme importance. Then when the challenge to open the scroll went out to all in heaven, earth, and hell (perhaps), and no one stepped forward to accept the challenge, John broke down into inconsolable weeping (v. 4),[35]

---

34. The title King of heaven obviously indicates his absolute supremacy over all. The King of heaven / King of earth construct arises most clearly from Ps 2. That precise title occurs once in Scripture: Dan 4:37.

35. In two words, the author expresses extraordinary passion. The verb of weeping (*eklaion*) is in the imperfect tense, suggesting onset and duration: "I began to weep and continued for some indeterminate but lengthy time." It is then heightened by the addition of the adverb, greatly (*polu*). The intended effect seems to be, as I expressed above, inconsolable weeping. The NIV renders it "I wept and wept."

dramatically indicating that the lack of a qualified champion would mean that somehow all is lost.

Following the sixth seal, a temporary halt is called (Rev 7:1–3). There was no similar break between the first and second seals, between the second and third, and so on. So following the sixth, readers are naturally expecting—because the author has led them to expect—to proceed immediately to number seven. But before things can proceed any further, God's servants must be sealed. That sealing is accomplished in 7:4–8. The angelic order to halt also provides a crucial clue as to the content of the seventh seal: "Do not harm the earth or the sea or the trees until . . ." (7:3). We should therefore expect to read of God's servants being sealed, and after that to read of harm or damage (*adikēsēte*, 7:3) to earth, sea, trees. Surely then it is more than random coincidence that in the first and second trumpets, there is severe damage to, if not destruction of, earth and trees (8:7) and seas (8:8). We must conclude the author expected us to understand that the seventh seal is now seven trumpets.

Further, chapter 8 opens with the eagerly expected breaking of the seventh seal. But instead of something dramatic, of stupendous moment, suitably climaxing the drama of Rev 5:1–5, we read of silence (8:1). Could that be the content of the seventh seal?[36] In addition to the arguments above, it is noteworthy that trumpeters are the first thing John saw (8:2). The first, fifth, and sixth seals were also introduced as visions; the second to fourth seals are probably to be understood as included in the first seal vision. The Greek *eidon* (I saw or looked) occurs six times in chapter 6, three times in chapter 7, then in 8:2 but not 8:1. The vision is the seventh seal, and it is trumpeters, not silence.

Is there some other explanation of the thirty minutes of silence? Perhaps the idea is that all heaven is virtually holding its collective breath. You could hear a pin drop. It is as if the attention of some may have drifted through the first six seals. But all know to pay utmost attention now: this is the big one.

If the seventh seal is not silence, what about the next thing John saw: seven angels with trumpets (Rev 8:2)? There is so much to commend this conclusion. Still, we must wonder then about verses 3 to 5: the matter of burning incense, the prayers of the saints, being hurled to earth, leading to thunder, lightning, and earthquake.[37] Are we to understand that to be

36. Poythress acknowledges that silence is anticlimactic, but still decides that that, rather than the trumpets, is the content of the seal (*Returning King*, 120).

37. This is the second of four statements in Revelation about these natural

the full extent of the seventh seal and the great wonder of the scroll? If so, why would the author not have held off mentioning the seven trumpeters until after this? I find these last two challenges rather strong, rendering the view considerably weaker than that the seventh seal is itself the trumpets. So for several reasons, positive and negative, it is most probable that the scroll extends all the way through the seven trumpets.

Then there is the content of the seventh trumpet (Rev 11:15–18). Nothing is more climactic and momentous. This is the moment of truth for creation: "The kingdom of the world has become the kingdom of our Lord and of his Christ; and he shall reign forever and ever!" (NASB). Still, the trumpet judgment does not end with that: it ends with the judgment of all the dead, both the faithful and the wicked (v. 18). Any judgment of the living might possibly be something less than final; but judgment of the dead cannot be other than final.

This should sober us all. I urge you, reader, to pause and worship humbly.

The First Four Seals: Riders on Variously Colored Horses

Let us now return to the beginning of the seals. We need to wonder about the first four (Rev 6:1–8) being a group, with so much in common, yet so different from those that follow. As noted in the previous section, John introduces visions with a typical prophetic formula, "I saw" (*eidon*). He does so three times in chapter 6: at verses 1, 9, and 12, at the beginnings of the first, fifth, and sixth seals, but not at the beginnings of the second, third and fourth horses. That is one argument for interpreting the four as a group.

The four colored horses must surely call to mind Zechariah's opening vision (Zech 1:8–17) and perhaps also his eighth (Zech 6:2–3). Of course there are some differences. But given John's inclination toward OT references and allusions, including the fact of his comfortable authority to take liberties to depart from strict replications, we should assign a high probability to the idea that he intended some significant similarity.[38]

---

phenomena (see also Rev 4:5; 11:19; 16:18).

38. Virtually all the commentaries agree John's image recalls Zechariah's visions. What to do with that fact is not as obvious.

Zechariah's eight visions are arranged in the form of a chiasm[39] with the first and eighth sharing in common the feature of colored horses, while the center pair, the fourth and fifth (chs. 3 and 4), focus on the complementary offices of high priest and governor, anticipating the Messiah in whom the offices of priest and king will be united, confirmed in the coda of the vision unit (Rev 6:9–15).

In those first and eighth visions, God commissions the horsemen to patrol the earth (ha'aretz, Rev 1:10–11; 6:7). In the beginning, God is angry (1:14–15),[40] but by the end, his wrath is satisfied (6:8).[41] His initial anger arose from his zeal for Jerusalem: the city was in rubble and no one (of the gentile nations) seemed to care about what God cares about (1:11–16). That's wicked; it arouses divine wrath and deserves divine judgment.

The comprehensive message of the most important of the eight visions—first and eighth visions, the extremities of the chiasm, and fourth and fifth visions, the vertex—is that God will raise up his Priest-King Messiah, the branch-man (Zech 3:8; 6:12), who will both punish the gentiles who despised God's chosen city, Jerusalem, and himself assume and fulfill the task to make her glorious. The operative issues for the interpretation of 6:1–8 then are that God is zealous over Jerusalem and that he will send Messiah to punish those end-time Babylonians who have defiled it. These points will be confirmed by further examination of details of the first four seal judgments.

First, the rider of the white horse is Messiah. The evidence for this and against alternative views is very strong.[42]

Next, I would like to take the reader on something of the same path I followed when I arrived at the following interpretation, considering the second, third, and fourth horsemen in reverse order. I think I should serve notice that this view is something I conceived entirely from my own

39. With the interesting wrinkle that instead of 2 and 7, 3 and 6 being mates, the mating goes 1/8, 2/3, 4/5, 6/7.

40. "So the angel who was speaking with me said to me, Proclaim, saying, Thus says the LORD of hosts, I am exceedingly jealous for Jerusalem and Zion. But I am very angry with the nations who are at ease; for while I was only a little angry, they furthered the disaster" (NASB).

41. "Then he cried out to me and spoke to me saying, See, those who are going to the land of the north have appeased my wrath in the land of the north" (NASB).

42. But in the interest of maintaining a brisk pace, that discussion is provided in appendix 1.

study of Bible texts. To my knowledge, it has not been proposed in any published works.[43]

Moving then to the fourth seal, the fourth horseman (Rev 6:7–8): he is empowered "to kill with sword and with famine and with pestilence and by the wild beasts of the earth" (NASB). Readers are supposed to wonder about this collection of agents of death: sword, famine, pestilence, wild beasts. It turns out these echo the language of Ezekiel (Ezek 14:21)[44] prophesying the judgment on Jerusalem (which came via the armies of Babylon) for her (Sinai) covenant defection. The main point is not how many (one quarter of *ha'aretz*), but the object of and reason for divine judgment: the tenants of Messiah's land[45] had violated the terms of tenancy and corrupted his land.[46] The Lord's coming (Rev 6:1–2) is God's judgment on the sinful inhabitants of his land, Israel, of the end time.

With the third horseman (vv. 5–6) comes a cry announcing an exorbitant price for wheat and barley, along with a prohibition against harming the olive and grape crops: "A quart of wheat for a denarius, and three quarts of barley for a denarius; and do not damage the oil and the wine" (NASB).[47] The author's point is not at all what virtually all commentators

43. Representative of the prevailing approach is this from Osborne: "These four horsemen flow together, as the action proceeds from the lust for *conquest* to *civil war* to *famine* to *pestilence and death*" (*Revelation*, 274; italics added).

44. "For thus says the Lord GOD, 'How much more when I send my four severe judgments against Jerusalem: sword, famine, wild beasts and plague to cut off man and beast from it!'" (NASB).

There are also several other passages that mention three of these, including some from Jeremiah. This one however most nearly mirrors John's statement. Ezekiel and Jeremiah seem likely in turn to draw the language of these particular four agents of divine punishment from Moses's song in Deut 32:24–25. Even as early as Exod 5:3, Moses recognized God might deploy sword or pestilence to punish Israel. Then as late as 2 Chron 20:9, four (not including wild beasts) are listed as disasters that could befall Israel.

45. The translations commonly say *earth*. But the Greek word *gē* could also be rendered *land* and refer narrowly to the promised land, Israel. It is also highly likely that John was thinking Hebrew while writing Greek, so that the word and idea he had in mind was *ha'aretz*, loaded with OT Israel connotations.

46. "I brought you into the fruitful land to eat its fruit and its good things. But you came and *defiled my land*, and my inheritance you made an abomination" (Jer 2:7 NASB; italics added). "I will first doubly repay their iniquity and their sin, because they have *polluted my land*" (Jer 16:18 NASB; italics added). Cf. Lev 18:24–25; Isa 8:8 ("your land, O Immanuel").

47. In Deut 7:13, grain, wine, and oil are staple crops, but also the representation of agricultural fertility.

say, that there is to be a great drought. Their confusion at explaining the last part about wine and oil[48] proves they are completely off the right track. The idea is rather that Messiah will initiate a new Joshua-type invasion to drive the end-time Canaanites out of his land and to claim the land for himself and his faithful followers: his millennial reign. That is, in Joshua's day an invading army would, as part of their conquering strategy, destroy the grain crops, which were going to have to be replanted the next year anyway, while sparing the durable trees and vines, since they would soon be the property of the invaders. If they were to destroy those, it would be decades before they would have reliable harvests from newly planted vines and olive trees.[49] His prohibition is, "Do not harm or damage or injure" (mē adikēsēs, exactly the same prohibition as in Rev 7:3). This certainly could imply the opposite action toward the grains, resulting in the spike in market prices.

John's point is not that Messiah will do this literally, but that he is coming as Joshua and will drive out the inhabitants of his land, because they have been corrupting it by their godless wickedness.

The second horseman ("it was granted to take peace from the earth, and that men would slay one another; and a great sword was given to

48. Osborne notes, "The emphasis here [v. 6] is almost certainly upon exorbitant prices caused by famine and the resultant rationing of the food supply" (Revelation, 280). He then addresses the conundrum of the "two somewhat minor items" (minor? really?) of oil and wine, that the horseman was directed not to harm them (mē adikēsēs), and summarizes five views thus (280–81):
   1. The poor suffer while the rich are not affected.
   2. The famine is moderate, affecting grains but not vines and olives.
   3. The oil and wine are sacramental and so symbolically represent believers being spared from the effects of the famine.
   4. A preterist view notes that during the first-century siege of Jerusalem, some rebels stole oil and wine from the temple.
   5. Domitian ordered the destruction of half the vineyards because of a grain shortage.

Osborne prefers number five. Beale notes that Domitian's order did not apply to olives. But as Osborne himself also notes, Domitian's order was never carried out; he rescinded the order under pressure (Beale, Revelation, 381).

49. See Deut 20:19f; 28:51; Judg 15:5 for statements that relate in different ways to the military strategy of destroying crops. See Josh 24:13, where God takes credit for giving Israel "vineyards and olive groves which you did not plant," with no mention of grains; also Deut 6:11; Neh 9:25. In the interest of full disclosure, in Nah 2:2, the prophet speaks of an enemy destroying the vine branches (not the vines themselves) of the Ninevites.

him," vv. 3–4 NASB) may then be an end-time Gideon,[50] who, though he bears a large sword, achieves his victory when he incites the enemy occupants to kill each other.[51] But surely John must also be thinking of Zech 14:13: "And on that day a great panic from the LORD shall fall on them, so that each will seize the hand of another, and the hand of the one will be raised against the hand of the other" (ESV).

The composite message of the four seals/horsemen then is that Jesus comes to reclaim the land that is rightly his. He does so as an end-time Gideon (red horse rider), an end-time Joshua (black horse rider), and an end-time Nebuchadnezzar (pale green horse rider).[52] Likewise, those he drives out are like Gideon's Midianites, Joshua's Canaanites, and covenant-defecting Judah of Nebuchadnezzar's day. We should probably also notice that while Gideon and Joshua drove out non-Israelite invaders and squatters, Nebuchadnezzar, the shadow-type of the fourth horseman, drove out wicked Israel. They had become the defilers of Messiah's land, just like the Canaanites before them, and shall be that again during the time of the seals, trumpets, and bowls.

When the Lamb receives the scroll, he begins immediately to exert all necessary force to carry out the implicit commission of the scroll—to claim the (Davidic) kingdom of *ha'aretz*.[53]

I doubt that the author intended for us to understand four successive strikes, as in the image of locusts in Joel 1:4 or, for that matter, that Messiah literally does any of the specific actions of the last three horses, but rather that Messiah is coming to do what each of these and all collectively represent: clear the land of his enemies. They are the ones to whom God had leased his land and who had been defiling it by their refusal to bow to him as its and their rightful Lord. That is the project of the scroll of seven seals and thus the overriding concern of chapters 6–11.

This interpretation is reinforced in two other features, curious expressions that cry out for consideration: "those who dwell on the earth" (Rev 6:10; 8:13; 11:10) and "to destroy those who destroy the earth" (11:18). The English reader needs to stop when reading such unusual

---

50. Or Zerubbabel? See Hag 2:22. See also Ezek 38:21; 1 Sam 14:20.

51. See Judg 7:22; 1 Sam 14:20; 2 Chron 20:23; Isa 19:2.

52. Yes, that seems to make him look like he is the rider on all four horses. Perhaps we are to think that he is the Leader and Commander of the foursome.

53. From that kingdom and capital, he will then extend his dominion to the ends of the earth. That is, all other nations will then bow and submit to his supremacy.

expressions and ask why the odd wording. Both will be addressed in the next section.

Those Who Dwell on the Earth = The Inhabitants of the Land

I have found that it can often be very enlightening to attempt to translate some of John's terms and expressions back into OT Hebrew.[54] The expression "those who dwell on the earth" (*hoi katoikountes epi tēs gēs*) can be quite easily represented as *yoshebei ha'aretz* (יֹשְׁבֵי הָאָרֶץ), which occurs numerous times in the OT, where it is commonly translated "the inhabitants of the land," referring originally to Canaanites and later to Israelites, as the occupants of the special land God promised to Abraham and delivered through Joshua. If only our NT translators had saved us that trouble and rendered John's Greek that way! In most, if not all, the OT examples, the word land, though translated earth[55] in Revelation, speaks narrowly of the promised land. I wonder to what extent the rendering earth in Revelation reflects a theological bias (against a future for literal, national Israel)—eisegesis, rather than careful exegesis. We should at the very least give serious consideration to the possibility that John was using

---

54. One of the more important ones, I believe, is included in my arguments for the identification of the rider on the first white horse. See appendix 1.

It seems that while John was writing in Greek, he was often thinking in Hebrew.

55. Throughout Revelation, John uses the common word *gē*, which can be used of the whole planet or the particular land of Israel promised to Abraham. Thus it corresponds wonderfully to the Hebrew *eretz*, or with its definite article, *ha'aretz*, which can also be used both ways. Unfortunately, the English language actually does us a disservice in that we are forced to choose between two words, earth and land, which speak of one or the other, not both. However, biblical authors of both OT and NT were blessed with simpler, more flexible vocabulary, which might refer to the planet or the promised land or even both. We need to be much more open to that fluidity when we interpret.

Zech 14:9–10 provides an interesting illustration of the problem.

In Rev 14:6, "those who dwell in the land" and "every nation" are taken by some translators as referring to the same. But the syntax not only allows but even favors the distinction and complementarity of the two: "to those who dwell in the land and to every nation" (*epi tous kathēmenous epi tēs gēs kai epi pan ethnos*). The whole statement seems redundant if both parts speak of the whole world and all mankind. On the other hand, if John is thinking in Hebrew, it makes good sense that between the two parts, he is referring first to the land of Israel and then to all the gentile nations.

Rev 20:9 seems to be one of the clearest uses of earth/land (*gē*) referring to the promised land of Israel, not earth.

the expression in that geographically restricted sense. I invite you to look at several selected examples from the Old Testament:[56]

> Then you shall drive out all the inhabitants of the land from before you, destroy all their engraved stones, destroy all their molded images, and demolish all their high places. (Num 33:52 NKJV)

> Therefore do not defile the land which you inhabit, in the midst of which I dwell; for I the LORD dwell among the children of Israel. (Num 35:34 NKJV; these two from Numbers are Moses to the people just shortly before they crossed the Jordan to take over the land.)

> And [Rahab] said to the men [the Israelite spies she was sheltering]: "I know that the LORD has given you the land, that the terror of you has fallen on us, and that all the inhabitants of the land are fainthearted because of you." (Josh 2:9 NKJV)

> And they said to Joshua, "Truly the LORD has delivered all the land into our hands, for indeed all the inhabitants of the land are fainthearted because of us." (Josh 2:24)

> And you shall make no covenant with the inhabitants of this land; you shall tear down their altars. But you have not obeyed my voice. Why have you done this? (Judg 2:2)

> Is not the LORD your God with you? And has he not given you rest on every side? For he has given the inhabitants of the land into my hand, and the land is subdued before the LORD and before his people. (1 Chron 22:18 NASB; David's charge to Solomon and other leaders of that next generation)

> Did you not, O our God, drive out the inhabitants of this land before your people Israel and give it to the descendants of Abraham your friend forever? (2 Chron 20:7 NASB)

> The earth[57] [land] is also defiled under its inhabitants, because they have transgressed the laws, changed the ordinance, broken the everlasting covenant. (Isa 24:5 NKJV)

56. The complete list is Num 33:52, 55; 35:34; Josh 2:9, 24; 7:9; Judg 2:2; 2 Sam 5:6; 1 Chron 22:18; 2 Chron 20:7; Neh 9:24; Isa 24:1, 5, 6, 17; 26:21; Jer 1:14; 6:12; 10:18; 25:29–30; Joel 1:14; 2:1; Mic 7:13; Zech 11:6. Also, Judg 1:11–33 uses very similar expressions, though not precisely this expression, and is perhaps for this reason especially helpful for appreciating the issue.

57. Here too translators may be imposing a theological bias. I think these oracles of Isa 24–27 make perfect sense with a narrower focus on the land of Israel.

> For behold, the LORD comes out of his place to punish the in-
> habitants of the earth [land] for their iniquity; the earth [land]
> will also disclose her blood, and will no more cover her slain.
> (Isa 26:21 NKJV)

> "For I will no longer have pity on the inhabitants of the land,"
> declares the LORD; "but behold, I will cause the men to fall,
> each into another's power and into the power of his king; and
> they will strike the land, and I will not deliver them from their
> power." (Zech 11:6 NASB)[58]

Originally the idea was that the pre-Israelite inhabitants of the land
that God promised to Abraham had by their wickedness defiled the land
God claimed as his (Num 33:52; cf. Gen 15:16).[59] Therefore they needed
to be driven out, so that he could give the land to his chosen people. As
God announced this plan to his people, he also added a warning that if
they ever became like those they drove out (Num 35:34; cf. 1 Kgs 21:26),[60]
then they too, themselves the new inhabitants of the land, would be in
jeopardy of being similarly expelled.

These inhabitants of the land were defiant of the Lord of the land;
they were his enemies and the enemies of his faithful people. Now in
Rev 5-11, God the King of heaven has decided the time has come to
clean house once and for all (forever), to drive out the wicked end-time
Canaanites (in fact, faithless Israel). They are the ones who caused the
martyrdom of the saints in the fifth seal (Rev 6:9-11).[61] That statement
carries in it the hinted assurance that God would in his time—in fact,
before the scroll seal judgments are finished—repay them with justice,
avenging his faithful ones. They were the objects of the terrors of the last

---

58. This one seems especially apropos, as this oracle (Zech 11:4-17) speaks of
God's future judgment on the nation Israel that has rejected its King (9:9).

59. Gen 15:16: "Then in the fourth generation they will return here, for the iniquity of the Amorite is not yet complete" (NASB).

60. 1 Kgs 21:26: "He [Ahab] acted very abominably in following idols, according
to all that the Amorites had done, whom the LORD cast out before the sons of Israel"
(NASB).

61. So also Rev 17:6, where Babylon is code for Jerusalem. This will be developed
below.

three trumpets, called woes (8:13).[62] And they were opposed to the two witness-prophets and joined in the celebration of their deaths (11:10).[63]

To Destroy Those Who Destroy the Earth (Land)

The very last statement of the unit, at the end of the seventh trumpet, is another which bears special attention: "to destroy those who destroy the earth [land]" (Rev 11:18 NASB). That seventh trumpet consists of two celebratory cries of saints. The first comes from voices identified only as being heavenly: "The kingdom of the world has become the kingdom of our Lord and of his Messiah,[64] and he shall reign forever and ever."[65] (This seventh trumpet is the second coming.) The second comes from the twenty-four elders, first echoing the point of the previous song, then rejoicing in the perfect justice of God's final judgment of the righteous and the wicked: "The nations were enraged [cf. Ps 2:1], and your wrath came [cf. Ps 2:9, 12], and the time came for the dead to be judged, and the time to reward your servants the prophets and the saints and those who fear your name [cf. Ps. 2:12], the small and the great, and to destroy those who destroy the earth/land" (NASB with adaptations).

This is the time when the dead are summoned for judgment, the faithful to be rewarded and the wicked to be condemned. This can only be final judgment.[66] But instead of styling the wicked as those who opposed his rule, or who refused to believe in Jesus, or some other common salvation formula, the author characterizes them as "the destroyers

---

62. "Then I looked, and I heard an eagle flying in midheaven, saying with a loud voice, Woe, woe, woe to those who dwell on the earth [the inhabitants of the land], because of the remaining blasts of the trumpet of the three angels who are about to sound!" (NASB).

63. "And those who dwell on the earth [the inhabitants of the land] will rejoice over them and celebrate; and they will send gifts to one another, because these two prophets tormented those who dwell on the earth [the inhabitants of the land]" (NASB).

64. Again, using the OT Hebrew word that John was translating. The language and idea echo Ps 2.

65. It is wonderfully appropriate that G. F. Handel chose this text for the most joyous song—"The Hallelujah Chorus"—of his enduring oratorio *The Messiah*.

66. Though not the great white throne judgment. This is the same judgment as Matt 25:31–46, the judgment of those wicked who lived through the great tribulation but were physically killed at the second coming, Rev 19:21, because they were deemed unworthy to enter Messiah's millennial kingdom. This judgment is final for them, though they yet await the great white throne, after the millennium (Rev 20:11–15).

[Greek present participle, *diaphtheirontas*] of the earth/land." Of course their eternal damnation is fundamentally the judgment for opposing their Creator and his chosen Messiah to the end. But the author's stated reason for their eternal condemnation is related to their abuse of God's and Messiah's earth/land. The evident point the author means to make here is that by opposing God, they oppose Jesus and his rightful claim to possess and rule *ha'aretz*, both the promised land and the whole earth. By opposing the true and rightful Lord of earth, they actually have been destructive of the promised land (and the planet), his precious creation (regardless of how green they lived or declared themselves to be).[67]

We would do well to remind ourselves how precious earth must be to the Creator. "In the beginning God created the heavens and the earth." He made only the two realms, and he is not going to allow one to be utterly lost. Earth is, along with humankind, his magnum opus. Sin and Satan have been ravaging earth since Eden, bringing it to the very brink of irreparableness. God has been biding his time, one might say, waiting for the perfect timing to step in. He has been extending much greater merciful patience than any of us would think reasonable. When he is fully fed up with evil's assaults on his precious earth,[68] his judging wrath will be poured out against the highest order sin and crimes, including, though not limited to, destroying his earth/land, because that is an expression of defiance of his supreme lordship (Ps 24:1), not to mention his unspeakable goodness (Gen 1:31).

How big a deal is creation to God? Rev 4:11 answers that question as well as any Scripture. The majesty of that scene culminates in the worship of the elders, "Worthy are you [King of heaven] . . . for you created all things," then loosely paraphrasing, "they (we) exist only because you created them (us)."[69]

Some of us evangelicals think—I know, because I recently realized this is what I had been thinking—that redemption is the big deal, and creation is little more than a hot, problematic issue because of the atheistic evolutionists. This verse would urge us to block out the noise of evolutionism and that debate, to focus on the wonder that behind our amazing

67. The first rule of Christian environmentalism is that Jesus is Lord of the planet. Only with that established are we ready to address water quality, etc.

68. We can say that earth is all that is not heaven (Gen 1:1), including the particular *eretz* promised to Abraham.

69. See also Ps 24:1–2. In Isa 8:8 and Ezek 36:9–12, the issue is especially the promised land.

creation is our even more amazing Creator. Take Rom 1:25[70] to heart, and determine not to be like the wicked ones described there.

If that seemed like an aside, I bring back the idea that prompted it: God loves earth, and therefore judging its destroyers (Rev 11:18) is a righteous and just concern to him.

The Sixth Trumpet

Before we wrap up this section on the structure of the scroll unit, chapters 6–11, we need to address another issue which is almost always misinterpreted: the sixth trumpet.

It is almost universally accepted that the sixth trumpet ends at the end of chapter 9.[71] The problem with this is that the author signaled the end of the second woe at Rev 11:14. So who is mistaken: John or modern commentators? It seems hard to argue against the notion that the sixth trumpet does not end until the author says it ends, which I insist is precisely the point of 11:14 and in fact the only reason for introducing the three woes back in 8:13. We ought at least to consider the author's representation to see if it makes sense. I will show what we lose by closing out the sixth trumpet at the end of chapter 9.

The trumpet judgments extend from chapter 8 through chapter 11. The first four are a set in which God's judgments are poured out on earth, the seas, fresh waters, and heavenly bodies. (The first four bowl judgments follow this same pattern; Rev 16:2–9.) The next two are a pair with progressive severity. The seventh is the second coming.

Chapter 9 seems at first to consist of a pair of similar judgments (vv. 1–12, fifth trumpet; vv. 13–21, sixth trumpet). But the last verse of chapter 8 cannot be ignored; it is there for a reason. After the first four trumpets but before moving on to the fifth, the author inserts the statement about the angelic announcement of three woes, corresponding to

---

70. "They exchanged the truth of God for a lie, and worshiped and served the creature rather than the Creator, who is blessed forever. Amen" (NASB).

71. Kistemaker, Ladd, MacArthur, Morris, Mounce, Poythress, and Stedman call 10:1—11:13 an interlude; Aune, Johnson, Caird, Tenney, and Walvoord agree.

Thomas at least acknowledges that some include 10:1—11:13 in the sixth trumpet. He cites three older works: Dusterdieck (1887), Bullinger (1909), and J. B. Smith (1961). He adds, "This conclusion is uncalled for, however, in light of the clear indication of 9:20–21 that the sixth trumpet has ended there" (*Revelation 8–22*, 58).

the final three trumpets.[72] Why? We will hold that question in reserve, and come back to it later.

The fifth trumpet is a plague of locust-scorpions, the sixth trumpet—that is, the portion of it that we find in chapter 9—is a plague of fire-breathing, lion-headed, snake-tailed horses. Contrary to the nature of locusts, these are forbidden to attack vegetation (v. 4). The locust-scorpions sting the inhabitants of *ha'aretz* who are not protected by God's seal (v. 4; cf. 7:4–8), inflicting excruciating pain for five months. It is non-lethal but so severe that the victims wish they could die (vv. 5–6). Following that, the fire-breathing, lion-headed, snake-tailed horses (two hundred million strong) attack and kill one third of mankind.

I urge you not to waste too much energy trying to make sense of that army of deadly fire-breathing, lion-headed, snake-tailed horses. It will make perfect sense to those who see it unfold before their eyes. But until then, it will continue to seem fantastical and to provide fodder for the Bible scoffers.[73]

The main point for us is the rhetorical effect of Rev 9:14–19, then also of verses 20–21. This is meant to build from the locust-scorpions of 9:1–11: as bad as they were, this is ten thousand times worse! The locust-scorpions afflicted nothing and no one but the wicked of mankind, those unclaimed and unprotected by God (lacking God's seal; 9:4). Those victims agonized and found no relief from the torment, but at least they eventually recovered (v. 5), only to face this next, much severer plague. The victims of 9:14–19—undoubtedly the same class, those unclaimed and unprotected by God—face their eternal judgment.

Chapter 9 concludes, however, not with mourning for the dead but with special attention paid to the survivors. The reader must not miss the obvious fact that these have witnessed and survived not just this most recent and most devastating plague but all the death and devastation described in the first to sixth seals and the first to sixth trumpets so far, and yet stubbornly—chillingly—they refuse to repent, bow, and cry out for mercy to the only one who could be responsible for all this. The greater part of verses 20–21 consists of numerous reasons[74] they should repent.

---

72. "Then I looked, and I heard an eagle flying in midheaven, saying with a loud voice, 'Woe, woe, woe to the inhabitants of *ha'aretz*, because of the remaining blasts of the trumpet of the three angels who are about to sound!'" (NASB, with adaptation).

73. There is not much we can do about that. "Do not answer a fool according to his folly, Or you will also be like him" (Prov. 26:4 NASB).

74. I count fourteen different charges.

The rhetorical effect of those verses is to pile up their guilt and to make the overwhelming case that the final judgment that awaits them is entirely deserved.[75] "Behold how wicked they actually are." As well, behold how restrained and longsuffering God has been toward them!

But as argued above, the author was not content to close out the section at verse 21. I urge you to read again those last two verses; read them slowly, aloud, to get the effect the author surely intended. Think of how ancient listeners would have been silently, progressively reacting through the oral reading of these indictments.

> The rest of mankind, who were not killed by these plagues, did not repent
>   of the works of their hands,
>   so as not to worship demons,
>   and the idols of gold
>   and of silver
>   and of brass
>   and of stone
>   and of wood,
>   which can neither see
>   nor hear
>   nor walk;
>   and they did not repent of their murders
>   nor of their sorceries
>   nor of their immorality
>   nor of their thefts. (NASB)

The second key point is that whereas back in Rev 9:12, at the end of the fifth trumpet, the author explicitly noted the end of the first woe, he does not similarly note the conclusion of the second woe at the end of the chapter. He does, however, add that statement—another chapter and a half later. The author, who went out of his way to add what might be considered an unnecessary clue to guide the reader through the final three trumpets—the three woes statement at 8:13 and the woe statement at 9:12 being completely unnecessary—does something quite unexpected. Following the plague of deadly fire-breathing, lion-headed, snake-tailed horses (9:13–21), he adds all of chapter 10 and the first thirteen verses of chapter 11 before telling the reader that the second woe—which,

---

75. The same point is made in the third bowl: "I heard the angel of the waters saying, 'Righteous are you, who are and who were, O Holy One, because you judged these things; for they poured out the blood of saints and prophets, and you have given them blood to drink. *They deserve it*'" (Rev 16:5–6 NASB).

according to 8:13, is the sixth trumpet—is concluded. This seems to be the only reason the author introduced the three woes in the first place: to keep us from erroneously seeing the sixth trumpet as concluding at the end of chapter 9. Certainly there must be a burden of proof on the position that argues that the trumpet ends at 9:21 and that the default position must be that it continues until the second woe statement at 11:14.[76]

Shouldn't we take another look at the possibility that the author might have been correct? What if the author meant to include everything from 9:13 to 11:13 in the sixth trumpet? How would that affect our understanding of this sixth trumpet? What do we lose by calling 10:1—11:13 an interlude rather than part of the sixth trumpet, as much as is 9:13–21? Shouldn't we at least explore what the expanded trumpet might then mean? I invite you now to seek with me to discover how 10:1 to 11:13 also belongs to the sixth trumpet.

Between the end of chapter 9 and the second woe statement (Rev 11:14), there are two (or three) scenes: a strong angel delivering to John a scroll he must eat (10:1–11), the command for John to measure the temple (11:1–2), and the career of the two witnesses (11:3–12). These last two are closely related and could be considered a single scene.

The key features of the tenth chapter are that John is given a scroll that he must eat (vv. 8–10), coupled with a command to prophesy again about many peoples of all kinds (v. 11). The burden of the scene concerns the time of the seventh and final trumpet, soon to be sounded (Rev 11:15–18), which will signal the conclusion of "the mystery of God" (10:7). All this is set up by a terrifying scene of a mighty and awesome-looking angel[77] descending from heaven (v. 1), who takes his stand on sea and land (v. 2), and when he roars, the seven thunders answer (v. 3).

John's reflexive response is to write the content of the seven thunders' message (which to John must have been verbal and sensible),[78] but, curiously, he is forbidden from doing so (v. 4). Presumably, John learned some new revelation. It seems God must have wanted for him to learn something and for us to know that he learned something—presumably it

---

76. I have not found any commentators acknowledging this burden of proof and providing evidence sufficient to meet the burden.

77. His similarities to the Lord Jesus in 1:12–16 are remarkable. But this one is, to use John's word, an angel; contra Beale (*Revelation*, 533).

78. Walvoord agrees (*Revelation*, 171).

must have helped him with his task as prophet—yet the content was for John and not us.[79]

The angel then announces with great emphasis,[80] "there will be no more delay (*chronos*)" (v. 6), cluing the reader that from here we will move quickly (literarily speaking) to the climax, the second coming, as described in the seventh trumpet.

But more than that, I think there is another important clue in that word *chronos*, time or delay. While it most frequently speaks of time in the NT,[81] most modern translations read, "There will be no more delay."[82] Comparing this to Rev 2:21,[83] it appears the author may have meant, no more time to repent. In the letter to the church of Thyatira, the Lord declared that he had given Jezebel time (*chronos*) to repent, but she refused. Why does God delay judgment when it is so richly deserved?[84] The theme of repentance seems to be the main idea in the sixth trumpet and appropriately so, as it is immediately followed by the final judgment (11:18). So this central verse of chapter 10, in the middle of the sixth trumpet, is also signaling opportunity to repent—the last chance.

In chapter 11, the brief temple measuring (vv. 1–2) and the two witnesses (vv. 3–12) are tied together by the repetition of three and a half years (vv. 2, 3) and the Jerusalem setting (vv. 1–2, 8). These are the days (three and a half years) when the beast (v. 7) "has his way with"[85] Jerusalem (v. 2). But he is not unopposed: he is frustrated by the two witnesses and his inability to silence them. Nor is he the main character, on center stage, in this section.[86] In this section, the spotlight is on those two wit-

---

79. Beale summarizes various published views (*Revelation*, 534–35). The best suggestion is that these thunders spoke of yet another round of seven judgments, much as the seventh seal opened into seven trumpets. This tenth chapter raises that question and answers that that is not to be. "There is to be no more delay." There is to be only one more trumpet which will mark the end of the scroll, taking us to the end of this age, the second coming.

80. "[He] raised his right hand to heaven and swore by him who lives forever and ever, who created heaven and what is in it, the earth and what is in it, and the sea and what is in it" (Rev 10:5–6 ESV).

81. Fifty-two out of fifty-four times.

82. In agreement with BDAG.

83. It occurs only two more times in Rev. 6:11 and 20:3.

84. Second Pet 3:9 comes to mind: "The Lord is not slow about his promise, as some count slowness, but is patient (*makrothumei*, longsuffering) toward you, not wishing for any to perish but for all to come to repentance" (NASB); which is also in a context of impending final judgment.

85. She is, after all, a prostitute.

86. He is not formally introduced until ch. 13.

nesses (seen nowhere else but in this section). In these last days before
the climax of history (the completion not only of the trumpets but of the
seven-sealed scroll),[87] God raises up two great prophets, giving Jerusalem
one last chance to repent: one Elijah-like, the other Moses-like. Were it
not for special divine protection (v. 5) they would not survive three and a
half hours, let alone three and a half years. The opposition to God—and
God's messengers—is fierce, as fierce as ever seen.

The author amplifies the importance of this event by allusion to important eschatological prophecies and prophets from the OT. First, the
three and a half years recall Daniel's seventieth week, which was divided
in half (Dan 9:26–27). Next, everything in verse 4 alludes quite clearly to
Zech 4, the fifth of Zechariah's eight night visions. Third, the witnesses'
powers described in verse 6 are widely recognized as echoes of Elijah's
and Moses's judgment powers. Finally, their resurrection after three and
a half days must surely be meant to identify them with their Lord.

The Moses reference—turning water to blood—suggests God's
judgment on the enemy of his people when he redeemed the people from
the enemy's clutches.[88] The Elijah reference—calling for drought—is also
about judgment on God's own spiritually adulterous people and call to
repentance, along with the faithfulness of a remnant. Zechariah's fifth vision (ch. 4) is mate to the fourth (ch. 3), which together anticipate Israel's
Savior as Priest-King.[89] The lampstands and oil may remain somewhat
mysterious, yet this much is plain: the redemption God is promising to
bring to Israel through a great Savior will be accomplished by the spiritual power (oil) and truth (light) of God himself (especially Zech 4:2–6).

Directly following the two witnesses section (Rev 11:3–12, set in
Jerusalem, v. 8), in 11:13 there is a catastrophic earthquake in the same
city—7000 fatalities—following which the author immediately directs
the reader's attention to the survivors.[90] In striking contrast to those at

87. And the second half of Daniel's seventieth week.

88. The predominant theme of Moses's Song of the Sea (Exod 15) is the utter destruction of the Egyptian army even more than Israel's miraculous passage through
the sea.

89. Note also the symbolic rite of crowning the high priest in Zech 6:11–13, clarifying the central issue of the combined eight-vision prophecy: Messiah will be Priest
and King.

90. "And in that hour there was a great earthquake, and a tenth of the city fell; seven
thousand people were killed in the earthquake, and the rest were terrified [*emphoboi
egenonto*, literally, became fearful] and gave glory to the God of heaven" (NASB).

the end of chapter 9, these repent faithfully, savingly.[91] After three and a half years of hearing the two witnesses and refusing to bow the knee to the true Messiah, these survivors will finally, and not too late, repent.[92] Here we are at the last hour, the last statement of the next-to-last trumpet of the last seal, the last chance before Messiah returns (the seventh trumpet, 11:15–18), and one group of survivors defies God to the end, while another group finally bows in reverential fear and ascription of God's rightful glory.[93]

Now we see that the sixth trumpet, from Rev 9:13 to 11:13, means something really significant and entirely appropriate. Now it clarifies that all the calamity of the first six seals and the first six trumpets, while being divine judgment, was simultaneously divine longsuffering. As over and over in the OT the prophets described God's heavy hand as simultaneously judgment, divine warning, and opportunity to repent,[94] so here, at the sixth of seven trumpets, is one last chance. The chilling revelation is that those with the most sins to repent will refuse to do so (9:20–21), while many Jews in Jerusalem will finally repent and submit faithfully,

---

91. Defense of the interpretation of "fear and glorify" as repentance is provided below.

92. There is no summary statement of the specific content of the prophecy/testimony of the two. But surely it must be the gospel: "Jesus is the true King; this beast character (v. 7) is an evil imposter. If you maintain your alignment with him, you will suffer his fate of eternal damnation. But if you align with Jesus, he will reward you with eternal life in his glorious kingdom."

We will learn from chs. 13 and 17 that Jerusalem of antimessiah's day will sell out to him and participate in his deadly persecution against Messiah's followers who refuse to submit to his lordship (refusing to accept the 666 brand).

93. I find it intriguing that in the original branch prophecy (Isa 4:2), there is attention directed to survivors in Israel/Jerusalem. Tellingly, these are faithful, in stark contrast to the population condemned in the previous judgment oracles. See also Zech 14:16, where surviving gentiles are all faithful worshipers of Yahweh, subject to the King in Jerusalem.

After hearing a report of tragic loss of life, Jesus also turns the focus back on the survivors and the necessity that they and all repent (Luke 13:1–5).

94. The theme of repentance is also found in the letters (Rev 2:5, 16, 21–22; 3:3, 19) and bowls (Rev 16:9, 11). The statement in Rev 2:21 shows mercy on God's part: "I gave her time to repent." Sadly, it is followed with a disappointing report: "She refuses to repent of her immorality." Compare Amos 4: five times (vv. 6, 8, 9, 10, 11) the prophet repeats, "Yet you have not returned [*shûv*, the most common OT word for repent] to me." Ominously, the last one is followed by the famous line, "Prepare to meet your God, O Israel" (v. 12).

savingly, to their true Messiah (11:13)—all this at the last hour before the great second coming.[95]

The Big Idea of the Scroll

The concern of the scroll then is *ha'aretz*, the earth/land: Who is to rule? Who is to claim its throne and reign forever? Jesus! Worthy is he to take the book and break its seals, for he was slain and purchased for God with his blood men from every tribe and tongue and people and nation (Rev 5:9). He purchased the redemption of his people by his sacrifice on the cross. The praise then continues: "[He has] made them to be a kingdom and priests to our God; and they will reign upon the earth" (Rev 5:10, in fulfillment of the original intent of Gen 1:26, 28). In order for them to reign, he must reign, for they are his faithful followers. In order for him to reign, he must wrest control of earth and earth's throne from the enemy usurper, Satan, the ancient serpent (Rev 12:9; 20:2; Gen 3:1ff), and his minions. He comes to evict the wicked, destructive tenants of his land, so that he can reclaim it and rule it forever. Such is the burden of the scroll and chapters 6–11. Such a burden is consistent with that of Ps 2.

Chapters 12-20: The Judgment of the Archvillains, Part 1

The other major segment of the larger body of the work is chapter 12–20. The big pieces in this span are the dragon and beasts (12–13), three visions (14), bowl judgments (15–16), Babylon (17–18), three cheers (four, actually; Rev 19:1–10), and the climactic coming of King Jesus, wrapping up history and the first creation (19:11—20:15).[96]

The big questions of this unit are:

- About what is chapter 14, and how does that fit with the rest?

- Who is the prostitute of chapters 17–18, and how does that fit with the rest?

- How does this whole unit hang together?

95. Perhaps we should see a parallel to the conversion of the one thief crucified beside Jesus (Luke 23:40–43).

96. There are several components to this last segment: his coming (Rev 19:11–16), final destruction of the beasts and their followers (Rev 19:17–21), the thousand years (Rev 20:1–6), final destruction of the dragon (Rev 20:7–10), and final judgment of all remaining rebels (Rev 20:11–15). Everything after his coming is resultative. His coming is the critical event introducing ultimate eschatology.

The thread that ties these all together is the careers of the archvillains, all culminating in their eternal destruction. These villains are the dragon (Satan), the beasts (antimessiah and the false prophet), and the wicked city (Babylon/Jerusalem). Their respective destructions then are described in reverse order: first that of Babylon, then the beasts, and finally Satan.

The Centrality of the Dragon (Satan) and Beasts in Chapters 12–20

The first mention of Satan is in the letters to the churches,[97] but he is not a central character in that literary unit of seven letters. His formal literary introduction comes in chapter 12. From chapters 12 to 20, that character is central in Rev 12:3—13:4 and 20:2-3, 7-10. He is an important player in the sixth bowl, though mostly a foreboding shadow over that scene. His prominence in chapter 12, carrying over into the introduction to the beast in chapter 13, makes him loom large. The special attention given to his thousand-year incarceration (20:1-3) and his final rebellion and judgment (20:7-10) provides significant frame to the entire unit of these chapters. It is probably not by accident that his identification in 12:9 and 20:1 by four and five identifiers[98] is also near the beginning and ending of the unit.

With the dragon's approving supervision, the first beast is formally introduced in Rev 13:1-10 and the second beast in 13:11-18. The first beast is prominent in chapter 16, the bowl judgments (vv. 2, 10, 13); chapter 17, the career of Babylon the prostitute (vv. 3-17); and chapter 19, his eternal demise (vv. 19-20). His image and number are also referenced prominently in 14:9 and 11; 15:2; 16:2 and 20:4. The second beast, the false prophet, is then associated with the first beast in 16:13 and 19:20.

---

97. The Smyrna church is persecuted by the Jewish synagogue inspired by Satan (Rev 2:9, 10). The Philadelphia church has to deal with a similar problem synagogue (Rev 3:9). The Pergamum church is in Satan's hometown (Rev 2:13). Some in the Thyatira church have embraced Satanic teachings (Rev 2:24).

98. "The great dragon was thrown down, the serpent of old who is called the devil and Satan, who deceives [literally, the deceiver of] the whole world; he was thrown down to the earth, and his angels were thrown down with him" (Rev 12:9 NASB).

"He laid hold of the dragon, the serpent of old, who is the devil and Satan, and bound him for a thousand years" (Rev 20:2 NASB).

The three are interrelated in their introductions in chapters 12–13 as well as 16:13; 19:20—20:1; and 20:10.

To summarize, after the formal introductions of the three in chapters 12 and 13, the first beast is the most prominent of the three in chapter 14; chapter 16, the bowl judgments; chapter 17, the career of Babylon the prostitute; and chapter 19, King Jesus's victorious return.

The Place of Chapter 14

Numerous details in this large section of chapters 12–20 cry out for attention; one that has proven especially challenging to interpreters is the function of chapter 14. The reason it was mostly overlooked above is that it is the least simple to describe as a whole. To refer to it as three visions is accurate literarily and structurally, but that does not provide any indication of its content. I will now give it somewhat extended attention, with the primary concern of supporting the macrostructure proposal.

The experienced student of Revelation will have noticed that I have not yet shown any awareness of a popular view that chapters 12–14 are a unit whose unifying feature is seven signs or seven something elses.[99] My approach throughout this book is especially to be positive in presenting my views, with minimal negative attacking of alternative views. This is one of those places where some negative criticism is required.

The following table displays representative examples of a seven somethings approach. One of the most obvious points is the mutual contradictions of these. There is irreconcilable disagreement as to the dimensions of the seven. The only agreement of note is the three consecutive elements: first beast, second beast, and the Lamb with the 144,000 (13:1—14:5). But there are either one, three, or five elements before these in the different lists.

---

99. Johnson, Morris, Ryken. Walvoord gives all of chs. 12–15 the heading "Seven Great Personages of the End Times."

Ladd calls chs. 12–14 an interlude (*Revelation*, 166). Poythress identifies "Seven Symbolic Histories": "the Dragon, the Woman, the Beast, the False Prophet, the 144,000, angelic announcers, and the Son of Man" (*Returning King*, 133). Beale argues there are only six in chs. 12–14, and the seventh is the opening of ch. 15 (*Revelation*, 784). He also wants to argue that Rev 15:1 is both the seventh sign and the beginning of the bowls section.

Signs	Ryken	Beale[100]	Johnson[101]	Morris	Walvoord[102]
1	The dragon's war (12)	12	The woman (12:1–2)	The woman and her son (12:1–6)	The woman Israel
2	The beast of the sea (13:1–10)	13:1–10	The dragon (12:3–4)	War in heaven (12:7–12)	The dragon Satan
3	The beast of the earth (13:11–18)	13:11–18	(The rest of ch. 12?)	War on earth (12:13—13:1a)	The man-child Christ
4	The Lamb and the 144,000 (14:1–5)	14:1–5	The beast of the sea (13:1–10)	The beast of the sea (13:1–10)	Michael and the angels
5	Angelic messages of judgment (14:6–13)	14:6–13	The beast of the earth (13:11–18)	The beast of the earth (13:11–18)	Israel the remnant of the woman
6	The reaping of the earth (14:14–16)	14:14–20	The Lamb and the 144,000 (14:1–5)	The Lamb and the 144,000 (14:1–5)	The beast of the sea
7	Reaping and judgment of the wicked (14:17–20)	15:2–4	The harvest of the earth (14:6–20)	The harvest of the earth (14:14–20)	The beast of the earth

The main (perhaps only) strength of a seven somethings approach is that it makes chapters 6–16 a continuous series of sevens: seals (6–8), trumpets (8–11), somethings (12–14), and bowls (15–16). The seals, trumpets, and bowls are unmistakable and undisputed. The question is,

100. Beale calls the section "Deeper Conflict" (*Revelation*, 621). He works from the vision formulas "and I saw" (*kai eidon*, Rev 13:1, 11; 14:1, 6, 14; 15:1, 2) and "and behold" (*kai idou*, Rev 12:3; 14:1, 14). One of several problems with this approach is that together these occur not seven but eight times in this section (the two expressions are duplicated in 14:1 and 14). So he excludes Rev 15:1. This plan requires too much help from the interpreter to make it work.

101. Johnson's position is very confused. His heading for chs. 12–14 is "The Seven Signs," but in the first paragraph of that section he indicates "at least seven signs are mentioned in chs. 12 to 19"; and "chs. 12 to 14 contain seven further images though only two are directly identified as signs." His opening comments on ch. 12 are, "In this chapter there are three main figures: the woman, the child, and the dragon. There are also three scenes: the first of the child (vv. 1–6), the expulsion of the dragon (vv. 7–12), and the dragon's attack on the woman and her children (vv. 13–17)" ("Revelation," 510–11).

102. Walvoord connects chs. 12–15 as "the seven great personages of the end times" (*Revelation*, 957), but as we see in his list, all seven are in chs. 12–13.

can we legitimately find or do we instead manufacture a seven in the space between trumpets and bowls?

There are at least two major problems with this. First, there is no consensus among the advocates of the approach as to what the some-things are or what numbers one through seven are. In fact, each one contradicts every other approach. Second, there is a glaring difference between the seals-trumpets-bowls on the one hand and the somethings on the other. In the case of the former, the author explicitly notified the reader there were seven of each[103] and proceeded to enumerate exactly seven of each,[104] such that there is no variation of opinion of interpret-ers as to what verses are the separate seals-trumpets-bowls.[105] I insist the seven somethings approach to chapters 12–14 is a failed approach that needs to be abandoned.[106]

The real challenges are to show how the segments of chapter 14 fit together internally and how chapter 14 fits between 13 and 15. I address the latter first.

Chapter 13 consists of the descriptions of the beast from the sea (Rev 13:1–10) and the beast from the land (13:11–18), antimessiah and the false prophet, respectively. The disturbing impression created in chapter 13 with its one-two punch of this very powerful, very evil tag team—a super tyrant and his enforcer—is that they appear certain to succeed in their plan to enforce universal loyalty to themselves and thus to become the indomitable lords of earth. They seem to hold all the cards. How can they be prevented from wiping out entirely the remnant of faithful followers of the Lamb-Messiah? They have all the power and no inner scruples encumbering them. Who can stop them? That is essentially the author's point in 13:3–4: "And the whole earth was amazed and followed after the beast; they worshiped the dragon because he gave his authority to the beast; and they worshiped the beast, saying, 'Who is like the beast, and who is able to wage war with him?'" (NASB).

Moving forward, chapter 15 is introductory, the literary build-up to chapter 16. Chapter 16 is about the seven bowl judgments against

---

103. Seven seals: Rev 5:1, 5; 6:1; seven trumpets: Rev 8:2, 6; seven bowls: Rev 15:1, 6, 7, 8; 16:1; 17:1.

104. Seals: Rev 6:1–17; 8:1; trumpets: Rev 8:7–9:21; 11:15–18; bowls: Rev 16:1–21.

105. Except for the question of where the sixth trumpet ends.

106. Beale cites Rissi (with whom he disagrees) "who sees attempts to discern any kind of sevenfold structure as 'much too ingenious and violent'" (*Revelation*, 621). I agree with Rissi.

the beast and his followers (Rev 16:2, 10). It is a depiction of gruesome, though not yet final, payback. (That final, crushing blow comes later, depicted in 19:17–21.) They deserve[107] every ounce of righteous judgment (16:5, 7) depicted.[108]

One could suggest that chapter 14 seems like an awkward intrusion of perhaps untimely or irrelevant material.[109] It is comprised of three blocks of material, each abruptly changing the subject from the preceding, lacking any explicit explanation of logical progression. Verses 1–5 depict the Lamb and his 144,000 purest, most faithful followers standing on Mount Zion. Verses 6–13 speak of a sequence of three angels flying in midheaven, delivering three fateful warnings to the inhabitants of *ha'aretz*. The last seven verses (14–20) describe a pair—almost twins—of harvests of the inhabitants of *ha'aretz* by heavenly beings.

How are we to make sense of these? Can this chapter then be demonstrated to be exactly the right interlude between chapters 13 and 15? Let's try it. (I suggest you turn there now and reread the chapter before continuing.)

First, there is a thread that ties these three together. There is something ultimate or penultimate about them all. The ultimacy of the third segment is the most obvious.

The 144,000 are sharing the glorious victory of their Savior. That's ultimate. The victorious Lamb has won Mount Zion, and these have been approved and honored by him to share in his rule (represented by standing). Further, they alone of the inhabitants of *ha'aretz* are privileged to learn the symphony commissioned by heaven's King for his pleasure (vv. 2–3). They are perfectly pure in every way (vv. 4–5). The reader must have begun with the assumption that these are the same ones previously

---

107. "They have shed the blood of saints and prophets, and you have given them blood to drink. It is what they deserve!" (Rev 16:6 ESV).

108. As a side note: the author is leading the reader to agree with him in celebrating God for his justness in pouring out frightening judgments on the wicked. Sometimes I worry that there may be a sentiment, or shall I say, a sentimentalism in some Christian circles today, of sympathy for the objects of God's wrath. I do not find this encouraged anywhere in Scripture. Of course, God takes no pleasure in the death of the wicked (Ezek 18:31–32; 33:11). And Paul wished he could swap places with Israel: they to Messiah's kingdom and he in their place in hell (Rom 9:3). But final justice is a good thing, and God is to be praised for accomplishing it perfectly.

109. Many find this chapter hopelessly disconnected. Ladd describes it as "a series of disconnected short visions" (*Revelation*, 188).

sealed, 12,000 from each of the twelve tribes of Israel (Rev 7:4–8).[110] By that sealing, God promised to protect them through the final scroll (seventh seal) judgment, the seven trumpets, and here we see that indeed they crossed the finish line victorious. This scene is a stunning and welcome sequel to chapter 13, where evil's complete and final victory seemed assured.

The three angelic messages[111] are, first, the eternal gospel[112] (vv. 6–7); second, the ominous announcement of the certain and irreversible demise of Babylon the great (v. 8); and third, the equally ominous threat that all who would acquiesce to the false prophet's demand to receive the mark of the beast, who threw in their lot with the beast, the antimessiah (instead of holding out for the true Messiah), are doomed, irredeemable. Their sentence has been pronounced; they are damned to hell for all eternity (vv. 9–11). These too concern the ultimate.

Here too, as with the rest of chapters 12–20, is continuity of the beast issue (Rev 14:9–11), providing evidence that this chapter belongs here and that the burden of these chapters is centrally related to the beast.

The gospel message (Rev 14:6–7) must be the message unto eternal salvation.[113] How likely is it that one hearing the message of this angel

110. Any suggestion that these two groups of 144,000 are not identical certainly must bear the burden of proof. What most probably did the author intend: that these are the same or different? Absent strong evidence, this default interpretation must stand. Mounce allows they may be different groups, and identifies these more with the innumerable multitude of 7:9–17 (*Revelation*, 268). But he offers no strong evidence.

111. Kistemaker (*Revelation*, 407–9) and Thomas (*Revelation 8–22*, 188) are mistaken when they say the number is four. The author counts out one-two-three (vv. 6, 8, 9). To be sure, there is a fourth voice, but that one is different: he issues instruction to John (v. 13), whereas the three were flying in midheaven making announcements to the inhabitants of *ha'aretz* (v. 6).

112. Though the author did not use the definite article, we need to ask, how many eternal gospels could there be? I see that the ESV, NASB, NET, and NRS all translate this "an eternal gospel," whereas the NIV, NKJ, and NLT say "the eternal gospel." Any intermediate student of NT Greek knows that the absence of the definite article does not necessarily indicate indefiniteness. It is grammatically ambiguous; the translation/interpretation decision depends entirely on context.

113. In agreement: Caird, Johnson, Kistemaker, Ladd, MacArthur, Poythress, Thomas. In disagreement: Mounce, Walvoord.

Walvoord seeks to distinguish this "eternal gospel" from "the gospel of grace" and "the gospel of the kingdom" (*Commentary*, 217). Sadly, he offers no comment on v. 7. In the BKC, however he adds, "the message is one of judgment and condemnation. . . . So the 'eternal' message seems to be a message of God's righteousness and judgment rather than a message of salvation" (*Revelation*, 964).

would comply and still be finally damned? That makes no sense. The gospel demand here is to fear and glorify God. This pair of verbs (or verbal ideas) also occurs together in 11:13 and 15:4.[114] It seems to be virtually synonymous with faithful and worshipful repentance.[115]

The second angelic message (Rev 14:8), the doom of Babylon, is the first hint of anticipation of chapters 17–18. (There is a second hint in the seventh bowl, 16:19.) This too seems to be a clue that the macrostructural unit extends on past the bowl judgments. Babylon the Great is indicted for complicity (with the beast) in the intoxication of the nations.

The primary point of the third message (Rev 14:9–11) was described above: followers of the beast are condemned; there will be no more offer of mercy. John's follow-up statement[116] suggests that resistance to the beast's siren seduction depends entirely on persevering, obedient faith in Jesus.

One last observation before leaving the angelic messages: ordinarily we think, "Cursed are those who die." John boldly turns that on its head.[117] There is great eternal hope for those faithful who pay with their

---

Mounce: "It is not the gospel of God's redeeming grace in Christ Jesus but, as the following verse shows, a summons to fear, honor, and worship the Creator" (*Revelation*, 273). What he does not address is how someone might comply with this demand and still fall short of eternal salvation.

Morris: "The words in fact constitute a last appeal for repentance from those about to be judged" (*Revelation*, 179). MacArthur: "As earth's darkest hour approaches, the angel will proclaim the good news that it is not too late. There is still time to repent" (*Revelation 12–22*, 86). Caird: "Whether it has an article or not, the word *euangelion* can only mean 'good news,' and it is improbable that John should have thought of using it in a cynical sense" (*Revelation*, 182).

In all probability, this is an instance of the idiom of anarthrous constuction with monadic [i.e., one of a kind] nouns (see Wallace, *Greek Gammar*, 248–49.) The gospel is one of a kind.

114. "In that hour there was a great earthquake, and a tenth of the city fell; seven thousand people were killed in the earthquake, and the rest were terrified and gave glory to the God of heaven" (Rev 11:13 NASB); "Who will not fear, O Lord, and glorify your name? For you alone are holy" (Rev 15:4 NASB).

115. Thomas: "To give God glory is an idiom of repentance, acknowledging his attributes" (*Revelation 8–22*, 203). The fourth bowl connects glorifying God and repenting (Rev 16:9). See also my comments in the verse-by-verse commentary at Rev 15:4.

116. "Here is the perseverance of the saints who keep the commandments of God and their faith in Jesus" (Rev 14:12).

117. "I heard a voice from heaven, saying, Write, Blessed are the dead who die in the Lord from now on! Yes, says the Spirit, so that they may rest from their labors, for their deeds follow with them" (Rev 14:13).

lives for their refusal to bow to the beast. Their faithfulness will not go unnoticed by their Lord. He will extravagantly share his gracious bounty with their likes. The chapter began with the scene of faithful ones who survived the beast's reign of terror. Thus some of the faithful will survive in their mortality, while others will not. But both are equally blessed in the end.

The chapter concludes with the pair of harvests (Rev 14:14–20). The following table displays the comparison of the various details of the two.

Verses 14–16	Verses 17–20
Son of Man (seated on white cloud)	Angel (from the sanctuary)
Sharp sickle	Sharp sickle
Grain (*therismos*): spring?	Vintage (*ampelos*): autumn
Dried (*exēranthē*)	Blossomed (*hēkmasan*)
Commanding angel: *from the sanctuary*	Altar fire tender
—	Wrath

Both describe a harvest by means of a sharp sickle.[118] The most significant differences are that the first harvester was Messiah (Son of Man) and the second an angel. The first harvest seems to be grain language (*exēranthē*), while the second is grapevine; and the second harvest is called wrath, while the first is not.

The similarities are very strong between this and Joel 3:13 ("Rush forth with the sickle, for the harvest is ripe! Come, stomp the grapes, for the winepress is full!"), which also speaks of grain (*qatzir*, harvest, in the above translation) and vintage harvests by use of a sickle. It also speaks of God delivering his people[119] while destroying his enemies, that is, the enemies of his people.[120]

The author seems then to be speaking of the deliverance of the faithful by the Son of Man, Messiah himself, and the slaughter judgment

118. Of course it must be remembered that farmers in that day did not have a wide assortment of tools. The few they had were undoubtedly as multipurpose as possible.

119. Verse 16, "But the LORD is a refuge for his people and a stronghold to the sons of Israel" (NASB).

120. Verse 2, "I will gather all the nations [*goyim*, gentiles] and bring them down to the valley of Jehoshaphat. Then I will enter into judgment with them there on behalf of my people and my inheritance, Israel, whom they have scattered among the nations; and they have divided up my land" (NASB).

of the wicked by angels.[121] Grapes provide an apropos image of bloody judgment.

The argument of chapter 14 then goes something like this. Chapters 12 and 13 are the foundation of the second part of the body of the book, which is chapters 12–20. In them, the archvillains are introduced with their character and mission. They are pure evil with no redeeming qualities, although the naïve godless—fools!—will be mesmerized by their charm, cleverness, and smooth speech and terrified by their power. Satan is shown to be like Captain Ahab, consumed by his mad passion to destroy Messiah (Rev 12:4). But whereas Messiah is caught up, rescued, to the presence of the King of heaven (12:5), Satan is expelled from heaven (12:9).

In his maniacal rage, Satan will recruit two likeminded inhabitants of *ha'aretz*, one from Rome (Rev 13:1) and one from Israel (13:11), to attempt to destroy Messiah's people, especially the faithful of Israel. They must be crushed, because they are the darlings of Messiah and the only ones who will stubbornly defy his efforts to supplant the Messiah as the dominant Lord of earth.

The impression of chapter 13 is that they hold all the cards; the faithful appear utterly powerless against these tormentors. But the abrupt new scene at the beginning of chapter 14 (vv. 1–5) looks into the future, immediately following their reign of terror, and assures the readers that God shall manage to protect the 144,000 he had sealed, so that in the end it is not antimessiah and that triumvirate but Messiah and his pure loyalists who are the last ones standing in Zion. The cause shall not be extinguished, but the good and rightful King will prevail.[122]

Given that determined and reassuring outcome, the author issues three complementary angelic messages especially for those in the time of antimessiah's tyranny. First the good news: it is not too late, now is the time to "fear God and give him glory." Only in this way can one be saved (Rev 14:6–7). Second, Babylon (which we learn later is the faithless Jerusalem of that day) will not long endure. So it is suicidal folly

---

121. Others see both harvests as judgment of the wicked: Beale, Caird, MacArthur, Thomas, and Walvoord. One might expect to find some suggestion of the rationale for this doubling with no meaningful difference, but it is lacking. Aune, Bauckham, and Ladd agree with me in this respect.

122. These 144,000 then shall be the seed population of his millennial kingdom. It is essentially the same scene as Rev 20:4–6, following the overthrow of the supervillains, though the saints in view there are martyrs from the great tribulation.

to embrace her and to fall in with her agenda (14:8). Third, the entire population of that day is warned not to submit to antimessiah and the false prophet's demand for irrevocable loyalty signified by a kind of brand (14:9; 13:16–18). That brand, 666, shall be deemed by the true King an irrevocable decision to defy and oppose him. To accept that brand is to volunteer for one's eternal death warrant (14:9–11).[123]

All living at the end of the tribulation, at the time of Messiah's great coming, have one of two harvests to which to look forward. Messiah will harvest his own before he leaves the rest to the death angel (Rev 14:14–20). This, along with the opening paragraph (vv. 1–5), will constitute the inauguration of Messiah's millennial reign.[124]

The seven bowls of judgment (chs. 15–16) continue the context of judgment on the beast and his followers (Rev 16:2, 10). That concludes with a link (16:19) to the next section, the judgment of the beast's faux bride, the prostitute Jerusalem (code name Babylon; chs. 17–18), counterfeiting Messiah's impending marriage to the new Jerusalem.

The destruction of all these archvillains of chapters 12–18 is described in reverse order. That of Babylon is first (chs. 17–18); of the beast and false prophet next (Rev 19:20); and then Satan the dragon, in two stages: temporary incarceration (20:1–3), then eternal consignment to the lake of fire (20:7–10). One final group is judged finally at the great white throne: all those not written in the Lamb's book of life (20:11–15).

---

123. Seemingly endless suggestions have been made to decode this number. In all probability, clever ones are being contrived as we speak. The simple fact is, there is not sufficient data—in the text plus history—for anyone today to say with confidence the precise historic referent intended by the author. I think the most certain point we can make is that the author is reassuring the reader that these beasts are not omnipotent: "the number [is that] of a man." The faithful reader is reassured: these beasts cannot triumph ultimately for they are less than divine. I also think that those faithful saints who are alive at the time of the fulfillment of this mark will be at a distinct advantage in the matter of interpreting this 666 prophecy and will be able to make a clear and confident connection between this text and contemporary events and persons. Until then, we must content ourselves with this minimal silhouette. Daniel and Peter both mention prophesying for the benefit of later generations (Dan 12:4, 9–13; 1 Pet 1:10–12).

124. Which is also what all of Matt 24:45—25:46 is about.

Chapters 12–20: The Judgment of the Archvillains, Part 2

Babylon (Chapters 17–18): Faux Bride of the AntiMessiah

Babylon is the code name for the one city singled out in this book for judgment, and the judgment is utter and final. Her crimes are prostitution, murder of saints, and consorting in a mock marriage with the Lamb's archrival, the beast, a.k.a. antimessiah. She is called the great prostitute (Rev 17:1; 19:2) and the mother of prostitutes (17:5). She is called Babylon the great, but that label is qualified as a mystery (*mustērion*, 17:5), hence the suggestion that this seems to be a code name.[125] She is also called the great city (17:18, plus five times in ch. 18). In these two chapters, plus the other verses mentioning this city, the author devotes almost 13 percent of the words of his prophecy.[126] This is a substantial component of the whole, so it bears considerable attention.

The main point of this present section is to develop the teaching of chapters 17–18 and their contribution to the unit of archvillains, chapters 12–20. Toward that end, it is necessary to make the case for the identity of the mysterious city. The identity issue will dominate the first part; the latter part will assume that identity and concentrate on developing the author's main ideas.

The Identity of Babylon the Great

Babylon is Jerusalem, not Rome. The problem with the Roman identity and all others is that the author provides no clues that point in those directions. All the clues in the book point to Jerusalem. Another fatal problem with the Roman identity is that the beast is Rome.[127]

Here's the idea: God is finally going to pour out justice on and against Jerusalem. He is going to bring her centuries-old rebellion to an end. He is going to use gentile forces to devastate her. But first she is

---

125. There is clearly a code name for the great city in Rev 11:8: "Their dead bodies will lie in the street of the great city which mystically is called Sodom and Egypt, where also their Lord was crucified" (NASB). Here too the Jerusalem of the tribulation is represented in extremely derogatory associations.

126. Of the 9851 words in the Greek text (BGT) of Revelation, 1184 are in chs. 17–18 plus the first five verses of ch. 19. Adding to that the words in Rev 11:8; 14:8; and 16:19 (another eighty words) brings the grand total to 1264, which is 12.8 percent of the total word count in the book, more than one eighth of the entire book.

127. Or more precisely, the king of Rome, per Dan 7.

going to engage in one final, most extreme act of spiritual fornication, deliberately selling out her birthright to an antimessiah and thus to pagan nations. She will even become the willing accomplice of the dragon himself. Along with antimessiah, she will commit greater than ever violence against the faithful, the followers of the true Savior of Israel and of the world, Jesus.

There are four leading proposals as to the identity of this Babylon the Great: Rome, Babylon, apostate Christendom, Jerusalem.[128] While their advocates present evidence they believe is substantial, I have decided, based on respectful reading of the authors' terms, that the cases for the first three are actually quite weak, while that for Jerusalem is strong.

Chapter 17 is perhaps the most challenging in Revelation (while ch. 18 is simple). Why the code name? Why so many symbols? Why the complication of heads (vv. 9–11)? That is, couldn't the author have written more simply, clearly? Is this supposed to be understandable?

Following is a discussion of the clues the author provided, some of which are more determinative of the specific identity.

First, this character is represented as both a woman and a city. As a woman. she is the beast's immoral consort, a prostitute, a counterfeit bride, and counterpart to the Lamb's wife. As a city, she is Babylon, the evil counterpart to the holy city, the new Jerusalem. As the beast is the counterfeit messiah and his enemy, so this trollop is the counterpart to the Lamb's pure bride. Both are cities. Both are identified with the rivals competing for the rule of earth. As such, her identity as developed by this author is inextricably intertwined with the beast, and so belongs to this larger division of the book dealing with the judgment of the archvillains.

Counterfeit to Messiah's Bride

The main idea is that this Babylon is the counterfeit bride,[129] as the beast is the counterfeit messiah (i.e., antichrist). The parallel is reinforced and

---

128. Identifications with representative advocates: Rome, too many to start with names; Babylon, MacArthur and Thomas; "the evil world system," Beale (*Revelation*, 843); "the archetypal head of all entrenched worldly resistance to God," Johnson (*Revelation*, 554).

129. As the counterfeit bride, she adorns herself with counterfeit splendor and beauty: "The woman was clothed in purple and scarlet, and adorned with gold and precious stones and pearls, having in her hand a gold cup" (Rev 17:4).

confirmed by John in the nearly identical wording of Rev 17:1 and 21:9 (NASB).

17:1	21:9
Then one of the seven angels who had the seven bowls	Then one of the seven angels who had the seven bowls full of the seven last plagues
came and spoke with me, saying,	came and spoke with me, saying,
Come here, I will show you the judgment of the great harlot who sits on many waters.	Come here, I will show you the bride, the wife of the Lamb.

He follows each of those with

17:3	21:10
And he carried me away in the Spirit into a wilderness;	And he carried me away in the Spirit to a great and high mountain,
and I saw a woman sitting on a scarlet beast.	and showed me the holy city, Jerusalem, coming down out of heaven from God.

Mother of Prostitutes

Another key clue is that she has prostituted herself to such a degree—more than any other—that John would style her "the mother of prostitutes" (Rev 17:5), the absolute worst of all prostitutes of all time.

Both of these make so much better sense if she is Jerusalem than any other suggestion. The irony washes out completely if the counterpart to new Jerusalem (Rev 21:9–10) is Rome or Babylon. Jerusalem, who should have given herself to Jesus, Son of David, instead rejected him—think triumphal entry and crucifixion—and will one day sell herself to history's most treacherous tyrant. In Daniel's prophecy of seventy weeks (Dan 9:24–27) and Zechariah's eleventh chapter about the contrasting shepherds, we are led to expect exactly that. The end-time (great tribulation) people of Jerusalem will sell out to antimessiah. It would not be stunning at all for John to learn that Rome or Babylon would cavort with such a one. But for Jerusalem to do so is disappointing and horrifying in the extreme.

Daniel 9 is very much about "your people and your holy city."[130] At the end of the sixty-ninth week, Messiah is cut off (v. 26); the seventieth week begins with antimessiah, "the prince who is to come,"[131] and "the many"—i.e., Israel—entering into covenant together (v. 27). This, I believe, is to what Paul is referring when he speaks of the apostasy coinciding with the advent of antimessiah (2 Thess 2:3). Rather than some apostasy within Christendom, Israel is choosing antimessiah instead of the real Messiah.

Zechariah 11 is the concluding statement of the burden (*massa'*) that is chapters 9–11. In vv. 4–14, we read of a dramatic oracle of Messiah being rejected by Israel as her shepherd, after which, and as consequential divine punishment, she is savagely abused by the wicked shepherd, antimessiah (vv. 15–17).

As Israel/Judah had been indicted by her ancient prophets for spiritual prostitution and adultery, because she rejected her true husband, Yahweh, and sought protection and provision from nations' armies and nations' gods,[132] so the prostitute of chapters 17–18 will turn to antimessiah for bounty, described in the future tense in Rev 17:4 and the past tense in chapter 18.[133] Whatever evil Rome and Babylon have done in history, it could scarcely be styled as greater prostitution than that of Jerusalem. No one ever prophesied of them the hopeful glories predicted for Jerusalem. Nor have they had anything approaching her divine privileges and opportunities.

This also helps explain John's amazement: "When I saw her, I wondered greatly. And the angel said to me, 'Why do you wonder?'" (Rev 17:6–7). John heightens his own amazement through the wording, literally rendered, "I marveled a great marvel" (*ethaumasa . . . thauma mega*). He sustains the reader's attention there by the follow-up question from the angel, "Why do you marvel (*ethaumasas*)?" How is it amazing, stunning, shocking if Rome or Babylon should appear as described in Rev

---

130. Especially vv. 16, 19, 24; also vv. 18, 26.

131. Cf. Dan 7:8, 11, 20–21, 24–26; 8:23–25.

132. A selective list: Isa 10:24; 30:2–3; 31:1–3; 36:6; Jer 2:17–18; Ezek 17:15; Hos 7:11; 12:1 (all Egypt); Ezek 23:5–9; Hos 5:13; 7:11; 8:9; 12:1 (all Assyria).

133. To be sure, the Greek verbs of 17:4 are perfect tense. But the vision is futuristic, in keeping with the sense of 1:19 and 4:1. The vision of ch. 18 is set in and anticipates the day following the prostitute city's demise, looking back on it.

17:1–5? On the other hand, it is bitterly stunning to see Jerusalem has come to this.[134]

More Clues: Babylon the Great, the Great City

The identity of this mystery prostitute is further confirmed by the designations Babylon the great and the great city. This is actually where the author provides the reader all the clues one would need to break his code.

In chapter 17, after introducing this character as the great prostitute (v. 1), he subsequently identifies her as Babylon the great (v. 5) and the great city (v. 18). These two are also found multiple times in chapter 18.[135] But both were used twice before chapter 17: the great city in Rev 11:8 and 16:19 and Babylon the great in 14:8 and 16:19. So we need to go back and look at those carefully.

In the first of these, Rev 11:8,[136] the author informs us that the two witnesses were killed (by the beast, 11:7) in the great city. Of course this is enigmatic, as the author fully knows. His next expression only heightens the mystery: "which mystically is called Sodom and Egypt." We are still in the dark. Finally, he eliminates all questions by adding, "where also their Lord was crucified."[137] He could not simply come right out and say they died in Jerusalem; that would yield so little rhetorical punch. By his cryptic description, he builds suspense and adds shock value with the code names Sodom and Egypt. When he finally clarifies, he does so by recalling Jerusalem's greatest wickedness: her having murdered her Savior, the ultimate Son of David.

The next time the expression occurs is in Rev 16:19.[138] The likelihood that he would change the referent at all must be judged small. The

---

134. Recall the glory and promise of the days of David and Solomon and even the minor but hopeful renaissance under Zerubbabel, Ezra, and Nehemiah.

135. The great city in Rev 18:10, 16, 18, 19, 21; Babylon in Rev 18:2, 10, 21. The two are linked in a compound designation in Rev 18:10, 21 (as well as 16:19).

136. "Their dead bodies will lie in the street of the great city which mystically is called Sodom and Egypt, where also their Lord was crucified" (NASB).

137. Upon subsequent reads of the whole chapter, one cannot help but notice that the opening scene is also set in Jerusalem (11:1–2). As well, the language of v. 4 is borrowed from Zech 4, in the middle of the eight-vision unit whose first three visions explicitly concern God's zeal for Jerusalem (Zech 1:12, 14, 16–17, 18–21; 2:2–5, 12). The previous discussion of the sixth trumpet develops the issue further.

138. "The great city was split into three parts, and the cities of the nations fell."

notion that he would do so without emphatically clarifying that he was shifting referent, such that no reader could miss it, is simply impossible; that would be a kind of equivocation, especially since he will use it so prominently in chapter 18. It must mean the same city in 16:19 as it did in 11:7. Certainly the burden of proof must be on any interpretation that denies this.[139]

The opening sentence of 16:19 makes reasonable sense when taking the great city to be Jerusalem. "The great city was split into three parts, and the cities of the nations fell." That is, the earthquake of verse 18 will damage the capital of Israel as well as the nearby cities of non-Israel, the gentile nations.[140]

The first time our author spoke of Babylon the great was in Rev 14:8. In the second angelic message of that chapter, we read, "And another angel, a second one, followed, saying, 'Fallen, fallen is Babylon the great, she who has made all the nations drink of the wine of the passion of her immorality'" (NASB). As we saw earlier, that fourteenth chapter provides crucial reassurance that despite the fearsomeness of the dragon and beasts (chs. 12–13), the final outcome is that God will rescue and bless the righteous and defeat and destroy the wicked, including the archvillains and all their followers—including this city. Yet her identity there (14:8) is cryptic. The angel's call is foreboding, ominous, but also suspenseful, as we must wait for clarity as to the identity of this character, the identity of this and the great city.[141] God is not unmindful of her guilt and will not fail to repay her. But John's focused treatment of Babylon and her fall is delayed until he has shown the reader the outpouring of the seven bowls (chs. 15–16).

It is in the last of those bowls in Rev 16:19 that he next uses the expression Babylon the great. Coincidentally, this is also the second time

---

139. Osborne is representative of many. He had already decided that the Babylon of ch. 17 is Rome and so drags that back to this reference (*Revelation*, 598). While he notes that some scholars say it is Jerusalem, based on the connection from Rev 11:7, he simply dismisses that without comment on the problem of the shift from 11:7.

140. As I suggest elsewhere, it is highly probable the author is referring here and in Rev 11:13 to a single earthquake wrecking Jerusalem and damaging other cities, presumably in the same seismic vicinity.

141. This word of the doom of Babylon is at the same time an implicit warning to come out from her, to any that would heed. See Rev 18:4, as well as the OT prophetic warning in Jer 51:6, 45. That in Isa 48:20 is a prophecy of hope that Judah will be redeemed from Babylonian slavery.

he uses the expression the great city.[142] As this verse is central to the final bowl and just three verses before the seventeenth chapter, the statement of doom is evidently intended as transitional into that main section of attention to Babylon.

The bowl judgments section begins, "Then I saw another sign in heaven, great and marvelous, seven angels who had seven plagues, which are the last, because in them the wrath of God is finished" (Rev 15:1 NASB). That is, the last loose ends of opposition to God's kingdom and kingship are about to be dealt with. The object of wrath in the bowls is the beast's followers and his kingdom.[143] The prostitute's role in the beastly program then is also exceedingly wicked in God's eyes, eliciting his righteous judgment.

Again in Rev 16:19, after noting "the great city was split into three parts, and the cities of the nations fell," John next announces, "Babylon the great was remembered before God, to give her the cup of the wine of his fierce wrath." This is a reiteration of the previous warning about Babylon the great (14:8). The reader is now freshly prepared for the ugly and horrifying scenes of chapters 17–18. As well, he is reassured of the justness of the coming judgment. Yet, the city's identity is still cryptic, and it remains so through the first seventeen verses of chapter 17. Not even the fact that the great city and Babylon the great are one and the same has yet been made clear.

However, unless continuity of reference is broken, the ending of chapter 17 resolves the suspense: "The woman whom you saw"—namely, the prostitute, Babylon—"is the great city" (v. 18). A natural reading of the book requires carryover of the previous identification of this expression: you broke the code earlier; now apply it here. Look at the nature of that verse. The next verse (Rev 18:1) begins, "After these things . . ." So 17:18 is a conclusion of the chapter, and it implies that the identity of the city remained cryptic until now. This is the gut punch John recognized earlier (v. 6) but just now gives the reader. This is designed to remove all doubt. But it only does so if the previous identification is carried forward.

142. "The great city was split into three parts, and the cities of the nations fell. Babylon the great was remembered before God, to give her the cup of the wine of his fierce wrath" (NASB).

143. Note especially Rev 16:2, 10.

So we are to read the identification of Rev 17:18 back into the earlier information about the prostitute, yet continue to recognize the dramatic suspense intended by the author in the way he composed his work.[144]

The Problem of Her Dominating the Kings of the Earth

The problem with this identification, however, is the rest of that sentence: "The woman whom you saw is the great city, which reigns over the kings of the earth." One naturally wonders, when did Jerusalem ever reign over earth's kings? We can see much more easily how that fits Rome or even Babylon. But Jerusalem never had greater international sway than in the era of David and Solomon. In the grand scope of history, that could scarcely be styled as reigning over the kings of the earth.

We are then to see this as another of the extraordinary predictions of this book. The day will come, near the end of history as we know it, the penultimate eschaton, the great tribulation (Matt 24:21), when Jerusalem will reign over the kings of the earth. These two chapters depict a flourishing city before and after her collapse. Jerusalem will sell out to the king of Rome, the fourth empire of Dan 2 and 7, and will be richly rewarded for it, such that she will become one of the most powerful cities in that part of the world.

Another Clue: Sitting

Now we need to consider other clues about this prostitute character. Let's go next to the issue of her sitting. In Rev 17:1 we see her sitting on many waters, which later are defined as "peoples and multitudes and nations and tongues" (17:15). In v. 3, we see her sitting on the scarlet beast, whose identity and career are expounded in vv. 8–17. Then in vv. 9–10, she is said to be sitting on seven mountains, which are also the seven heads of the beast, and they are seven kingdoms, five past, one present, and one future. Pretty obvious, right?

A first point to make is that sitting often speaks of being enthroned, that is, being seated on a throne. Many biblical references could be cited (Matt 20:21; Ps 110:1; Rev 4–5—no less than seven times).[145]

---

144. It is hard to say that the author has provided any clues in support of any of the other interpretations.

145. And I believe many are wonderfully enlightened by this, such as Ps 2:4; Heb 1:3, 13; 8:1; 10:12; 12:2.

So now the first sitting makes sense: she sits on—that is, she reigns over—many waters[146] (v. 1), that is, people groups, not just Jews (v. 15), and the kings of the earth (v. 18). Somehow, she dictates to these nations and peoples and kings; she decrees what is proper and what is improper. She threatens those who oppose her with death. We are horrified but not surprised by the volume of blood—innocent blood of God's saints—on her hands (Rev 17:6; 18:24; 19:2). In this regard, she is very much like the beasts (13:7, 15–17).[147] In fact, I think John is indicating that the false prophet, the second beast, is mayor of Jerusalem or prime minister of Israel.

The other two sittings go together and seem hard to imagine actually happening. She sits on the beast (v. 3) and on his heads (vv. 9–10). It seems to go something like this: she holds some kind of sway over him, antichrist, perhaps as a prostitute has seductive power over a client.[148] But as a prostitute is also vulnerable, so here the client (the beast) snaps and turns on her. She has used her wiles to get him to do her bidding. But after a while, he tires of her arrogance and attacks and destroys her (v. 16).

I continue to be pained by teachings on Hebrews that note that the Lord sat down after he completed his priestly ministry, yet fail to notice the extremely important point that his sitting is enthronement at the second highest throne of all, the right hand of his most exalted majesty (esp. Heb 1:3; 8:1; 10:12). That is, that author's concern is to reiterate the teaching that he is not just Priest but King. And the author of Hebrews explicitly directs our attention to Ps 110:1 as early as Heb 1:5.

146. It is also interesting to consider the point of the metaphor of waters here. For a city to be situated on many waters (such as a great river) is a splendid advantage. Abundant water means that agricultural abundance would be relatively easy, making the populace relatively prosperous, which in turn allows for greater leisure, which means educational and cultural and technological advancement.

Babylon was so situated, as was Rome; Jerusalem however was/is not. This does not undermine the present interpretation, however.

147. Let us not forget that the true King on the throne of heaven and his Son, the true Messiah, the true and rightful King of earth, likewise demand submissive loyalty on pain of eternal death (Ps 2:9–12).

148. My mind goes to Samson and Delilah, though she is not called a prostitute (Judg 16).

Connecting This Beast to Daniel 2 and 7

Next, there is good reason to identify this antimessiah beast as prophetic (end-time) Rome, based especially on Dan 2 and 7. This is where John's prophecy gets even more complicated. But I have to dive in.[149]

In Rev 17:7, John says he will explain the mystery of the woman (and of the beast with seven heads and ten horns), but spends the rest of the chapter explaining the heads and horns of the beast. That is, building on the clues of vv. 1–6, all the reader needs further to understand the woman is to understand the beast with heads and horns and her relationship to them.

The beast of Revelation is the composite of a transhistorical phenomenon of Daniel's chapter 2 statue and his chapter 7 cluster of beasts, and he is the final iteration of it. It is going to take some time to develop this, so please be patient. You may want to slow your reading pace for this. First I'll discuss some features in Revelation, then in Daniel.

When John formally introduces the beast in Rev 13:1–10,[150] he first notes the seven heads and ten horns (with ten crowns) and next likens him to leopard-bear-lion (13:1–2). All but the seven heads are clear allusions to the beasts of Dan 7:3–8, all of which were kings/kingdoms.[151]

That transhistorical phenomenon is described in Dan 2 and 7. Daniel declares King Nebuchadnezzar's dream as having been a manlike statue with a fundamental holism about it,[152] yet comprised of four components, each made of progressively less valuable metallic material: gold head, silver chest and arms, bronze abdomen and thighs, iron legs with iron and clay feet and toes (Dan 2:31–33), referring to a succession of kingdoms whose commonality is that they rule over Israel/Jerusalem: Babylon, Medo-Persia, Greece, Rome. In Dan 7, the account of Daniel's

---

149. I have added an appendix on the book of Daniel which you may want to read next before proceeding here.

150. He was previously mentioned in Rev 11:7, but I believe the author means for us to regard ch. 13 as the formal literary introduction to the character. In terms of a stage and spotlight, in ch. 11, he was relatively incidental, at the side of the stage, while the witnesses were primary; in ch. 13, he was summoned to front and center in the spotlight.

151. As are also the metals of the ch. 2 statue.

152. "You, O king, were looking and behold, there was a single great statue; that statue, which was large and of extraordinary splendor, was standing in front of you, and its appearance was awesome" (Dan 2:31 NASB).

dream of four beasts[153] corresponds to Nebuchadnezzar's statue point for point, while embellishing the final manifestation of the fourth empire. Chapter 2 sets the framework of the program of history from Daniel's day to the ultimate, the day of the endless and glorious kingdom of God (Dan 2:44). Chapter 7 builds on that in several ways, but especially in the second and final phase of the fourth empire.

The fact that the fourth empire of chapter 2 is in two distinctive phases (iron legs with iron and clay feet and toes) anticipates the two-part complexity of the fourth beast of chapter 7, the last part being the pen-ultimate, that is, the antimessiah, while the son of man (so, the Messiah, Son of David) and the eternal kingdom are the ultimate.

Watch this about the fourth empire in chapters 2 and 7. In both cases, it is the direct successor to the third; that is, it follows it immedi-ately, just as the third followed the second and the second followed the first with no gaps. Here is why that is significant. The ultimate empire—that is, the stone from chapter 2 and the son of man and saints of chapter 7—directly succeeds only that latter part of the fourth empire. The stone does not smash into the gold, silver, bronze, or even the iron, but the iron and clay (Dan 2:34); likewise, the saints replace the little horn in particular (7:21–22; compare vv. 13–14). Notice also that the little horn of chapter 7 is said to arise after the ten horns (7:24). That is, the visions of chapters 2 and 7 describe consecutive history from Daniel's day into the Roman Empire, but then they both jump historically to the last days before the advent of the glorious King and the kingdom of God. (This jump is also seen in the gap between the sixty-ninth and seventieth weeks in 9:24–27.) That glorious, eternal kingdom is the ultimate; the last days before that are then the penultimate kingdom, the last days of history as we know it.

So here is what the author means for us to understand about the great tribulation. Jerusalem will come to be led by one who will join in alliance with antimessiah, the leader of end-time Rome, who will broker peace (think, peace at any price) for Israel with her neighbors (Dan 9:27). That leader of Israel is the false prophet of Rev 13, who enforces on Israel submissive compliance (or else) toward the antimessiah, the beast, the leader of an end-time iteration of Rome. This alliance will produce a time of unprecedented prosperity, especially for Jerusalem (Rev 17:4; 18:3, 7, 15–16, 19, 22–23). This is when Jerusalem comes to "have a kingdom over

---

153. Actually, that part is just the first scene of his four-scene vision/dream.

[literal translation of *echousa basileian*] the kings of the earth" (17:18). Jerusalem will flaunt her glory, causing the other nations in alliance with antimessiah (the ten horns; 17:17) to become fed up and to ravage her, as described in 17:16 and 18:8. Her demise will be sudden and utter, the judgment of God. And it will be one of the final events of the tribulation, having been central to the seventh bowl (16:19).

Why These Code Names (Great City, Babylon) for Jerusalem?

The Great City

In whose eyes is Jerusalem great? As soon as we ask that question, the answer is obvious: God's. In whose eyes were Rome and Babylon great? Humanity's. The psalms taught the faithful of Israel to regard Jerusalem as "the city of the great King" (Ps 48, especially v. 2) and to hope that "God will establish her forever" (v. 8). Is the book of Revelation about humanity's ideas about the end of history? Is it about humanity's evaluation of good and evil? What is the prophesied final destiny of that city? She is Messiah's darling fiancee, one day to be his bride and wife. That's the greatest city.

Babylon

We have not yet considered the OT prophecies against Babylon, especially in Isa 13–14 and Jer 50–51. We can be sure John was very familiar with the OT, including these major statements, and that he expected his readers (i.e., the faithful rabbi-types responsible to read and explain his work) also to know and understand them.

The big idea there is that God is reassuring Israel that he will not fail to pour out catastrophic, ultimate judgment on literal Babylon. Israel is to take consolation in that. Such is a necessary part of the ultimate redemption of Israel.

The great imperial enemies of Israel in biblical times were Egypt, Assyria, Babylon, and the rest of those identified in Daniel: Medo-Persia, Greece, Rome. Babylon stands out for Jeremiah not only because she was the contemporary enemy, but also because she wreaked the greatest destruction on Israel. She destroyed Jerusalem and the temple and brought an end to the Davidic monarchy, from which Israel has never recovered. Additionally, Babylon was the equal in wickedness and immorality to any of those others. God through the prophet admits in Hab 1:13 that in Babylon he chose as his instrument of judgment on Israel (Judah) a nation more wicked even than Judah.[154]

The Teaching of Chapters 17–18

God chose Jerusalem to be the site of the throne of his glorious earthly vassal, Messiah Jesus. Spectacular prophecies have been made and preserved of the ultimate glories of both King and city. One of the saddest narratives of history is Jerusalem's failure to rise to those lofty hopes and instead to descend to the level of her pagan neighbors and suffer indignity after painful indignity. That failure is directly correlated to her stubborn faithlessness and disobedience to God most extremely manifested in her rejection of his great Son.

As bad as her story has been through the centuries, the worst is yet to come. But it won't last long. God will punish her one last time, and the wicked Jerusalem will never recover. From her ashes, God will bring forth the Jerusalem of the greatest prophecies.

The bitter irony of Rev 17 is that in the penultimate day of history Jerusalem shall become the moral peer of ancient Babylon. She who had the greatest national promise in history—one of her own sons is destined to rule the world—not only spurned his loving overtures, rejecting him and demanding his crucifixion, but will at the end of history as we know it choose history's most villainous tyrant as her lover. That is so much worse than ordinary prostitution: she will become the world's mother of prostitutes.[155]

She must, like Babylon, descend to the lowest depths—her penultimate destiny—and from there be ultimately redeemed and transformed into the most glorious city of the greatest King.

154. "Your eyes are too pure to approve evil, and you can not look on wickedness with favor. Why do you look with favor on those who deal treacherously? Why are you silent when the wicked [Babylon] swallow up those [Judah] more righteous than they?" (Hab 1:13 NASB).

155. If you have never done so, I strongly urge you to do a search of Jerusalem or Zion in the Psalms and OT prophets. It is really important to God, especially in eschatological passages. To call attention to just two instances, Jerusalem is prominent in Zechariah from beginning to end, and Ps 48 predicts magnificent glory commensurate with the glory of God himself.

Appendix 1

The Rider of the First White Horse

Identifying the rider of the white horse in Rev 6:1–2 should not be as difficult as the church has made it. God did not intend that John write in mysterious, arcane terms, not where the meaning is so crucial not just to the generation living in the days when these events will be fulfilled but to all generations. I am convinced that the earliest readers were not confused nor divided in their understanding of John's point in chapter 6.

John left clues. Sure, he wrote in figurative and sometimes coded language. But the faithful[156] recognized the clues and did not manufacture false ones.

I am going to go to some lengths in this section, because the issue is so disputed, and many arguments have been put forward by a number of advocates. I want to begin with what I consider to be very strong, literary points which decisively excel those supposedly supporting alternative views.

Let's consider the clues.

First, this is the first scene following the exchange of the scroll from the Father to the Son, from the King of heaven to the Lion-Lamb. Second, the horse is white. Third, the horse is the first of four colored ones. Fourth, the rider is armed with a bow. Fifth, he has a crown. Sixth, that crown was

---

156. It is slightly misguided to ask, what did the original readers understand? By that we normally mean readers like today's readers: anyone from the masses who might choose to open and read for oneself. That never happened. Nor did original authors ever intend or expect that would ever happen.

In the quest for the sender's (author's) intended meaning, often it is helpful to approach the question from the perspective of the original readers. I submit however that we are to conceive of the author's intended readers in terms of what I call faithful rabbi-types. What I mean by that is that, first of all, as the Hebrew Scriptures (the Old Testament) were entrusted to the custody of the priestly and scribal class, if you will, so were the new Scriptures. Copies were not available to the general populace of the community of the people of God (OT Israel, NT church). Also, the authors of all the Scriptures would never have understood that their writings would be read by the church at large in any medium other than their *hearing* them read aloud by another (which is reflected in Rev 1:3). The ideal then was that those readers would be faithful interpreters and teachers. They were virtual rabbis, even if that is technically anachronistic, trusted custodians expected to preserve the scrolls, study, and teach, much like Ezra, who "devoted himself to the study and observance of the law of the LORD, and to teaching its decrees and laws in Israel" (Ezra 7:10 NIV).

given to him. Seventh, he went out conquering and to conquer. Eighth, this is the first but not the only white horse rider in the book.

Clue #1: "This is the first scene following the exchange of the scroll from the Father to the Son." Nowhere in the preceding section is the reader led to expect the imminent appearance of the antimessiah; on the contrary, one is led to expect the imminent movement of the Savior (Lion-Lamb) from heaven to earth. That is what Rev 1:7, the warnings in chapters 2–3, and the drama of chapter 5 imply.

Clue #2: "The horse is white." White speaks of genuine holiness, purity, new creation. The author uses the word white seventeen times.[157] Aside from this place, every one of those is undisputed: it refers to that which is truly pure, perfected, righteous. This by itself leads to a clear prima facie interpretation and implies a weighty burden of proof on alternative interpretations.

By the time the reader gets to chapter 6, he or she has read the word white seven times (Rev 1:14 [2x]; 2:17; 3:4, 5, 18; 4:4). In these, there is no ambiguity, no debate as to the symbolic value of whiteness. The author has established that value as perfect, whether it is of God himself (1:14) or his saints (2:17; 3:4, 5, 18; 4:4). The reader should be stunned by finding John now using it of wickedness, especially the wickedest man of all history. Nor is white an odd or unlikely symbol for purity; on the contrary, it is intuitively assumed as such.

One objection[158] is a reference to 2 Cor 11:14, where Paul teaches that Satan disguises himself as an angel of light. But the legitimacy of the application of that truth about Satan to this passage is suspect at best: different books, different authors, different issues under discussion. This author speaks multiple times of Satan, and not once does he leave his identity in doubt. Twice, he compounds four and five terms of clarification, even when not seemingly required: "the great dragon . . . the serpent of old who is called the devil and Satan, who deceives the whole world"; "the dragon, the serpent of old, who is the devil and Satan" (Rev 12:9; 20:2).

As well, this author seems to use the color red in a coded way, using it consistently[159] in reference to this same Satan and his associates.

157. Jesus's appearance—Rev 1:14 [2x]; stone—2:17; garments—3:4, 5, 18; 4:4; 6:11; 7:9, 13, 14 (the verb *leukainō*, not the adjective); 19:14; cloud—14:14; horse(s)—19:11, 14; throne—20:11; and of course this one, the white horse, in 6:2.

158. Beale (*Revelation*, 377), speaking for himself and many others.

159. The red horse of Rev 6:4 is the lone exception. In that place, the unit of the

In Rev 12:3, Satan is called a great red (*purros*) dragon, and in 17:3, the antimessiah is described as a red (*kokkonis*, scarlet) beast. The prostitute is also clothed in that same scarlet. One might say, this is their gang's color.

I suggest that this author is constructing his point in a style not unlike a melodrama, in which the villain is clearly recognized by his cape (commonly black on the outside, red inside) and handlebar moustache or, in this case, by his color. That is, whereas the real-world Satan can and does disguise himself, in John's drama, his villain is assigned a stereotypical costume so as to signal the audience clearly. None of his characters is permitted to disguise himself or herself before God's eyes; John is giving his readers God's perspective on these matters.

Clue #3: "The horse is the first of four colored ones." This clue was addressed earlier in the discussion of the first four seals.

Clue #4: "The rider is armed with a bow." That is, he is prepared for battle. One question is whether he is actually dangerous or not. Some have argued that because the author does not also mention arrows, he is militarily powerless.[160] However, if the author were writing in terms of more modern weaponry, what would readers assume if it was stated that he was carrying a gun? I think they would assume bullets; they would not demand the author say the gun was loaded. There is an attested figure of speech known as synecdoche.[161] Furthermore, there is ancient Israelite precedent for using precisely this figure—a bow with no mention of arrows—to speak indisputably of deadly weaponry.[162]

Clue #5: "He has a crown." As already noted, there are several characters in this book with crowns. So this is not an especially disambiguating clue. Still, a couple comments are in order.

There are two different Greek words the author uses that are rightly rendered crown: *stephanos* and *diadēma*. The former is used in Rev 2:10; 3:11; 4:4, 10; 6:2; 9:7; 12:1; 14:14; the latter in 12:3; 13:1; 19:12. BDAG, the premier authoritative NT Greek–English lexicon, defines *stephanos* as wreath, crown,[163] *diadēma* as royal headband, crown. Some argue

---

four colored horses becomes the more controlling factor.

160. MacArthur, *Revelation 1–7*, 179.

161. In which the part is used for the whole. For instance, in "man does not live by bread alone," bread stands not only for bread but for food generally.

162. Isa 13:18; Jer 46:9; 50:29; 51:3; 2 Sam 22:35 (= Ps 18:34).

163. Some suggest a *stephanon* is not a royal crown. But in John 19:2, 5 (from the same author), *stephanon* is the word for the crown of thorns Jesus was made to wear

that the two white horse riders (here and 19:11) must be different characters, since the first wears a stephanos and the latter many diadems (*diadēmata*).[164] And since the character in 19:12 is agreed by all to be the Lord, they insist this rider is another, the antimessiah.[165]

That argument actually defeats itself. The only crown the beast is said to wear is the diadem (Rev 13:1, seven *diadēmata*). If 6:2 is antimessiah, are we to understand that he (this rider and the beast of ch. 13) can wear both kinds of crown, but the true Messiah cannot? Applying their own argument then, this rider in 6:2 cannot be the beast. Furthermore, the Son of Man, a King, wears a *stephanos* in 14:14. Their logic better supports the position that this is Messiah than that it is antimessiah.

Clue #6: "That crown was given to him." Here I am calling attention to a somewhat obscure feature, the verb *was given, edothē* in Greek.[166] This specific form is recognized by virtually all experts to be what is called the divine passive. That is, though there is nothing unusual about the form (aorist passive indicative from *didōmi*), the contextual sense in every instance is that the implied giver is God.

For instance, in Rev 9:1, when an evil angel fell from heaven, "the key of the bottomless pit was given to him." Who but God could give that? Then in vv. 3 and 5 of the same passage, "out of the smoke came locusts upon the earth, and power was given them," and yet "they were not permitted [same verb] to kill anyone, but to torment for five months." Again, who but God could grant such power and then who but God would impose such a restriction?[167]

Of course, while this is a clue, it does little to rule out any of the leading interpretive options. I included this discussion for the sake of completeness.

Clue #7: "He went out conquering and to conquer." This is another of those curious expressions that cry out for special attention. It is such an odd construction. It is not only unlike our way of speaking, it is quite

---

(along with a purple robe), mocking his claim to be a king (v. 3).

164. MacArthur, *Revelation 1–7*, 178.

165. Beckwith, Bruce, Caird, Johnson, Mounce, Swete, Walvoord.

166. It occurs twenty-one times in eighteen verses in Revelation. The complete list of those references is Rev 6:2, 4, 8, 11; 7:2; 8:3; 9:1, 3, 5; 11:1, 2; 13:5, 7, 14, 15; 16:8; 19:8; 20:4.

167. In many of these, God is driving the evil players to carry out his will. "It was given" (*edothē*) to characters in Rev 9:1, 3, 5; 13:5, 7, 14, 15 (nine hits out of twenty-one total).

unlike the known writing style of this author or any NT author. But if we explore the idea of translating this back into Hebrew, it seems perhaps to allow for a construction that is a very common idiom in the OT.[168] A notable example of that idiom is in Gen 2:17, "in the day that you eat from it, you shall surely die." The last four words of this English rendering represent just two words in Hebrew, and they are both forms of the same verb.[169] Crudely, literally, the Hebrew could be rendered "dying, you shall die." The thrust of the idiom is to express a thought with emphasis and certainty, hence the translation above.

It is quite possible John has this idiom in mind, as he is thinking in Hebrew while writing in Greek. In fact, this seems the most probable explanation. In this case, his expression could be rendered as the exclamatory clause "He shall most certainly triumph!" That is something John would say of Jesus, but no others. The point is to confirm to the reader that this rider is the final victor and that this moment is the beginning of the end.

Clue #8: "This is not the only white horse rider in the book." The only other time John mentions white horse/s is in Rev 19:11 and 19:14. The structural location of the Rev 19 horse compared to this one strongly suggests a correspondence and even an inlcusio, a literary framing device to indicate the beginning and ending of a section. That is, chapter 6 marks the beginning of the extended section dealing primarily with earthly judgments, and 19:11 marks the climax of the great conflict of the book. The default or prima facie interpretation must be that the two are to be identified together, rather than that they should be antithetical.

---

168. Deut 15:11: "You shall freely open your hand" (NAS); "make sure you open your hand" (NET); lit., "opening you shall open"; Gen 22:17: "I will surely/greatly bless [barek abarekka, blessing I will bless] you and I will surely/greatly multiply [harbah arbeh, multiplying I will multiply] your seed"; Gen 37:8: "His brothers said to him, 'Are you indeed to reign [hemalōk timlōk] over us? Or are you indeed to rule [mashōl timshōl] over us?'"

How were these translated in the LXX? Gen 22:17 uses the Greek eulogōn eulogēsō, present participle, future indicative; but Gen 2:17 uses thanatō apothaneisthe, noun, future indicative.

One example of a NT quotation of the OT is in Acts 7:34, "I have certainly seen" (idōn eidon, aorist participle, aorist indicative), translating Exod 3:7 (raōh raiti).

So it seems there was no standardized Greek grammatical construction to represent the Hebrew idiom.

Beale agrees this may be the explanation for the odd construction, but still concludes the rider is evil (Revelation, 378).

169. מוֹת תָּמוּת, môt tamût.

Of course, we cannot simply dismiss the possibility of antithesis. But the author would surely take some pains to rule out the otherwise more probable connection—which he did not. Absent strong arguments to the contrary, these two horsemen must be understood to be one and the same.

To summarize: the most definitive clues are the whiteness of the horse and the Hebraic expression "conquering and to conquer." The whiteness factor is so important as to settle the question by itself. The common dismissal of it is eisegetical, not exegetical.

Arguments Raised against This Rider Being the True Messiah

Some argue that because the Lord is armed in Rev 19:15 with a mouth-sword (sharp, *rhomphaia*), the character in 6:2, being armed with a bow, cannot be the same character.[170] This must be judged a weak argument. The point is not the particular weaponry but the fact that, in both cases, the white horse rider is armed for war. As well, in both cases, that warrior turns out to be the ultimate victor. One must also not ignore the fact that in 14:14, the Son of Man wields a sickle for his work of harvesting the earth. We should also note that the beast and false prophet are nowhere described as armed with any weapon: not when they are killing saints in 11:7; 13:7, 15; nor in their final battle in 19:19–20. See also 13:10, where people die by a sword, though that sword is not said to be wielded by the beast.

Some argue that Christ cannot open the seal, then be the one that appears, and then continue to open each of the remaining seals.[171] That is to impose too strict of a realism standard. This is heavenly, spiritual, symbolic imagery. As well, the opener of this seal is the one by whom the kings (and others) feel menaced, such that they hide in caves (Rev 6:15–17).

But the scene of chapters 4–5 indicates the author not only can but did do precisely that. Who is the Lion-Lamb of Rev 5:5–6? No one doubts that it is Jesus. Who is John's guide showing him around this heavenly throne room? The same: Jesus. (For support, see the commentary below at 4:1.)

---

170. MacArthur, *Revelation 1–11*, 178.

171. MacArthur, *Revelation 1–11*, 178.

Some argue that the fact that an angel (one of the four cherubim) gives the command to come precludes the possibility that he who comes is that angel's Lord. The simple answer is that while the voice is that of an angel, the authority behind it is the King on the throne of heaven. The command is virtually an announcement.[172]

Some suggest that the conquering in Rev 6:2 is somehow evil. That thought has no merit whatever. Certainly the author did use this word of victories for the villains in 11:7 and 13:7. But other than those, the author uses this verb only of divine victories.[173] Victory is not a bad thing when God is the victor. So the argument is circular and fails.

To argue that this (the beginning of the seven seals, the beginning of the tribulation) is not the time of the Lord's coming[174] is eisegetical. There is nothing in the statement nor in the near context that confirms or suggests that thought. The only way one can arrive at that conclusion is to import it from someplace else or from one's theological commitments into this place.

That is not to say that theology must never influence interpretation. It is often legitimate to interpret from an author's known theology. Yet a careful reader must also consider the possibility that what he thinks an author believes may not always be so; and an author may, in an instance like this one, be expressing a wrinkle or nuance to his theology, one which is not yet an element of the reader's theology. That is, if we would just consider this passage from a slightly altered perspective, we might be able to learn, grow, and improve our theology.

The interpretation that this is not an individual, Messiah or antimessiah, but a corporate entity or a spirit of conquest suggests that there is something unlikely about identifying various literary characters in Revelation as individuals. We must, however, keep in mind that Daniel explicitly identified the gold head as Nebuchadnezzar himself (Dan 2:37–38). Then in chapter 8, the referent of his goat (that is, its first horn; Dan 8:5–8, 21) is by all accounts Alexander the Great, and the despicable

---

172. Paul may be making the same point in 1 Thess 4:16: "For the Lord himself will descend from heaven with a cry of command, with the voice of an archangel." That commanding call (*keleusmati*) that the Lord should descend is through the voice of an archangel. The one issuing the loud call in Rev 6:1 is one of the four cherubim. We know so little about either of these classes or species of angel that it is certainly possible they may be the same.

173. The complete list of occurrences of the verb *nikaō* (conquer) is Rev 2:7, 11, 17, 26; 3:5, 12, 21 [2x]; 5:5; 6:2 [2x]; 11:7; 12:11; 13:7; 15:2; 17:14; 21:7.

174. MacArthur, *Revelation 1–11*, 178; Walvoord, *Commentary*, 127.

person of Dan 11:21 is Antiochus Epiphanes. It is very common biblically that kings and their kingdoms are referenced somewhat interchangeably.[175] This fact should also be recalled when considering the identities of the beasts.

Many interpreters think that the mission of the next three horsemen being judgment makes it "problematic to view the first rider's mission as redemptive," and so not likely Jesus. Wilson, however, seems to have no problem with the mission of the white horse rider of Rev 19:11 being judgment, not redemption.[176] Besides that, judgment and redemption commonly go together. The redemption of God's faithful saints commonly entails the associated divine activity of punishing the wicked who have been tormenting the saints. The saints of 6:9–11, just a couple seals after the white one, petition their Lord to avenge them on their tormentors as part of their salvation. The great Song of Moses or Song of the Sea, Exod 15:1–18, celebrating the salvation of Israel through the parted Red Sea, focuses mostly on the destruction of the Egyptian forces in the sea.

Finally, assuming for the sake of argument that this rider is Jesus, how does this work out in reality? How does he come seemingly at the beginning of the tribulation (Rev 6:1–2) and come at the end (19:11)? Is it all right for me to say I'm not sure? I have been convinced for several years that both riders are the same. With your forbearance, I will share some of my thoughts.

How does Jesus ride the white horse in Rev 6:1–2 and ride it again in 19:11? Is the author saying that the whole seven-year tribulation is his coming? I think so.

Acts 1:11 says he must return in the same way (manner, fashion, *tropon*) he left. There, his departure must have been gradual; he seems to have ascended relatively slowly. Presumably his ascension endured for at least some seconds. It does not seem that he simply disappeared. He was lifted until he disappeared from view into a cloud (Acts 1:9). However long it took, it was something more than zero and less than infinite moments. Viewed this way, one might consider that his return might not necessarily take exactly the same length of time; it would be close enough if it were also something between instantaneous and eternal. So

---

175. One might also recall how often in Shakespeare a king or other noble will be called by the name of his domain. For instance, King Lear speaks of "the Princes, France and Burgundy" (*King Lear*, act 1, scene 1, line 46) referring to the King of France and the Duke of Burgundy.

176. Wilson, "Revelation," 289.

why couldn't his return take seven years? In God's time, what difference is there between seven seconds and seven years?

As well, his ascension seems to have been in two phases: first visible, then cloudy, no longer visible. So his return should also be in those phases. First there is the real but cloudy phase. Then there is the visible second phase. The rapture of 1 Thess 4:17 is in the clouds, in the first phase. The destruction of the antichrist, at the end of the tribulation, is accomplished by "the brightness [epiphaneia] of his coming [parousia]" (2 Thess 2:8), after he emerges from the cloud, in the second phase.

It makes sense that Jesus the Lamb, upon finally receiving the scroll for which he has been waiting for centuries to possess,[177] would begin embarking on this mission immediately.

Still, the point of the four horses, the first four seals, is more the program of his coming than particular events, plagues, or calamities. As argued elsewhere, the point of the Zechariah visions, and the first and last in particular, those with the colored horses, is God's zealous intention to restore Jerusalem himself. So as also argued above, the seven-sealed scroll is about Jesus coming to claim his kingdom real estate, the land of Israel and its capital, Jerusalem. That requires that he drive out the contaminating inhabitants. A correlative purpose, as he is a just King, is to avenge the wrongful deaths of his faithful followers (fifth seal). That process continues for the entire seven years—during the cloudy phase—giving people who survive the successive catastrophes opportunity after opportunity to repent and embrace him as the rightful King.

I think that fits with the images of God visiting judgment on Israel and gentile nations (as well as visiting Israel for salvation). The Hebrew verb paqad is commonly translated (by NASB) as visit when speaking of God's acts in salvation and as punish when speaking of judgment.[178] It is

177. Connect Mark 13:32 ("But of that day or hour no one knows, not even the angels in heaven, nor the Son, but the Father alone") to Rev 5:1–7.

178. For instance, "who keeps lovingkindness for thousands, who forgives iniquity, transgression and sin; yet he will by no means leave the guilty unpunished, visiting [Qal participle, paqad] the iniquity of fathers on the children and on the grandchildren to the third and fourth generations" (Exod. 34:7). The idea here is that when God punishes Israelites and their descendants for violation of the Sinai law, it is as if he personally pays a call on them. Perhaps it is even more: perhaps he actually visits them when he pours out said covenant punishment.

"You visit [Qal perfect, paqad] the earth and cause it to overflow; you greatly enrich it; the stream of God is full of water; you prepare their grain, for thus you prepare the earth" (Ps. 65:9 NASB). In this case the visitation is for blessing, salvation. The psalmist expresses it as if every time there is agricultural fertility, God has personally visited to

truly God; he the omnipresent one is truly present. Perhaps what John has in mind is that Messiah visits judging punishment on the inhabitants of his land in chapters 6–11, culminating that visitation with his bodily presence (Rev 11:15). Likewise in chapters 12–19, he visits the same judging punishment on those who foolishly, wickedly throw their lots in with antimessiah. This also culimates with his second coming (19:11), the brightness phase. At every stage of this process he was warning survivors, giving genuine opportunity after opportunity to repent, before the last opportunity expires.

---

bless the ground with rain. And again, could he be saying it is more than "as if" God visited?

In neither case, however, did God show up bodily, especially since the incarnation had not yet happened.

A few other references for my readers' consideration are Isa 23:17; Jer 27:22; 29:10; Luke 1:68; 7:16; 19:44; 1 Pet 2:12.

Appendix 2

Overview of Daniel

The author of Revelation draws images and ideas from many parts of the Old Testament. But his dependence on and development of Daniel stands out and calls for special attention. So it seems appropriate to add at least a brief overview of Daniel.

Two key features of the macroscheme of Daniel are the unique structure and the extraordinary attention to the theme of kingship.

A third powerful key to the book is the recognition that its eschatology is more penultimate than ultimate. That is, whereas most of the eschatology of the Old Testament is given to the promise of the glorious ultimate kingdom that God will bring about through Messiah, Daniel's eschatology is especially about the last state of world affairs and especially Israel's place in that day, just before that great, climactic coming—what we now know to be the second coming—of Messiah, the Son of Man.[179] Since Revelation is also more about the penultimate than the ultimate, that may well explain why John found the themes and message of Daniel crucially important to his book.

Structure

The outstanding structural feature of the book of Daniel is the language. Although every other book of the Old Testament is written in Hebrew (with a handful of brief Aramaic intrusions), half of Daniel is in the cousin language, Aramaic. The book begins, as hearers of an Israelite prophet's word should expect, in Hebrew. But Daniel surprises his readers by switching at what is for us Dan 2:4 to Aramaic. He continues in Aramaic until what is for us 8:1. From there to the end, he writes in the customary Hebrew.

Evidently this document was meant to be handled by a bilingual readership. If Aramaic was the lingua franca of the Medo-Persian empire (especially in the West), Hebrew remained the beloved ethnic language

---

179. One other feature, though less profound, is that each of the first nine chapters is a complete, discrete episode whose punch line is at the end. Chapters 10 to 12 consist of a final episode plus an epilogue for the entire book. That final episode (roughly 11:2—12:3) also concludes with a punch line which is its main point.

of only one minority group, Israel. They were the only people bilingual in Hebrew and Aramaic.

As this book was read to the Jewish community, the hearers would have immediately recognized the language shift (at Dan 2:4), and when the reader began what is for us chapter 8, they would just as easily have shifted with the author back to their historic national language, Hebrew. It would of course fall to the custodian, the faithful rabbi-type,[180] to interpret the author's purpose for that unprecedented communication device and factor that into his explanation and exposition of the book's message to the people.

Once the language shift is provisionally identified as the author's structural device of the macroshape of the book,[181] the interpreter must then seek to discover the author's purpose and message according to this framework, a message which must corroborate his initial hypothesis of the macroshape.

It turns out there is an amazing chiasm in that Aramaic block (chs. 2–7). There are remarkable similarities and correspondences between chapters 2 and 7 and between 3 and 6. The point of comparison between chapters 4 and 5 is especially in their contrast as counterpoints.

Literarily, the stories of the fiery furnace (ch. 3) and the lions' den (ch. 6) are virtual duplicates. Think about it: in both of them, righteous, innocent Jews are condemned to death for behaving faithfully in violation of royal decrees and refusing to compromise. In both cases the execution is carried out, and the bullets bounce off. The genuine lethality of the means of execution is then demonstrated on subsequent victims. Finally the king that condemned and carried out the execution of the faithful ones issues a decree demanding respect for the Jews' God, the God of Israel.

These stories seem to be in every meaningful way complete duplicates of each other: chapter 6 adds nothing new or different beyond

---

180. See footnote 156.

181. The alternative structural plan of Daniel held by many commentators—chs. 1–6, stories; chs. 7–12, visions—is based on other literary features, namely, that supposed schema of stories and visions plus the indications of chronological progression up to ch. 6, followed by a new chronological progression beginning at ch. 7. As well, there is a shift from third person narration to first person.

One problem with this approach is that it treats the language shift as virtually accidental, meaningless. In fact, it splits the Aramaic block into its two sections. Another problem is that it yields no big idea for the book other than the very generic idea that Israel's God is superior.

what was already in chapter 3. They are there to make a key point (with perhaps subpoints) and make it emphatically, but also to cry out to the reader for recognition of the duplication and thus to balance each other in the chiasm.

Chapters 2 and 7 likewise exhibit significant duplication. The main idea of both is that the ultimate kingdom of God will come to earth following a sequence of four gentile empires (ruling over Israel) and following immediately a final form of the last empire. But this time, the sequel chapter 7 expands upon the basic framework laid out in chapter 2.

Chapter 2 begins with a very lengthy account of the threat accompanying the king's dream and demand of trustworthy interpretation (Dan 2:1–30). Daniel then discloses both the dream and its interpretation (2:31–45), and the king is more than completely satisfied: he honors Daniel and his God (2:46–49). Key features of the meaning of the dream are that from the time of Nebuchadnezzar until the eternal glorious kingdom—what we mean by heaven, the new creation (v. 44)—there would be four successive empires, represented by the four metals of the statue, and that the fourth would somehow be in two stages (the iron legs followed by the iron and clay feet and toes). Significantly, when the stone kingdom destroys the statue, it does not make direct contact with any part of the statue except the iron and clay (v. 34), the second phase of the fourth empire. The result is that the entire statue is pulverized, annihilated, destroyed forever (vv. 35, 44).

Chapter 7 represents the same four empires, now as lion, bear, leopard, and monstrous beast. The vision is described in verses 1–14 and its interpretation in verses 15–28. As in chapter 2, the fourth empire is represented in two phases. This time, the second phase is in the final little horn of the fourth beast/empire (v. 8), which then becomes the main character in verses 19–26. As with the statue, here also the glorious kingdom brings that final phase of the fourth kingdom, the little horn (vv. 24–26), to its end, and so the entire sequence of beast kingdoms is ended forever. New information that goes beyond the simple sketch in chapter 2 is provided in verses 8, 20–22, and 24–25.

Chapter 7 also introduces the Champion King as "one like a son of man" (vv. 13–14). The significance of that title is that he corresponds to the four beasts (vv. 3–8), taking the reader back to Gen 1, where the earth (*ha'aretz*) was to be ruled by man (*adam*), not the beasts. Man (male and female) was created to be king of earth (vv. 26, 28). But in Gen 3, he effectively forfeited the throne, so that the planet has been topsy-turvy ever since. Satan usurped the vacated throne. Dan 7 then notes that Israel, the promised land (*ha'aretz*), shall be under beast rule (think of the creatures of the fourth and fifth days and the first part of the sixth day of Gen 1), gentile powers, until the second Adam, the son of man, is set loose by the Ancient of Days, the King of heaven, to overthrow that final monster, antimessiah, and free his faithful ones to reign with him (7:27) over the earthly kingdom of Dan 2:44.

As now seen in chapters 2–3, 6–7, the strong probability of an author-intended chiasm encourages us to consider some similar correspondence between chapters 4 and 5. There we have the stories of Nebuchadnezzar's pride, insanity, humility, and faithful praise juxtaposed to Belshazzar's blasphemous pride and demise. Where Nebuchadnezzar is last seen humble, restored to royal glory and praising the God of Israel (Dan 4:34–37), Belshazzar is last seen[182] slain and the Babylonian kingdom overthrown (5:30–31). One humbled himself before Daniel's God and was exalted; the other exalted himself against Daniel's God and was humbled in the extreme.[183]

Significantly, the author includes statements in chapter 5 that connect back to chapter 4, reinforcing the literary companionship of the two. In Dan 5:18–21, the author recalls in words of Daniel the events described in chapter 4, noting especially Nebuchadnezzar's faithful humility, and rebukes the present king for his refusal likewise to humble himself (vv. 22–23). Daniel effectively rebukes him, "You should have known better; you should have learned this crucial lesson from the life of Nebuchadnezzar."

Now we are ready to synthesize the big, complex idea of chapters 2 to 7. The extremities, chapters 2 and 7, set the program of the section and of the entire book, which is about the schema of the course of history leading to its climax, the ultimate glorious kingdom. Neither chapter 2 nor 7 directs significant attention toward the first, second, or third empires. They simply indicate that there must be these empires. The attention on the fourth empire and especially its final phase indicates the author's primary concern for the penultimate day-era of history. The outstanding feature of that day will be the antimessiah, the most tyrannical despot

---

182. Remember that Daniel puts the main point of chapter episodes at the end.

183. "Everyone who exalts himself will be humbled, and he who humbles himself will be exalted" (Luke 14:11; 18:14 NASB). This principle is repeated several times in the OT and NT.

of history, but whose notoriety is specifically defined by his disposition toward Israel.

The inner chapters (4, 5) assure the faithful reader that in every generation, including that penultimate one, Israel's God is supreme; all the gentile emperors must humbly bow to Israel's God or suffer destruction. Of course, there is also the implied exhortation to every generation of Israelite readers to renew and redouble their allegiance to the true eternal King who specially chose her.

In the mediating chapters (3, 6), the heroes stand for the faithful of Israel during the generations of inversion (when beasts run the planet, and Israel is the servant, not the master). God is promising that he will not allow the genocidal wrath of man[184] to extinguish his people.

Chapters 8 to 12 seem also to be a chiasm, with chapters 8 and 10–12 the extremities and 9 the vertex. The climaxes of chapters 8 and 11 are the same: focus on the antimessiah, the penultimate world ruler (King Jesus being the ultimate). Chapter 9, the midpoint, delineates something of a calendar for the course of history until the end. A key feature of that calendar is that while a definite number of years is predicted (seventy times seven), there is also an indefinite period of time between the sixty-ninth and seventieth weeks, putting that calendar on pause between Messiah's first coming, at the end of the sixty-ninth (v. 26), and the advent of antimessiah on the world stage. Once the calendar is restarted, however (v. 27), the penultimate begins and continues for the final week (seven years), before the great hope, the ultimate kingdom, arrives. But those seven are a resumption of the 490, which were about the course of the four empires that God raised up to punish and purge Israel.[185] So now we know what the two phases of the fourth empire were about: the first phase extended through the sixty-ninth week; the second phase is manifested in the seventieth week.

Chapter 8 is about Antiochus IV Epiphanes;[186] but he is just there to serve as a type of the final archvillain, the little horn of chapter 7, the

184. And Satan, as seen in Rev 12.

185. Thus forming the second Israel of Rom 9:6, which is also the Israel of God of Gal 6:16. But when I say second, I refer to the Greek word order, which the NASB reverses. Somewhat literally, "not all the ones from Israel are Israel." That is, not all biological descendants of Jacob/Israel are among the ultimate chosen ones to populate the redeemed nation.

186. The Greek (Seleucid) king, the final king of the bronze of Dan 2, the leopard of Dan 7, whose domain included Israel, 175–165 BC.

one commonly known as antimessiah or antichrist. The grand vision of chapter 11 returns to Antiochus in verses 21–35, who then morphs into antimessiah in verses 36–45.

The final chiasm, chapters 8–12, then focuses on the penultimate world ruler and the timeline for the course of the four empires.

Before we leave this section, we must address what purpose the language shift serves. It would be ludicrous to suggest that part of the book is to be read by one audience and the rest by another. It would be insulting to the divine Author, not to mention the human author, to say that it was a random accident. The entire book is for a single readership, the only readership of that day that was bilingual in Hebrew and Aramaic. It reinforces the point that until the coming of the Son of Man, Israel will be forced to live in a gentile-dominated world, whereas the ideal world is the reverse: Israel should be the head nation. The ultimate state of the world is still what all the previous prophets have said.

The King-Kingdom Theme

The words king(s) and kingdom(s) occur 235 times in Daniel. I hope you are stunned. Related vocabulary pushes the total number of words in Daniel that directly relate to the theme to more than 300.[187] Simple arithmetic yields a quotient of an average of twenty-five occurrences of the vocabulary in every chapter.[188]

The book is about the great contest of history for the dominion over *ha'aretz*, earth and the promised land. As long as the throne of earth is occupied by anyone other than its rightful Lord, the circumstances of history and people will be less than ideal.

Another fact that needs to be brought out is the kingship of God is fundamental to the special revelation of the nature of God. This needs to be stated, because it was much more important and implicit to the ancients than we appreciate. Undoubtedly, our life under non-monarchic

---

187. The attention in Daniel to kings and kingdoms far exceeds that in all other books of the Bible. In Daniel, king*: 235x; reign, Aramaic: 2x; reign/rule, Hebrew *malkut, malak*: 4x; Heb *shaphat*: 2x; Heb *mashal*: 2x; royal (*m-l-k*): 4x (Heb, 1x; Aram, 3x); rule/rule, Aram *shalit*: 11x; dominion, *shaltan, mashal*, domain: 16x; throne, Aram: 3x; sit/seat (in the sense, enthroned), Aram: 2x; prince, *sar*: 11x; prince, *nagid*: 3x; queen, Aram: 2x.

188. Other books in which it is a primary theme include (in addition to the obvious Samuel, Kings, and Chronicles) Psalms, Matthew, Luke, Acts, Revelation.

governments has led to a widespread demeaning view of monarchy as a quaint relic from a primitive time of human history. But there was only one view of God from the garden of Eden through New Testament times and revelation, and that is that he is King of heaven and earth. That is, God has revealed himself to his prophets and people as that King. That is how he wants his people to see him and relate to him. The great visions of Isa 6, and Ezek 1, and Rev 4 attest emphatically to the same.

The Message of Daniel

The big idea of the book of Daniel is first to tacitly affirm the previous prophecies[189] of ultimate messianic glory for Israel. This it does especially by implying that the prophecies are given as truth.

To those, it adds information that will be especially valuable to those saints living through the worst of times (the great tribulation, Matt 24:21), when the antimessiah is acting in accord with the will of Satan, attempting to exterminate the woman, Israel, who birthed the Messiah (Rev 12–13). By reading Daniel and seeing that point after point has been fulfilled throughout history, they will be buoyed by the evident truth of the prophecies and thus also the hope that the worst of times will only last for half a week, that is, for a relatively short period of time.[190] They will be able to compare the predictions of the profile of antimessiah to his actual character and career, further confirming their recognition that their redemption is drawing near (Luke 21:28).[191]

---

189. Daniel could not have been written in its final form before about 536, the last datable event in the book being the final vision in the third year of Cyrus (Dan 10:1). It certainly is not from the Maccabean era, as far too many scholars assert without evidence. Nor is the book from the dates of the episodes.

So the author and his earliest readers were already knowledgeable of most of the OT, not to mention the historical fact of the fall of the Babylonian kingdom. Thus the first transition predicted in chs. 2 and 7 was already realized history when the book was finished.

190. Note that Revelation speaks five times of a period of three and a half years, all in chs. 11–13: 11:2, 3; 12:6, 14; 13:5.

191. The book is obviously for the author's generation, Jews in the early years after Medo-Persia overthrew Babylon. But it is also for every generation since. It is then fascinating to contemplate how the faithful would rightly have read it in the next generations after Alexander and after Antiochus and after the rise of Rome. But this is not the place to explore those readings.

Thus it also serves as encouragement and exhortation to every generation to be faithful to the Yahweh of Israel and the Bible. All must and shall bow to him either as loyal servants or as cringing victims of his righteous wrath.

Appendix 3

Armageddon (Rev 16:16): If Not Megiddo, Then What?

> And they gathered them together to the place which in Hebrew is called Har-Magedon. (NASB)
>
> καὶ συνήγαγεν αὐτοὺς εἰς τὸν τόπον τὸν καλούμενον Ἑβραϊστὶ Ἁρμαγεδών.

ALL RECOGNIZE THE WORD *harmagedōn* is a transliteration of the Hebrew *har*, mountain, plus something (-*magedōn*).

Traditional view: Mount Megiddo
Alternate view: Mountain of Assembly

Problems with the traditional view:

1. Megiddo is not a mountain. At most it is a *tel* (hill). The OT refers to Megiddo not as a mountain but a plain (2 Chron 35:22; Zech 12:11), which is vastly different from a mountain.

2. Aside from this one statement, Megiddo is otherwise of no significance prophetically.[192]

3. The original spelling in Rev 16—Armagedon rather than Armageddon—does not quite match what we would expect (one *d* instead of two).

To take the disputed root (*m-g-d*) back to the Hebrew presents a complication, in that there are two different letters in the Hebrew alphabet which could be represented in Greek by the *gamma*: the third letter, *gimel*, or the sixteenth letter, *ayin*. The *g* sound is commonly recognized as being the rough equivalent of *gimel*, and that is the normal transliteration for it. The *ayin*, however, is often represented in transliteration by a sort of apostrophe, and its pronunciation is a sound we don't have in English or other Western languages, described by linguists (phonologists) as pharyngeal. The cities we know as Gaza and Gomorrah have as their first

---

192. The name occurs in Josh 12:21; 17:11; Judg 1:27; 5:19; 1 Kgs 4:12; 9:15, 27; 2 Kgs 23:29–30; 1 Chron 7:29; 2 Chron 35:22; Zech 12:11.

letter not the *gimel* but this *ayin*. So in some words, at least, it has con-ventionally been decided that the closest English letter to the *ayin* is *g*.[193]

To transliterate the Greek back to Hebrew using the *ayin* yields a word completely different from Megiddo, the word assembly.[194] If that is the case, then what John wrote is "the Mountain of Assembly." It turns out that that is an expression that the prophet Isaiah used in a remarkably apt prophecy, Isa 14:13. There Babylon, the Satan-like character, says,

> I will ascend to heaven;
>   I will raise my throne above the stars of God,
> And I will sit on the *mount of assembly* (בְּהַר־מוֹעֵד, *har môʿed*)
>   In the recesses of the north.[195]

This seems to allude to a common ancient Near Eastern mytho-logical concept of a mountain where the gods gather and plan. This light bearer character (Lucifer, v. 12[196]) aspires to domination there, in heaven. Having been kicked out of heaven (Rev 12:7–9), however, his mount of assembly is now on earth rather than in heaven.

In this case, Megiddo is not in view at all, nor does a battle take place at this time. It would be anticlimactic to have the battle of the great day of God Almighty, which surely must be seen as ultimate, during the penul-timate bowl. Terms in the seventh bowl speak of ultimacy—*gegonen* (it is done), the plagues—while also transitioning to the judgment of Babylon.

Could it be indicating that the judgment of Babylon is located at the very end? Or perhaps that dealing with Babylon is complementary to the bowls: judgment on the followers of the beast? Of course these judg-ments are warning, not final. They still leave survivors and afford them opportunity to repent. The battles in Rev 19:19–21 and 20:7–10 leave no enemy survivors.

The sixth bowl seems instead to be the summoning of the kings of the earth (no armies are mentioned here) to a council of war (rather than to war or battle itself) with the anti-trinity of the dragon, the beast, and

193. The LXX also transliterates the first letter of those two city names with *gamma*.

194. A problem with this view is the ending of John's word, *-ōn*. But Hebrew often added endings requiring strange explanations and perhaps sometimes defying mod-ern explanation.

195. Isa 14:4–21 is the prophecy that Judah's later destroyer, Babylon, will eventu-ally come to an end. This is in the form of a taunt that the redeemed and regathered Israel would one day raise over the humbled king of Babylon.

196. This is still Babylon, in her king. But the prophet likens him to the leader of the rebel angels, Lucifer, the light bearer.

the false prophet (Rev 16:13). Verse 15 assures the faithful reader that despite this ominous preparation, the Lord will catch them unprepared, naked.[197]

---

197. See further comment in the verse-by-verse commentary below.

PART 2: OUTLINES

Simple Outline

I. Prologue 1:1–8

II. The things which you have seen 1:9–19

III. The things which are 1:20—3:22

IV. The things which shall take place after these things 4–22

    A. The Lamb-King's commissioning in heaven 4–5

    B. The Lamb-King's coming to earth 6–20

        1. Reclaiming his rightful domain, earth: eviction of the defiling tenants of his earth/land (seals and trumpets) 6–11

        2. Wrath directed against archvillains 12–20

    C. The glorious, eternal reign of Father and Son: new heaven and earth 21:1—22:5

V. Epilogue: the imminence of his coming 22:6–21

Complete Outline

I. Prologue 1:1–8

    A. Introduction 1:1–3

        1. Description of the document 1:1–2

        2. Blessing on the obedient reader 1:3

    B. Salutation 1:4–6

        1. The parties 1:4a

2. Greeting 1:4b–6

   a) Well wishes from Trinity 1:4b–5a

   b) Doxology 1:5b–6

C. Summary of the message: announcement of the coming One 1:7–8

II. The things which you have seen 1:9–19

  A. Introduction 1:9–11

    1. The circumstances 1:9–10

    2. The initial directive 1:11

  B. The vision 1:12–18

    1. The vision proper 1:12–16

    2. John's reflexive fear 1:17a

    3. The Lord's consolation: he is life itself 1:17b–18

  C. The command to write: the structural plan 1:19

III. The things which are 1:20—3

  A. Introduction 1:20

  B. Ephesus 2:1–7

    1. Destination 2:1a

    2. Identity of sender: holds the stars, walks among lamps 2:1b

    3. Commendation 2:2–3

    4. Rebuke 2:4

    5. Exhortation 2:5

    6. Second commendation 2:6

    7. Promise 2:7

  C. Smyrna 2:8–11

    1. Destination 2:8a

    2. Identity of sender: first and last, resurrected one 2:8b

    3. Commendation 2:9

    4. Exhortation 2:10

    5. Promise 2:11

  D. Pergamum 2:12–17

    1. Destination 2:12a

    2. Identity of sender: wields sword 2:12b

    3. Commendation 2:13

        4. Rebuke 2:14–15

        5. Exhortation 2:16

        6. Promise 2:17

    E. Thyatira 2:18–29

        1. Destination 2:18a

        2. Identity of sender: Son of God, fiery eyes, bronze feet 2:18b

        3. Commendation 2:19

        4. Rebuke 2:20–23

        5. Exhortation 2:24–25

        6. Promise 2:26–29

    F. Sardis 3:1–6

        1. Destination 3:1a

        2. Identity of sender: holds seven spirits, stars 3:1b

        3. Rebuke 3:1c

        4. Exhortation 3:2–3

        5. Commendation 3:4

        6. Promise 3:5–6

    G. Philadelphia 3:7–13

        1. Destination 3:7a

        2. Identity of sender: holy, true, holds key 3:7b

        3. Commendation 3:8

        4. First promises 3:9–10

        5. Exhortation 3:11

        6. Summary promise 3:12–13

    H. Laodicea 3:14–22

        1. Destination 3:14a

        2. Identity of sender: faithful and true foundation of creation
           3:14b

        3. Rebuke 3:15–17

        4. Exhortation 3:18–19

        5. Promise 3:20–22

IV. The things which shall take place after these things 4–22

    A. The Lamb-King's commissioning in heaven 4–5

        1. Vision of heaven's throne room 4

            a) Introduction: John's arrival in vision 4:1

b) Description of the majestic scene 4:2–8a

(1) The King 4:2–3

(2) His entourage 4:4–8a

(a) Twenty-four elders 4:4

(b) Holy Spirit 4:5

(c) Four living beings 4:6–8a

c) Praise of the King 4:8b–11

2. Vision of the seven-sealed scroll and the Lamb 5:1–12

a) The scene 5:1–7

(1) Introduction of the scroll 5:1

(2) Dramatic introduction of the Lamb 5:2–6

(3) The Lamb's claim of the scroll 5:7

b) Praise of the Lamb 5:8–12

(1) By the living beings and elders 5:8–10

(2) By innumerable angels 5:11–12

3. Summary: praise of the King and the Lamb by all creation 5:13–14

B. The Lamb-King's coming to earth 6–20

1. Reclaiming his rightful domain, earth: eviction of the defiling tenants of his earth/land (seals and trumpets) 6–11

a) Six seals 6–7

(1) The first four seals: colored horses 6:1–8

(a) White: the ultimate conqueror 6:1–2

(b) Red: sword, killing each other 6:3–4

(c) Black: damage to grain but not trees 6:5–6

(d) Pale green: death by sword, famine, pestilence, wild beasts 6:7–8

(2) Fifth seal: martyrs under altar 6:9–11

(3) Sixth seal: cosmic disturbances, divine wrath 6:12–17

(a) The phenomena 6:12–14

(b) The terror upon all 6:15–17

(4) Interlude 7

(a) The command to pause 7:1–3

(b) Sealing of 144,000 Israelites 7:4–8

(c) Multitude of martyred saints in heaven 7:9–17

(i) The vision 7:9–12

(ii) Their identity 7:13–14

(iii) Their blessing 7:15–17

b) Seventh seal: seven trumpets 8–11

   (1) Introduction 8:1–6

      (a) Seventh seal: silence, seven trumpets 8:1–2

      (b) The censer of prayers thrown to earth 8:3–5

      (c) The seven trumpeters prepared 8:6

   (2) The first four trumpets 8:7–12

      (a) First: one third of land burned 8:7

      (b) Second: one third of sea polluted 8:8–9

      (c) Third: one third of fresh waters polluted 8:10–11

      (d) Fourth: one third of heavenly bodies darkened 8:12

   (3) Introduction to last three trumpets (woes) 8:13

   (4) Fifth trumpet: locust-scorpions from the pit, non-mortal wounds 9:1–12

      (a) Their advent 9:1–3

      (b) Their commission 9:4–6

      (c) Their description 9:7–11

      (d) Summary: end of first woe 9:12

   (5) Sixth trumpet: last chance for repentance 9:13—11:14

      (a) Army from East 9:13–21

         (i) Their release 9:13–15

         (ii) Their deadly threat 9:16–19

         (iii) Survivors' refusal to repent 9:20–21

      (b) The mighty angel and the little scroll 10

         (i) Introduction 10:1–4

         (ii) The angel's message: the end is near 10:5–7

         (iii) John's filling with that message 10:8–11

      (c) The two witnesses 11:1–13

         (i) Measurement of the temple 11:1–2

         (ii) Ministry of the two 11:3–6

         (iii) Death of the two 11:7–10

         (iv) Resurrection of the two 11:11–12

         (v) Earthquake: survivors' repentance 11:13

(d) Summary: end of second woe 11:14

(6) Seventh trumpet: second coming; mission accomplished: the kingdom of earth is won! 11:15–19

2. Wrath directed against archvillains 12–20

a) Dragon introduced 12

(1) The woman and the dragon 12:1–6

(a) The woman in labor 12:1–2

(b) The dragon poised to devour the child 12:3–4

(c) Mother and child delivered 12:5–6

(2) The dragon's defeat in heaven 12:7–12

(a) His expulsion 12:7–9

(b) Anticipation of God's final victory 12:10–12

(3) The dragon's persecution of the woman 12:13–17

(a) His frustrated efforts against her 12:13–16

(b) His redirected efforts against her faithful offspring 12:17

b) Beasts introduced 13

(1) The beast from the sea 13:1–10

(a) His description 13:1–3a

(b) His blasphemous rule 13:3b–8

(i) Amazement and adoration of inhabitants of *ha'aretz* 13:3b–4

(ii) His brazen blasphemies 13:5–6

(iii) His deadly, intolerant rule 13:7–8

(c) Warning to the reader 13:9–10

(2) The beast from the earth/land 13:11–18

(a) His description 13:11

(b) His enforcement of loyalty to the first beast 13:12–17

(c) Warning to the wise: 666 13:18

c) Preview and warnings 14

(1) The 144,000 with the Lamb on Mount Zion 14:1–5

(a) Their position 14:1

(b) Their heavenly song 14:2–3

(c) Their purity 14:4–5

(2) Three angelic messages 14:6–11
    (a) First: eternal gospel 14:6–7
    (b) Second: Babylon's fall 14:8
    (c) Third: doom of the beast's followers 14:9–11
(3) Blessing of the faithful even in death 14:12–13
(4) The harvests of the earth 14:14–20
    (a) First harvest 14:14–16
    (b) Second harvest 14:17–20
d) Seven bowls 15–16
  (1) Preparation 15:1–8
    (a) Introduction 15:1
    (b) Tribulation martyrs' song 15:2–4
    (c) Seven angels' reception of bowls 15:5–8
  (2) Command to pour them out 16:1
  (3) First bowl: sores on the beast's subjects on earth 16:2
  (4) Second bowl: death in the sea 16:3
  (5) Third bowl: bloody rivers and springs 16:4–7
    (a) The plague 16:4
    (b) Affirmation of God's right to judge 16:5–7
  (6) Fourth bowl: scorching sun 16:8–9
    (a) The plague 16:8
    (b) The response: blasphemy 16:9
  (7) Fifth bowl: darkness and pain on the beast's kingdom
    16:10–11
    (a) The plague 16:10
    (b) The response: blasphemy 16:11
  (8) Sixth bowl: dried Euphrates, Armageddon 16:12–16
    (a) The river dried 16:12
    (b) The kings summoned (war preparations) 16:13–16
  (9) Seventh bowl: earthquake and hail 16:17–21
    (a) Report of the finality 16:17
    (b) The earthquake: God punishing Jerusalem (Baby-
    lon) finally 16:18–20
    (c) The hail 16:21

e) Wrath directed against the counterfeit bride 17–18
  (1) Babylon's rise and fall 17
    (a) Introduction to her judgment 17:1–2
    (b) Description of the prostitute 17:3–6
      (i) Her mount: the beast 17:3
      (ii) Her adornment 17:4
      (iii) Her name 17:5
      (iv) Her drunkenness 17:6a
      (v) Parenthesis: John's amazement 17:6b
    (c) Signification of the beast 17:7–17
      (i) Introduction 17:7–8
      (ii) The seven heads 17:9–11
      (iii) The ten horns 17:12–17
        (α) Submission to the beast 17:12–13
        (β) Opposition to, and destruction by, the Lamb
          17:14
        (γ) Destruction of the prostitute 17:15–17
    (d) Positive identity of the prostitute: the great city
      17:18
  (2) Her fall 18:1–24
    (a) The announcement of her fall 18:1–3
    (b) The warning to escape her fate 18:4–8
    (c) The world's lament over her fall 18:9–19
      (i) Kings of the earth 18:9–10
      (ii) Merchants 18:11–19
    (d) The symbolism of her termination 18:20–24
f) The two woman-cities contrasted 19:1–10
  (1) Heaven's joy over Babylon's judgment 19:1–5
  (2) Heaven's joy over the Lamb's bride's readiness for
    the wedding 19:6–9
  (3) John's misguided exuberance 19:10
g) The Lamb's triumphant return 19:11—20:6
  (1) His arrival described 19:11–16
  (2) The battle 19:17–21
    (a) Invitation to the bird feast 19:17–18
    (b) The enemy forces arrayed 19:19

(c) The enemy forces destroyed 19:20–21

    (i) Beast and false prophet summarily dispatched to Hell 19:20

    (ii) Enemy armies slaughtered, birds feasting 19:21

  (3) Lamb's thousand-year reign 20:1–6

    (a) Satan's incarceration 20:1–3

    (b) Blessed reign of resurrected saints with the Lamb 20:4–6

h) Satan's end 20:7–10

  (1) Final rebellion 20:7–9

  (2) Final destruction 20:10

i) Final judgment of all enemies: great white throne 20:11–15

C. The glorious, eternal reign of Father and Son: new heaven and earth 21:1—22:5

  1. The new creation 21:1–8

    a) The vision: all-new heaven, earth, Jerusalem 21:1–2

    b) Angelic announcement: divine cohabitation, end of sorrows 21:3–4

    c) Statement of the King (God the Father) himself 21:5–8

      (1) It is certain 21:5

      (2) Free, satisfying water 21:6

      (3) "I claim the overcomers" 21:7

      (4) "I dispatch the wicked" 21:8

  2. The new Jerusalem 21:9—22:5

    a) Introduction: descending from heaven, glorious like precious stone 21:9–11

    b) Its walls, gates, and foundation stones 21:12–21

      (1) The gates (tribes of Israel's names) and foundations stones (apostles' names) 21:12–14

      (2) Measurements of its walls 21:15–17

      (3) Materials of the walls, gates, and foundation stones 21:18–21

    c) Its luminary and temple: God himself 21:22—22:5

      (1) Summary 21:22–23

      (2) Its international renown without contamination 21:24–27

(3) Its river of water of life and tree of life 22:1–2

(4) The blessedness of the King's servants 22:3–5

V. Epilogue: the imminence of his coming 22:6–21

    A. Review of the main message: Jesus is coming soon 22:6–7

    B. John's misguided exuberance again 22:8–9

    C. Discrimination between righteous and unrighteous 22:10–15

    D. Final invitation 22:16–17

    E. Warning against tampering with the book 22:18–19

    F. Final announcement of the Lamb's coming soon 22:20

    G. Benediction 22:21

PART 3: ARGUMENT

SEVERAL POINTS SHOULD BE made at the outset of the study of Revelation. First, it ends with the description of the new heaven and earth and Jerusalem (Rev 21:1ff), the eternal reign of God the Father and Son (shared with saints; 22:3–5), and a threefold announcement (22:7, 12, 20) by the Lord Jesus himself of his soon coming (echoed by invitations to the reader, v. 17, and John's prayer, v. 20). All that is immediately preceded by description of the final judgment of the devil and all the wicked (20:11–15), which itself is preceded by ultimate battles. Could anything be more obvious than that this book is about the conclusion of history and its giving way to eternity? Along those lines, the book seems to achieve its climax in the account of the coming of the Lord in 19:11ff. These factors point toward the conclusion that the book means to address and explain ultimate issues of history as we know it.

Such ultimate concerns could then be more precisely described as ultimate and penultimate. Ultimate should include final judgment and eternal dispositions of the righteous and the wicked, with special attention to the glories of eternal life for the redeemed. God has seen fit also to reveal some details of events and characters that will dominate the world scene in the last days just before the ultimate (such as antichrist and the great tribulation).[1]

---

1. Eschatology is the branch of systematic theology that is about last things. But it turns out last things consist of what could be called ultimate last things and penultimate last things, last-last things and next-to-last things. The ultimate is when the great promises and our great hope are actually fulfilled. Those promises are about our ultimate salvation. They also include the crucial component of judgment against the stubborn, incorrigible enemies of God and of his people. That is the day of the LORD as prophesied in both OT and NT. It is God's day of climactic visitation: his coming to earth to bring perfect justice against wickedness and perfect deliverance of the chosen saints.

But there is also penultimate end times prophecy declaring truth about events and

His coming is the great climax of the whole program of the first creation and is the end of the penultimate, the beginning of the ultimate. His coming inaugurates the rollout of all the concluding chain of events determined to wrap up this creation before the full delivery of the new creation, the new heaven and earth, the glorious eternal kingdom.

Second, two themes predominate: coming, which is especially about the Lord's second coming, and king/kingdom. A next tier of themes includes judgment, worship, repentance, conquest, and witness.[2]

The book is about the same thing the prior sixty-five canonical books are: the coming of the Savior, the seed of the woman, of Abraham, of David. He comes to repair the damage done to his precious creation and to effect the redemption of his chosen people. The fact that he comes twice in no way minimizes the importance of the fact that the coming described in Revelation must be that which has come to be known as the second coming. It is eminently appropriate that canonical revelation would conclude with a final information dump about the most important event in history since creation and the first coming. That this book is centrally about the Lord's second coming is prominently indicated by the author at the beginning and ending, is developed throughout all the major sections, and is itself the book's climax.

This author consistently represents this coming One as King. So he comes to claim his rightful domain, earth, which has been corrupted by the abusive pretender and usurper, Satan, and his followers ever since Eden. The ruling situation is that the throne of heaven is and has always been securely maintained by God the Father, the King of heaven. But earth, created to be ruled by humanity, has been topsy-turvy since the fall. This book is about the final resolution of that ultimate conflict of the ages, with earth in the end being remade and ruled by heaven's chosen vassal, God the Son, the Son of Man.

---

persons in the last few days leading up to the second coming of the Lord. This is especially what are commonly known as the great tribulation and the antichrist.

Most OT end times prophecy is about the ultimate; most NT end times prophecy is about the penultimate, including most of the book of Revelation. We have glimpses of ultimate end times in Rev 7:9–17; 11:15–18; 14:1–5, 14–20; and from 19:11 to the end. Most of the material from chs. 6 through 18 is penultimate, including the seals, trumpets, bowls, the two beasts, and the judgment of Babylon.

The greatest body of penultimate prophecy in the OT is in the book of Daniel, which may be why it is so important to the book of Revelation.

2. These need to be traced and analyzed individually. But as they seem to intertwine, they must also then be synthesized.

As well, most end times prophecy in both the OT and NT is centered around Israel and particularly Jerusalem. So we should not be surprised that that is also the case with Revelation. Israel is God's chosen people, and Jerusalem is the city of David and of the great Son of David.

The penultimate prophecies of Rev 6–19 are especially about judging and purging Israel in the time of the great tribulation, the seventieth week of Dan 9:24–27. God determined and promised long ago that he would eventually and ultimately purify and redeem Israel. But that will not be fully realized until the last days and hours before the Messiah returns. The horrors of the seven years of the seventieth week (especially the seal, trumpet, and bowl judgments) will be God's pressure on that generation of Israel to repent and bow in humble faith and allegiance to her King, Jesus. God's pressure on his enemies, including wicked Israel, is a kind of reverse persecution. If persecution is pressure on nonconformists to get in step with the regime, so God demands absolute allegiance and threatens, not idly, to crush forever persistent defiance in the face of Calvary's grace and God's longsuffering through many centuries, not to mention his undeniable supremacy over creation (Rom 1:19–21). The elect will finally be broken of their stubbornness; the rest will just be broken and crushed. Revelation speaks in several passages in several ways of the need and opportunity to repent. Of course, that goes for the rest of the world, too, but Revelation gives primary attention to Israel, exposing its wickedness, as God demands the worship he is due.

All the other important themes—including judgment, worship, repentance, conquest, and witness—descend from these two. Jesus is coming to claim his throne. He will judge his enemies and reward his loyal followers. The exhortation to the faithful readers, especially those of the penultimate day, is to persevere in faith and testimony in the face of persecution, which for some reaches the extreme form of martyrdom.

Third, the entire book, not just the letters of chapters 2–3, is to and for the seven churches (Rev 1:4, 11; 22:16). But it is also for all churches from John's day to today and to the day of fulfillment, the time between Daniel's sixty-ninth and seventieth weeks, churches which are comprised of Jewish and gentile Christians. The churches are not the Israel of the seventieth week, but are nevertheless in need of this revelation as to how God intends to wrap up history and the consolation that he will give those who suffer unjustly.

As well, it is a rare church in John's day or ours that is not populated by true and false followers of Jesus. So this book is a warning to all churches and all Christians that the coming King of Israel, the Lord of the churches, does not countenance false or halfhearted devotion by them. (Recall numerous statements of God's impartiality, including 1 Pet 1:17.) The scenes of pressure on the Israel of the penultimate day are meant then to put the fear of God in the hearts of all in the churches from John's day to the end.

Fourth, the author indicates in his opening statement that the events described must soon take place (Rev 1:1), that the time is near (*engus*; 1:3; 22:10) or the events will occur soon (*tachu, en tachei*; 2:16; 3:11; 22:6, 7, 12, 20; these last three being the Lord's announcement that he is coming soon). To state the obvious, these reinforce the previous point that the book is about the future, but also that the grand climax will creep up on the last generation and catch the unrepentant unprepared.

Fifth, the structure of the book must be considered carefully. In some ways, it is quite transparent: letters to the churches (chs. 2–3); heaven's throne room (chs. 4–5); seals and trumpets (chs. 6–11); introduction to the dragon (ch. 12) and beasts (ch. 13); bowls (chs. 15–16); Babylon (chs. 17–18); climactic judgments (chs. 19–20); new heaven and earth (chs. 21–22). The challenging question is how to organize these—or rather, how the author meant them to be grouped. Various factors have been noted by interpreters, and various approaches have been championed.

This study sees Rev 1:19 as providing the broad plan: chapter 1 (that is, especially the vision of the Lord in 1:9–20) being the things which the author saw; chapters 2 and 3, the things which are; and the rest of the book (perhaps leaving out the epilogue, 22:6–21, as a final section), the things which will happen after these things. But that still leaves more than 80 percent of the book in the third section.

There are the two white horses and riders in Rev 6:1–2 and 19:11. These define the beginning and end of this largest block of material in the book, chapters 6 to 19–20. The rider must be the same in both places, Jesus, the rightful King. The climax to the whole drama is 19:11–21; chapters 20–22 are the falling action, including the happily ever after.

There is a strong connection between the throne room (chs. 4–5) and the following section with the introduction and opening of the seven-sealed scroll. The sevenness demands literary continuity, even with the gap between the sixth and seventh. The seventh seal must be seen as consisting of the seven trumpets, so that that entire section is a continuation of the scroll seals, thus yielding a literary unit from chapters 6 through 11: the scroll. The seventh trumpet (Rev 11:15–18) has the quality of finality, ultimacy, and the next verse acts as a transitional buffer. Likewise the material that follows is new in a number of ways.

The material that follows is an introduction of the archvillains—the dragon (ch. 12), the two beasts (ch. 13)—who had not yet been formally introduced. These are literarily connected. The bowl judgments (chs. 15–16) focus on these and their followers. The prostitute Babylon (chs. 17–18) is also entwined with the first beast. So the author seems to shift at chapter 12 to the topic of archvillains and to continue on that concern through chapter 19.[3] Chapter 19 provides the climax of the building dramatic tension, the second coming (v. 11). Chapter 20 completes the climax with the fate of the devil heightened, as he is treated separately from the beasts (Rev 19:20).

One more big impression: our author means that we should above all be impressed—amazed!—with God, that he is spectacularly glorious. That glory includes such perfections as his infinite power, absolute righteousness, and limited patience. It is the height of folly to oppose him who is all-powerful. It is his very nature to run a kingdom of righteousness, and so he will certainly bring all moral agents of all time to answer to him in his holy court. That reckoning is delayed, as he is patiently giving people opportunity to repent before their day in court. He has, however, set the day for that reckoning; his patience will run out. It is the height of folly to procrastinate repentance, as none of us knows the day of our death or of the Lord's coming.

We must be very careful not to get so caught up in bizarre images and debated interpretations that we lose sight of God. All revelation is God revealing himself. There is nothing grander, and so there is nothing more important. Knowing God is the bullseye of all of life. He is the only reason there is life and a wonderful eternal future. He is the great prize. The kingdom will be glorious, because the King is glorious.

This book opens with a prologue in which the author asserts his work as the true account of important future events, which carries the promise of a blessing for those who order their lives accordingly (Rev 1:1–3). Next comes an epistolary greeting, in which there is reference to several themes of the book, but especially those of the Lord's coming

---

3. The very common approach of identifying a group of seven somethings in chs. 12–14 must be rejected for obvious and strong reasons. The main reason is that whereas the author spoke explicitly of seven seals, trumpets, and bowls (chs. 6–8, 8–11, 15–16), he did not here speak of seven anything nor did he enumerate anything as he had done in each of those three groups of seven.

and reigning (1:4–6). The final piece of the prologue is a summary of the central message of the book (1:7–8), the coming of the Lord leading to great repentance.

The divine source of the book is emphasized in the command to write (Rev 1:9–11), and its impact is magnified by the majestic and fearsome description of the speaker (1:12–18). Most significant in the symbolism are his likeness to the great Judge of Dan 7 and the great Revealer of Dan 10–11 and his special association with the churches. Verse 19 provides the outline for the structure of the work.

The immediate movement to the Lord's words to his churches (chs. 2–3) indicates his special concern for his own. His glorious person, a feature of which begins each letter, commands the attention of the churches. He exercises the power of a judge—to the faithful, more like a loving and strict father—in each case, presenting the facts of their performance ("I know your works") both positive and negative, and prescribing a course of action for improvement, often a threat of judgment for failure, and always a promise of participation in his glorious triumph for those who obey. The behavior he seeks is unfailing and uncompromising loyalty to himself, even in the face of fierce opposition and pressure to defect.

Having shown the Lord's attitude toward his own churches, he turns to the larger burden of the work, his conquest and judgment of his enemies. The background for that begins with the scene in heaven (chs. 4–5). In the first part, the scene is set, depicting the majesty of the heavenly Father in the description of him and his entourage and his absolute dominion over creation, his magnum opus (ch. 4). The second part introduces more directly the judgment that follows, with the focus on the scroll and the Lamb (ch. 5). It is his prerogative alone to open the scroll's seals because of his atoning self-sacrifice.

The next several chapters are clearly structured around the sevens of seal (chs. 6–7), trumpet (chs. 8–11), and bowl (chs. 15–16) judgments. There may be progression of intensity of the judgments from the seals to trumpets to bowls. There is a fairly obvious four-three pattern in the groups of seven judgments.

The first four seals involving four colored horses harken to the first and eighth of Zechariah's vision unit, Zech 1:8–17 and 6:1–8. These speak of God's zeal for Jerusalem (see especially Zech 1:14). The scroll, which includes the seven trumpets, is about the rightful King reclaiming his land and his holy city. God's people have been suffering deadly persecution at the hands of the wicked inhabitants of the land, so that they cry out for justice in the fifth seal (Rev 6:9–11). The terror expands in the sixth seal to cosmic disturbances on a supernatural level, leading to attempts to hide from heaven's King and the Lamb, the undoubted source of certain judgment (6:12–17). Before the seventh seal is opened, there is a pause, beginning first with a clue as to the content of that seventh seal—harming of earth, sea, trees—(7:1–3), then two complementary scenes that reveal God's special protection of his own saints from the effects of the plagues; first the Jews, second the gentiles, first the ones on earth and in their mortality, then the others in heaven and following their martyrdom (7:4–17). The breaking of the last seal brings all heavenly beings to the edge of their seats, so to speak ("silence for about a half an hour"), looking to see what might emerge as the last seal is broken and the scroll is at last fully opened (8:1).

What comes forth is the answer to the prayers of the saints for the completion of their salvation and vengeance on their tormentors (Rev 8:2–6), in the form of seven trumpet judgments. The first four trumpets bring judgment through calamities in all aspects of the natural world: earth, the seas, fresh water, heavenly bodies (8:7–12). As if that were not enough, the last three are so much severer that they warrant a special announcement (8:13). The fifth and sixth are a complementary pair. In them, demonic forces are permitted to attack the unprotected, non-elect men; in the first, merely inflicting excruciating pain (9:1–12), whereas in the second actually killing (9:13–19). The refusal of the survivors to repent (9:20–21) demonstrates God's justice in pouring out such judgment. While the sixth trumpet may appear to end in chapter 9, the author signals that the content of chapter 10 and the first fourteen verses of chapter 11 are also part of it (the end of the second woe, 11:14). What the ending of the sixth trumpet adds is clarification that the sixth trumpet, and hence all the trumpets, is an opportunity to repent. Whereas the survivors of the carnage in the second half of chapter 9 stubbornly refused to repent, the survivors of the great earthquake in Jerusalem "feared and gave glory" to God, an expression used twice more of faithful repentance (14:7; 15:4).

In chapter 10, a strong angel, whose appearance conveys divine authority, commits to John a message of the imminent conclusion to judgments, confirming the idea of a last chance to repent.

Next the measuring of the temple of God and the career of his two witnesses describe a specific timeframe—the second half of Daniel's seventieth week (three and a half years; Rev 11:3)—during which two special witnesses prophesy in Jerusalem and survive constant threat of martyrdom only by unique divine protection (11:3–12). Immediately upon the removal of that protection, their martyrdom, their resurrection and heavenly rescue three and a half days later, there is a catastrophic and deadly earthquake in Jerusalem, leading to widespread repentance among the survivors (11:13). It is then that the author means for us to see the sixth trumpet as finally concluded (11:14).

As it turns out, this was effectively the last hour or last chance for repentance before the Lord's triumphant second coming, claiming what he came for: dominion over earth. The seventh trumpet speaks in ultimate terms of that historic development issuing in final judgment of the righteous and the wicked (Rev 11:15–18).

What ties the next group of segments together is the thread of judgment on the enemies of Israel, the chosen people of God (chs. 12–14). The opposition was satanic in source—aroused by the threat of the Savior coming from Israel to overthrow him—and frustrated in its intent (Rev 12:1–6). Satan's expulsion from heaven portends his eventual final defeat but also explains his great rage in view of the shortness of his time (12:7–12). Confined to earth, his efforts are directed against Israel but again are frustrated, so that he thrashes against her faithful offspring (12:13–17). He then raises up his human agents, the beasts from the sea and land, to perform his work. The former climaxes a long train of oppressors of Israel, exercising intimidating powers and demanding absolute loyalty to himself (13:1–10). The latter enforces the same by deception and coercion (13:11–18). This chapter creates the impression that these characters are indomitable (especially 13:4, 16–17). The opening paragraph of chapter 14, however, demonstrates first that the Lamb will ultimately win and rule Zion and second that God shall have successfully protected the 144,000 (7:4–8) from the dragon and beasts' deadly ferocity. In contrast to their identification with the Lamb in his conquest of Zion, the rest of the earth, those who submitted to the dragon and his goons, will surely suffer the wrath of God. This is the message emphasized by the compound (three) angelic announcements and the twofold harvest of the earth (14:6–20).

In the bowl judgments that follow (chs. 15–16), the object of divine wrath is especially the kingdom of the beast. The preparatory events focus on the truth of God's unique position as deserving of worship (Rev 15:2–4), and the righteousness and finality of the judgments (15:5–8). The object of those judgments is identified in the first and fifth bowls: the subjects of the beast's kingdom (16:2–11). The survivors validate the justification for the judgments by refusing to repent and cease their blasphemies.

The sixth bowl is Armageddon (Rev 16:12–16). But it is not a battle, as traditionally understood. Nor does it have anything to do with Megiddo. It is rather about a war council at a mythic mountain of assembly (Hebrew, *har-moed*; cf. Isa 14:13). The point is that, despite all the evildoers' preparations for the anticipated ultimate conflict, they will not be ready (16:15; caught in their pajamas, so to speak).

The seventh bowl is God raining down terror—from the air, using lightning, hail, and the greatest earthquake ever—and still the survivors blaspheme and refuse to repent (Rev 16:17–21). These last two bowls also set the stage for the remaining judgments against Babylon (chs. 17–18; cf. the reference to Babylon in the earthquake and hailstorm) and the Lord's return (19:11).

The next to be judged is Babylon the great, a.k.a. the mother of prostitutes, the mother of the abominations of the earth/land, and the great city (Rev 17:5, 18). First John describes her, especially as to her relationship with the beast and the kings of the earth, her extravagant self indulgence, and her deadly opposition to saints (Rev 17:1–6). Next he expresses that he was extremely shocked: he is stunned that this city of promise has come to this deplorable state (vv. 6–7). Then he provides the angel's description of the beast (vv. 8–11) and the ten kings (vv. 12–17), as well as their eventual destruction of her in fulfillment of God's purpose (vv. 16–17). Finally, in verse 18, he provides the final clue eliminating any remaining question as to her identity: she is Jerusalem (the great city; cf. 11:8).

Chapter 18 represents her demise in the dramatic form of a funeral dirge. Every section of the entire chapter—the announcement of her impending fall (vv. 1–3), the warning to individuals to escape her fate (vv. 4–8), the lament (vv. 9–19), and the symbolization of her destruction (vv. 20–24)—points to the certainty and finality of that fall, and obviously that multiplied compounding is meant to underscore the message.

The first ten verses of chapter 19 go together, juxtaposing the two leading ladies, Babylon, old wicked Jerusalem, prostitute girlfriend of the antimessiah, and new Jerusalem, the spectacularly beautiful bride of the Messiah. All of heaven rejoices at the ending of chapter 18, the prostitute's utter destruction (vv. 1–5, hallelujah three times). Then the celebration continues with another hallelujah as all eyes are on the Lamb's bride-to-be (vv. 6–9). When John hears the revealing angel speak of the blessing on those invited to the wedding banquet, it seems his exuberance gets the best of him and he mistakenly bows to the messenger (v. 10).

The book has been building from the beginning toward its literary climax (as the future history it presents is building toward its climax) in the coming of the Lamb (cf. Rev 1:7). That return is gloriously portrayed by the description of his appearance (19:11–16). As expected by his earlier presentation as judge (cf. 1:13–16) and here as warrior, as well as by the deadly animosity of his enemies, he immediately engages those enemies in order, bringing on each the judgment of second death (19:17—20:15). The first of those is the beast and his false prophet, while their toadies, the kings of the earth (Ezekiel's Gog and Magog, Ezek 38–39), suffer their first death (19:17–21). The dragon is next, being subjected first to temporary (one thousand years) confinement, while the saints enjoy participation in Messiah's millennial reign (20:1–6). After the dragon is allowed a final moment of freedom, at which time he leads a final rebellion, he too is committed eternally to the lake of fire (20:7–10). The third enemy to be judged finally is the world of unbelieving men (20:11–15).

When the judgments are all past, the positive effects of the Lamb's coming are described (Rev 21:1—22:5). He first brings about a new creation, without any taint of sin or its effects (21:1–8). Provision for the saints is made by the new Jerusalem, heavenly, beautiful (21:9–11), secure (21:12–21), especially made to honor God's saints of all ages (patriarchs' and apostles' names). But most of all, it will be a place where God dwells and reigns among his people: his presence eliminates the need for a temple or luminaries (21:22–23). His very presence means a glory that draws holy people to the city like a magnet (21:24–27). The prosperity and health of the residents are symbolized by the river of the water of life and the tree of life (22:1–2). In sum, it will be a place of perfect benefit (22:3–5).

John's epilogue appears to be a scattered review of the main points of the book, designed as a final exhortation to the readers (Rev 22:6–21). Its main emphases are the imminence of the climactic return of the Lord (vv. 7, 12, 20), and an underscoring of the validity of the whole. To the unbeliever, it offers an invitation to turn in submissive faith to the Lamb. To all, it predicts the final discrimination between the righteous and unrighteous and pronounces a warning against tampering with the book. The closing benediction of grace upon the reader was never more meaningful than in the light of the Lord's coming.

PART 4: VERSE-BY-VERSE COMMENTARY

Chapter 1

1—OPENS WITH A TITLE, "The Revelation of Jesus Christ," whose *of* phrase is both subjective and objective genitive. That is, the book is both from and about Jesus. For *from*, see the next clause ("which God gave to him to show to his servants") and Rev 22:16; for *about*, see 1:7, 13–17. As well, one cannot help but see that he is the central protagonist of the entire book. Of course it is also about things that must soon take place. But these things are all associated in one way or another with him and his coming.

Chain of revelation: God → Jesus → angel → John → us his servants.

Servant (*doulos*) = subject-vassal of the King. The concept comes more from the OT and the ancient Near East than from Greco-Roman culture (bondslave, per NASB). See 1 Chron 18:2, 6, servants bringing tribute.

"Things which must soon take place": here in the first sentence of the book is the first of ten short time statements, two of which are in these first three verses and five in the last chapter (Rev 1:1, 3; 2:16; 3:11; 12:12; 22:6, 7, 10, 12, 20). Five are quotes of the Lord Jesus, "I am coming soon/ quickly." All the others are closely related. It has now been more than nineteen centuries. So what sense did the author intend? I suspect it was along the following lines: the first sixty-nine of Daniel's seventy weeks were past even for the author, so only one remains. Thus we are sixty-nine seventieths of the way through the biblical timeline culminating at the ultimate, the Lord's glorious (second) coming. That seventieth week will be the final seven years of penultimate history. See also comment at 6:11.

As well, several "day of the LORD" statements in the OT prophets insist it is near. Zeph 1:14: "Near is the great day of the LORD, near and coming very quickly" (NASB). John uses the same two key words that the LXX uses again and again: *eggus* and *tachei*. See also these, where the day of the LORD is said to be near: Isa 13:6; Ezek 30:3; Joel 1:15; 2:1; 3:14; Obad 1:15; Zeph 1:7. If the day of Yahweh was near to prophets in the eighth century BC, it is certainly more near to John in the first century AD. (See also comment at Rev 6:11 in refutation of preterism.)

2—Testify = swear as before a judge; all that he saw = eyewitness of prophetic visions.

Testify: 4x here (and 3x in ch. 22); testimony: 9x (testimony of Jesus [Rev 1:9; 12:17; 19:10; 20:4], their testimony [6:9; 11:7; 12:11]).

Linked with Word of God (1:2, 9; 6:9; 20:4).

This book is not only about the Lord's coming to claim his crown, but it is also about his subjects' testimony, especially in the face of deadly persecution. They swear to their tormentors that Jesus is King, as God has declared. They fear God's wrath, not that of humans or Satan (see Matt 10:28.)

3—"Read and hear" speaks of the normal way people received Scripture before Gutenberg: one would read aloud, an audience would hear the reading.

"Hear and keep" sounds similar to James's concern to be doers, not just hearers of the Word (Jas 1:22–25; see also Luke 11:28; Matt 28:20). This book is not just information, but mandate. That is because God is the speaker, and whatever he says, whenever he the King speaks, he speaks law. (That is how Paul can speak of the law of Christ in Gal 6:2 and 1 Cor 9:21 and of the gospel as the law of faith in Rom 3:27.)

That one promises to bless those who faithfully attend to this book. Biblical blessing always implies its antipode, a curse; and they respectively speak ultimately of life and death (cf. Deut 30:19).

The point about the importance of this book is reiterated in eight of the sixteen verses of the epilogue (Rev 22:6, 7, 8, 9, 10, 16, 18, 19).

4–6—Stereotypical though unique epistolary introduction: author, intended readership, well wish, divine source, doxology. The reader is to understand that the entire book is an epistle addressed to all seven churches.

4—"Who is": the self-existent eternality of Exod 3:14 ("I am") is expanded to include past and future (though the future is in the present tense of come). This is repeated in Rev 1:8 and 4:8. There is also a variant description of the beast in 17:8 (see comment there).

The Greek grammatical error (*apo* + nominative) probably preserves a standardized formula, "he who is": "from he [instead of him] who is," as in verse 8.

Sevenfold Spirit (see also Rev 3:1; 4:5; 5:6): by its placement in this Trinitarian formula, this is obviously the same who is more commonly known as the Holy Spirit. Further, there can be no doubt John is affirming the full deity of the Holy Spirit. (Some might find the author's frequent attention to Father and Son without Holy Spirit a bit curious; 5:13; 6:16; 7:9–10; 14:4; 22:3. That is probably best explained as the suzerain-vassal construct as laid out in Ps 2 where the Father is King of heaven and the son is King of earth.) Why he used this unique expression would require comparative study of the four instances. It is likely he found some precedent for the expression in the sevenfold spirit of the branch-son of Jesse (poetic for David) in Isa 11:2.

"Before the throne" anticipates chapter 4, where God the Father is seen as the King of heaven. This throne room setting is referenced several more times.

5—Messiah is the quintessential faithful witness; cf. 1 Tim 6:13, "Christ Jesus, who testified the good confession before Pontius Pilate" (NASB). He confessed that he is Messiah (see Matt 26:63-64), the essential affirmation of the gospel. He is firstborn as forerunner and firstfruits assuring the eventual resurrection of his spiritual family (1 Cor 15:20, 23).

Side note on Matt 26:63–64: the high priest asks, "Are you the royal hero of Ps 2, the Messiah, Son of God?" Jesus answers, "Yes, but don't forget about Dan 7:13 and Ps 110:1. I am all of these." To the same effect, see Luke 22:67—23:3.

This book is also his sworn testimony (Rev 22:20).

All earthly kings, and by extension all their subjects, must and shall submit to his supreme rule, whether voluntarily or involuntarily. See Phil 2:10–11. Whereas the expression King of kings occurs in Rev 17:14 and 19:16, here we read Ruler [*archōn*] of the kings, which obviously means the same. The expression the kings of the earth, coupled with the designation of Jesus as ruler over them, also alludes to Ps 2, where the kings of the earth (v. 2) were informed that, contrary to their clamorous designs, they must finally bow to God's chosen ruler of earth, enthroned in Jerusalem. So this is but the first of many references and allusions to Ps 2 in this book of Revelation.

As elsewhere, the good news of Jesus does not terminate at the resurrection (firstborn of the dead) but on his reigning (ruler of the kings). See also Acts 2:32–36; 1 Cor 15:24–28; Phil 2:9–11; Eph 1:20; 2 Tim 2:8; Heb 12:2; 1 Pet 1:21.

Not only was his death ultimate victory, not defeat, it was also valuable for the redemption and forgiveness of many. His redemptive self-sacrifice was voluntary (John 10:15–18) and the ultimate expression of love (Rom 5:8).

The word blood, *haima*, appears nineteen times in twelve chapters. It is the Lord's blood shed on the cross four times (here and Rev 5:9; 7:14; 12:11); it is faithful martyrs' blood six times (6:10; 16:6; 17:6 [2x]; 18:24; 19:2); and it appears in judgment statements against God's and the saints' enemies (8:7, 8; 11:6; 14:20; 16:3, 4, 6; 19:3).

6—Kingdom of priests (Exod 19:6; 1 Pet 2:9). But here we are not just in, we are his kingdom, and we are the holy ones, priests, privileged to approach the holy heavenly King. He is the eternal, glorious, dominant one; we are his glorious kingdom, the greatest element of all the new creation. Our extreme privilege of reigning with him is indicated in many places (Rev 3:21; 5:9; 20:4–6; 22:3). His dominion shall be glorious and eternal (Dan 7:13–14).

7—Without saying Son of Man, John references Dan 7:13: "Behold, with the clouds of heaven One like a Son of Man was coming, and he came up to the Ancient of Days and was presented before him" (NASB). Of course, John does say Son of Man later in Rev 1:13 and again in 14:14.

He couples that to Zech 12:10, "I will pour out on the house of David and on the inhabitants of Jerusalem, the Spirit of grace and of supplication, so that they will look on me whom they have pierced; and they will mourn for him" (NASB). "All the tribes" seems to refer to Zech 12:11–14, where one tribe of Israel and a couple families are named.

The coming in Daniel refers to the son of man (cf. Rev 1:13) to be presented before the Ancient of Days, who confers on him eternal dominion over all the earth. That is, Daniel's son of man is the Adamic king (think of Gen 1) who replaces the beast kings of Dan 7:1–12. They had ruled over Israel; he will reverse that, as he is the son of David who will rule not only Israel but, like David, the surrounding nations as well.

Exceeding David, his rule will extend to encompass the entire planet and continue forever.

This verse is not parenthetical or an aside (contra NET Bible notes): it is the central thesis of the book. Jesus is coming to reign, and Israel will at long last recognize him, repent, and embrace him as her Son of David King. Rev 11:13 speaks of that final rush of national repentance. Stephen in Acts 7:12–13, 35–36 predicts Israel's faithful recognition at the second coming.

8—This is the first of three alpha-omega statements (also Rev 21:6; 22:13). Here he adds expressions of eternality (see comment at 1:4) and omnipotence. Almighty (*pantokratōr*) likely represents the Hebrew *tsebaoth*, as Lord God likely represents *Yahweh Elohim* or *Adonai Yahweh* (both of which are common in the OT).

9—"Partaker in the tribulation and kingdom and perseverence" (NASB) is a case of parataxis, where the parallel nouns connected by *and* are mutually modifying. The sense is something like "we share together today in the kingdom, though our experience today is one of tribulation, to which we respond with perseverance." (We must remember that in the great son of man statement in Dan 7:14, we read "to him was given dominion, glory, and a kingdom," where the idea is a dominating and glorious kingdom.)

On the pairing of Word of God and testimony of Jesus, see also Rev 1:2; 6:9; 20:4; cf. 12:11, 17. John's banishment was for refusing to recant, for maintaining his testimony about Jesus—he is the ultimate King—which we know by divine revelation (Matt 16:17).

Witness/testimony is described as faithful in Rev 1:5; 2:13; 3:14.

10—Wasn't John in the Spirit daily? I think this should be spirit, meaning this was a spiritual vision (as also Rev 4:2; and of course the Holy Spirit is not excluded or unimportant). John is not the initiator, nor is this merely his imagination. God gave him a very unusual experience of a truly spiritual nature.

Lord's day may be double entendre. Sunday is not as important as the day of the Lord, though this is not the usual wording for either one. God took him in this spiritual vision to that day.

John uses the noun trumpet six times and its verb ten times, twelve of those in chapters 8–9.

11—From that future day, the Lord himself directed John to write to the contemporary churches. ("Write" also in v. 19.) "What you see" speaks often in this book of the typical prophetic experience of having a vision of divine origin. As well, hearing (v. 10) is common for prophets receiving a verbal message to proclaim. See for instance Rev 8:13; 22:8 for both together.

12—First he heard, then he turned so he could see, then he saw (a vision).

Lampstands must recall the idea of menorahs (Hebrew; LXX *luchnia*, the same word as John uses here), perpetual light in the temple. See Exod 25:31–40.

In verse 20, we learn the menorahs are the seven churches. The churches—particular, real, local churches—are the light of the world (Matt 5:14). But they are such only as they are exclusively and absolutely devoted to Jesus, the Light of the world (John 8:12; 9:5). They are precious (gold). But, as we shall see in chapters 2–3, they are not today invulnerable to corruption and disintegration.

13–16—This is a spiritual vision, hence the symbolic value of the whole and the parts is the author's concern.

The Lord Jesus is described by nine features: robe, sash, hair, eyes, feet, voice, hand, mouth, and face. The overall impression is of the supremely glorious and awesome one.

13—Son of Man is in the midst of these menorah-churches.

Many English Bible readers will see "a son of man" and wonder if this is "the son of man," as Jesus referred to himself, not realizing that the expression as we find it in Revelation (here and in Rev 14:14) is actually more faithful to the original in Daniel than what we find in the Gospels and Acts ("the son of man"). John's expression is virtually identical to the Greek of Dan 7:13 (*hōs huios anthrōpou*), which is itself a faithful translation of the Aramaic original. The only variation is that John uses *homoion*, whereas Daniel LXX uses *hōs*; see Rev 1:15; 2:18, where these are used interchangeably.

Rev 1	Daniel	Other
Son of Man (one like; cf. Rev 14:14) (= ultimate King)	7:13—one like a son of man	
Floor-length robe (= esteemed leader)	7:9—Ancient of Days (= ultimate judge) Vesture white as snow 10:5—Dressed in linen	
Gold belt/sash across torso (= priest perhaps, dignity)	10:5—Girded with pure gold	
White head/hair, as wool, snow (= age, wisdom, honor)	7:9—Hair as wool	Lev 19:32 Honor the elderly
Flaming eyes (= penetrating knowledge, judgment)	10:6—Eyes as flaming torches 7:9—Throne blazing	
Feet like glowing, burnished, polished bronze (= purity, power, right to judge)	10:6—Arms and feet like bronze	
Voice like many waters (= commanding authority)	10:6—Voice like tumult, roaring	
Right hand holding seven stars (= authority over church)		
Tongue like two-edged, sharp sword (= execution of judgment by a word)		Isa 49:2; Heb 4:12
Face bright as the sun (= inscrutable glory)	10:6—Face like lightning	

16—He holds stars: identified in verse 20 as angels of the respective churches.

17–18—John's response—falling at his feet as if dead—is very similar to that of Daniel (Dan 10:9).

First and last is surely synonymous with alpha and omega (v. 8). "Living ... dead ... alive": perhaps the *kai* (the common word for "and") preceding "dead" could be understood as close to "though" (NET renders it "but").

"Fear not": those who have nothing to fear are those who fear faithfully and bow (Rev 15:3–4); those who have the most to fear are those who brazenly decline to fear and refuse to bow (6:15–17).

Beginning with the last line of verse 17, it is hard to conceive of a stronger statement of indomitable eternal life and the power to confer it. The last couple words—"and of Hades"—then add the power to impose death in its ultimate degree.

I was dead, but look at me now: does this look like dead? Who else should have the power (keys) over death and the grave (Hades), eternal death, but the one who defeated them by rising? The Bible is not about small issues: it is about ultimate life. We must give supreme attention to this one who alone conquered death to live eternally.

19—Write past, present, future—so say most translations. Some (ESV, NLT), however, see the latter two as epexegetic of the first: what you have seen concerns the present and future.[1] That is a less likely sense of the Greek construction.

This formula seems to indicate the author's macrostructure for the entire book: that which he has seen is the vision he just described, hence chapter 1; that which will take place after these things is everything from chapter 4 to the end (as the wording in Rev 4:2 is largely identical to this). The things which are then could reasonably refer to the letters to the churches (which were in John's day) in chapters 2–3.

20—Angels, not pastors. See the discussion in the introductory comments to chapter 2.

Chapters 2–3

The letters to the seven churches in chapters 2–3 are perhaps the most preached part of the book. In addition to the complete commentaries on Revelation, numerous published works have been devoted to this unit. For that reason, I will not seek to duplicate those, but rather I refer the reader to them, many of which offer much valuable information, especially in regard to the historical and cultural factors pertaining to the separate cities. I intend to call attention to what I regard as some of the most relevant literary features for gaining a grasp of the big idea of the unit.

---

1. Aune, *Revelation*, 1:117.

What is the point of the letters in the argument of the book? Jesus is coming. He has just been seen as fearsome and glorious (Rev 1:12–16), so much so that John nearly died just from seeing him (v. 17). He is fabulously longsuffering and forgiving, yet his patience has an end; there is a predetermined date set by the Father (Matt 24:36; Acts 1:7). At the end, there is terrifying judgment on all who shall have refused every opportunity to repent. (See discussions of repentance in this commentary at Rev 9:20; 16:9.) If that is how history will end, and if the timing of the end is soon and like a thief (3:3; 16:15), the people of the churches are warned that they will not escape if they are unrepentant. ("For it is time for judgment to begin with the household of God; and if it begins with us first, what will be the outcome for those who do not obey the gospel of God?" 1 Pet 4:17 NASB; cf. Ezek 9:6.)

There was then and there always will be pressure on Christians, including the false professors in our churches, to back away from their faith confession. In its extreme form, we call it persecution. So we all need constant encouragement, exhortation, and warning to remain faithful and to support one another in this common struggle.

Most of the churches are warned that some in their churches are presently straying. Some may be false professors, unrepentant, in line for the kind of judgment that is coming on the world as described in the following chapters. It is not yet too late for them to repent genuinely; but a day is coming when that will change. The church's Lord does not play favorites. He who will judge the wicked world will judge any in the churches who have not repented. (On God's impartiality, see Acts 10:34; Rom 2:11; Gal 2:6; Eph 6:9; Col 3:25; 1 Pet 1:17; Deut 10:17; 2 Chron 19:7; Job 34:19.)

As well, those churches must cooperate in warning their members. Churches that do not collectively repent are subject to being snuffed out as flickering lamps (Rev 2:5).

The persecuted faithful in the churches are also reassured that in his coming, the Lord will avenge their innocent suffering.

One of the features of all seven letters is a statement of overcoming. Overcoming (from *nikaō*, win, triumph, defeat, conquer, overcome) is spiritual victory in spiritual conflict. There are only winners and losers, and the stakes are always life and death.

"For whatever is born of God overcomes the world; and this is the victory that has overcome the world—our faith. Who is the one who overcomes the world, but he who believes that Jesus is the Son of God?" (1 John 5:4–5 NASB)

"They will fight against you but will not overcome you, for I am with you and will rescue you, declares the LORD" (Jer. 1:19 NIV).

The Lord Jesus, the Lion-Lamb, is the great Conqueror (Rev 5:5–6; 6:1–2; 14:1; 17:14; 19:11ff). He won the ultimate victory by his voluntary death and resurrection. That triumph becomes the triumph of his loyal followers. They triumph never by their own exploits or virtues but only by his (12:11).

All seven: "To the angel of" most likely means an angel, not a pastor. This is certainly unusual, whichever way we take it. There is no definitive local clue to settle the question, hence the debate.

Pastors? The idea would be the prophetic messenger of the church. But there is no support and no precedent for this sense. There is the occasional reference in the OT to prophets as messengers, *mal'ak*, the Hebrew equivalent of the Greek *angelos*, angel (Isa 44:26; Hag 1:13; 2 Chron 36:15). For John to intend that here, we would conclude the Lord had a single prophet designated at each church. While the idea of a senior pastor is common in churches today, it is at variance with the consistent NT pattern of a plurality (i.e., never singular) of elders, pastors, and bishops at churches.

Angels? This must be the default interpretation, based on common usage.

The word *angelos* occurs sixty-seven times in Revelation. Outside of these statements (including Rev 1:20), there is no debate whether those references are human or angel as traditionally understood. Satan's angels (12:7, 9) are called stars (12:4), as are these (1:20).

Angels were associated with nations in Dan 10:13, 20–21; 11:2; Michael being Israel's. (See comment at Rev 12:7.) That author calls them princes of the respective nations. (On other strange teachings about angels, see 1 Cor 11:10; Eph 3:10; similarly, on spirits, see 1 John 4:1–3, 6; 2 Chron 18:21–22.)

But what could that mean? Why here? Why now? My best guess is that it serves to heighten the awareness of the primacy of spirituality in the churches. It calls attention to heaven's spiritual view of these and all churches. As well, it calls attention to the critical place of word ministry. Beyond that, the author makes nothing of it.

One problem with the angel view (no less with the pastor view): in Rev 2:10, the address begins in the second person singular (as do they all) but shifts to plural for the second sentence, then shifts back to the singular for the last sentence. Taken strictly then, the angel is warned not to fear what he is about to suffer; some of the members will soon be imprisoned, tested, and endure ten days of tribulation; and finally the angel is urged to remain faithful and promised to receive the crown of life. It is probably best to understand that the singular addresses are for the church collectively, while not all in the church will directly suffer the impending persecution.

This then may well provide an important clue that all the churches are seen as collective wholes, though the individuals will have different experiences. That being so, the idea of faithful mutual responsibility must be pervasive, the idea of all being the keepers of all their brothers (an idea I see as fundamental in the exhortations in Hebrews, especially Heb 3:12; 4:1, 11; 12:12–15).

All seven: "He who has an ear, let him hear what the Spirit says to the churches [plural]." Each reads all seven's mail, as well as the entire book. (The introduction is an epistolary greeting addressed to all seven churches [Rev 1:4]). All are to take warning from the threats and comfort from the promises.

The hearing ear refers to spiritual hearing, analogous to spiritual seeing (with eyes of the heart, Eph 1:17). The image of spiritual sight (and blindness) and hearing (and deafness) originated in Isa 6:10 and is repeated many times in OT and NT.

There is to be no compromise with wicked influences that have crept into the church (cf. Jude 4).

Every church and all members must be faithful to the end (Rev 2:25).

All the overcomer promises amount to eternal life. Thus the point is that God will sift false from true saints in the churches; all and only true believers are overcomers.

Virtually all commentators suggest the order of the letters fits a likely itinerary of a courier delivering the book to the churches.

Chapter 2

1–7—Ephesus: So much good (vv. 2–3, 6), but one little flaw threatens to bring the church to ruin (v. 5): loss of first love (v. 4).

1—The Lord holds every church (angel) and walks among all. Readers-churches must not fail to personalize this. It is meant to instill both comfort and fear simultaneously.

2–6—The asset side of their ledger is substantial, with eight items: deeds, toil, perseverance, intolerance toward evil men, both testing and rejecting false apostles, endurance without weariness (vv. 2–3), hating Nicolaitans' deeds (v. 6)—all commendable. They were zealous for the truth. Most of these commendations are quite general: all churches should embrace and seek to live such values. They were right not to put up with evil men in the church. They were rightly discerning in challenging and rejecting false, lying claims of apostleship. They were commendably strong on truth (while culpably weak on love).

It is noteworthy that the author, the one dictating these letters, does not expand on any of these except that in the second half of verse 2. All these assets are expected, so their presence, while commendable, is not heroic, above and beyond the call of duty.

4—The liability side: they had left their first love. What is this first love? Is it vertical—toward God—or horizontal—toward one another? Since the author did not rule out either one, and since there is (especially in another writing of this author) an unbreakable connection between the two (1 John 4:20), it is probably best to say both. After all, is it even possible to stop loving one another, yet continue to love God? Or the reverse? 1 John 4:7–21 strongly denies such a possibility.

The Ephesians were very busy—deeds, toil, perseverance (v. 2)—perhaps Martha-like; so busy, they seem not to have prioritized Mary-like adoration of the Lord (see Luke 10:38–42). Naturally, that fervent love for him would wane and, inevitably, so would their love for one another.

They were not directed to let go of the assets, especially zeal for truth, in order to shift all focus to the liability, lack of love.

5—Remedy: repent. Stated twice, both affirmatively and negatively, this is no mere suggestion. It is imperative. This church is headed toward disintegration; it must reverse course and do so soon. The entire book emphasizes the point that opportunity to repent will run out once the Lord returns.

Remember. As a married couple that is headed toward divorce may get back on the right track by reviewing memories, returning to places and activities from their courtship and honeymoon days, churches may benefit from looking back at their best days (not just recent offenses), to remind themselves of the core values of focusing on the Lord and their special love for one another.

Faith is fixating on the Lord, which inevitably leads to love.

Threat: removal of the lamp, which amounts to ceasing to be a true church in which the Lord reigns (v. 5), not unlike Ezekiel's vision of the temple vacated by God in his glory (Ezek 10).

The words are "or else I am coming and I will . . ." The idea is, "when I come, I will . . ." He is coming, whether they repent or not.

6—Nicolaitans: the Ephesians hate their deeds (while some in the Pergamum church subscribe to their teaching; Rev 2:15). Beyond this, we know nothing of their identity, doctrines, or deeds.

7—Tree of life = eternal life. See Gen 2:9, the tree Adam and Eve did not choose to eat; Gen 3:24, from which they were banished; Rev 22:2, freely provided in the new creation.

8–11—Smyrna (shortest letter; one of two without any condemnation): the Lord knows their persecution felt as poverty (though they are spiritually rich) and slander by satanic synagogue (cf. Rev 3:9). More suffering is coming (imprisonment for some, "ten days"). Don't fear (dread), be faithful, even if you (someone) suffer ultimate persecution.

8—First and last is synonymous with alpha-omega (Rev 22:13) and with the beginning and the end (21:6); it is coupled with "him who was and is and is to come" (1:8). It speaks of eternality, hence of assured ultimate triumph. That eternality was tested by the cross and proven true: he is indestructible. He lives forevermore (1:18). And so he shall reign forever (11:15).

9—Outwardly (materially) poor; inwardly (spiritually) rich.

"Tribulation and poverty" sounds very similar to the Hebrew hendiadys "poor and needy" (*ani weebyon*), which occurs at least twenty-nine times in the OT. See for instance Ps 37:14; 40:17. It speaks of the faithful who are typically humble and thus especially vulnerable to abuse by the powerful, the proud.

Blasphemy has the sense of slander, false accusations: falsely accusing and slandering God. As noun and verb, this word also occurs in Rev

13:1, 5, 6; 16:9, 11, 21; 17:3, all associated with the first beast and his associates. In chapter 16, it is the expression of unrepentance.

It was coming from the Jewish synagogue. But they could hardly be called true Jews if they were so hateful toward Messiah's people, the church. They belong in fact to Satan, who is shown later to be consumed with bloodlust to destroy Messiah Jesus and his loyal followers (Rev 12:3–4, 10–17).

10—You have not seen the end of suffering; more will surely come. Do not fear that prospect. Even if you die, I promise you the life of a king (crown) forever.

On the shift from second singular to plural and back to singular, see comment above under "to the angel."

12–17—Pergamum: The Lord knows they live in Satan's capital city, where he has his throne room. Yet even on their worst day—when a brother was put to death—they were steadfast in faith (v. 13). Nevertheless, they have two problem groups: one that holds to the teaching of Balaam (v. 14), who coaxed Israel into cohabiting with Moabites and joining in their idolatrous worship (Num 25:1, 3, 5; 31:16); the other that holds to the teaching of the Nicolaitans (v. 15; see comment at Rev 2:6).

12—"Sharp double-edged sword" from his mouth (see Rev 1:16): by his word, he judges with the power to put to death (as in 19:15). The power of God's word goes back to creation, Gen 1, and is taught throughout OT and NT.

13—The verse begins and ends with "where you live . . . where Satan lives." It is not that Satan lives among them, but that they live in his lair.

Satan has a throne; it is on earth (cf. Luke 4:5–6; John 12:31; 14:30; 16:11; Eph 2:2). In this case, it was even in Pergamum.

The pressure to deny their Lord must have been enormous. That is the point of persecution. But this church stayed true by holding fiercely (*krateis*; also in vv. 14, 15, 25; 3:11; see comment at Rev 2:15) in the darkest days.

Antipas (of whom nothing more is known) and Jesus (Rev 1:5) were faithful witnesses when threatened with death.

14–15—A short list of complaints: two problem groups within the church, one associated with Balaam, the other with the Nicolaitans. Both hold fiercely (*kratountas*, cognate to the noun *kratos*, strength, might) to their respective errors (see further at v. 24), just as the church holds fiercely to the Lord's name (v. 13).

16—He demands the angel—i.e., the church—repent, and threatens to come and wield the sword of his mouth (v. 12) against them; that is, to execute eternal capital punishment by his word. They must confront and deal decisively with both of these problems. These must be utterly purged out of the church; they must not be condoned or coddled.

17—On spiritual manna, see John 6:31–35. The phrase there, "the true heavenly bread" (v. 32), is probably the best definition. That is then further explained as referring to Jesus himself (vv. 33, 35). He is the eternally satisfying (spiritual) nutrition.

Beale is probably correct in opining "there may be no single background for the 'white stone.'" He then identifies a couple probable associations. "A white stone was commonly associated with a vote of acquittal . . . or a favorable vote . . . . A white stone sometimes was also used as a pass of admission to special occasions."[2] Both of these fit nicely in John's promise for overcomers. White is used consistently in Revelation of glorious perfection. This is certainly a prized reward.

On the new name, see Rev 19:12 and comment. Here it seems to suggest something of the glory in the new creation: these saints are destined to be entirely redeemed, utterly new.

18–29—Thyatira (longest letter):

Brief, crisp commendation (v. 19): deeds of love, faith, service, endurance, and their works have been continually improving—many similarities to Ephesus—followed by more lengthy warning (vv. 20–23). The false teacher is Jezebel and her teaching is "the deep things of Satan" (v. 24). The church should have expelled her long before. It is hard to say which John means: has she been leading or has she merely been attempting to lead true saints (*tous emous doulous*, literally, my servants, v. 20) into compromise with idol worship and its immoral practices, a virtual definition of paganism (cf. v. 14)? She is a stubborn, unrepentant adulteress whom he will consign to a different bed, her death bed. He will also kill her illegitimate offspring and pour out great tribulation on even those saints who have joined themselves to her, who will not repent and distance themselves from her (v. 22). The Lord here identifies her; it is now up to the church to isolate her and pull away from her, leaving her exposed to the Lord's judgment (vv. 22–24).

2. Beale, *Revelation*, 252–53.

18—"Son of God" = Vassal-King of earth (Ps 2:7; 2 Sam 7:14; who of course is also the second person of the Trinity); see vv. 26–27, quoting Ps 2:9. Eyes and feet together speak of real justice and judgment. With his eyes, he sees even the secrets of the heart (see v. 23; Ecc 12:14; Luke 8:17; Rom 2:16; 1 Cor 4:5). With his feet, he can trample the guilty. That image is seen from the other side in Dan 7:7, 19, where the antichrist crushes his opponents by trampling.

19—The congregation collectively exhibits several commendable qualities, indicative of genuine faith. In fact, they are even growing stronger, indicative of dynamic faithfulness. This must be true of a significant number of the members of the congregation, at the same time as others compromise with false teaching and come under the Lord's threats which follow.

20—This church's major fault is misguided tolerance: they have condoned a teacher he calls Jezebel. The point is not her real name, but the association with the infamous wife of King Ahab. (See especially 1 Kgs 18:13; 19:1–2; 21:1–26; 2 Kgs 9:22.) She falsely claims to speak as a prophetess with a new word from God. She teaches and deceives—a hendiadys meaning her distinctive doctrine is false and misleading. It has as its goal and result pagan behaviors and practices. These practices—fornication and eating that which had been sacrificed to idols—are scarcely distinguishable from those inspired by Balaam (see comment at vv. 12–17 above).

21—God's longsuffering is extreme. He gave her plenty of time to change her mind and her ways. This only served, however, to prove her thoroughly hard-hearted, just like Pharaoh, the survivors in Rev 9:20–21, the followers of the beast in chapter 16, just like Satan, who will have one thousand years to consider his option to repent (20:1–3, 7–10).

22—Poetic justice: she loves spending time in bed (of adultery); I will make her so sick, she cannot get out of bed.

23—She thinks she has successfully brought forth a next generation like herself, but even that will be destroyed; she shall have nothing to show for her wicked ways. (More or less literally translated, "I will kill her children with death.") The faithful of all seven churches will see and learn crucial truth about the Lord. Searching hearts and rewarding the godly also come out of the fiery eyes and bronze feet.

24–25—Distancing themselves from her is all he demands of those who have not followed her, but he urges them to hold fast until he comes. Here the faithful do not even hold loosely (*echousin*) to Jezebel's doctrine.

They are then commanded to hold fiercely (*kratēsate*) to as much as they rightly know of truth. He cannot pass up another opportunity to remind us that he is coming ("until I come").

26–27—Overcoming consists of and requires keeping his works to the end of one's mortal life; that is, respecting him as Lord-King by complying with his every demand.

Overcomers will share his rule over the nations. This is remarkable: the Lord promises them the high honor of ruling, with the same words with which the High King of heaven commissioned him (Ps 2:8–9; see also Rev 3:21; 5:10; 2 Tim 2:12).

28—Morning star = Venus? Many connect this to Num 24:17, "A star will come out of Jacob" (Balaam). "The image of a star from Jacob became a stock messianic expression in intertestamental Judaism."[3] Compare Rev 22:16, "I am . . . the bright morning star."

Chapter 3

1–6—Sardis: Dead or dying church, despite a reputation (name) for life.

Faux liveliness: their works look impressive, when they are actually lifeless. Many people look at this church and think that's life; but the Lord knows otherwise. We need to be more concerned about God's assessment than people's.

Name (*onoma*) is the key word in this letter: vv. 1, 4, 5 [2x].

The first name means reputation (v. 1 ESV, NET, NIV); their public reputation is lively, whereas the truth is the opposite. They get this reputation/name from the surrounding society, but God contradicts that assessment: "You are [in fact] dead."

The second name is the people—literally, names, rendered people, individuals, persons—in the church who have not defiled themselves by compromise with the world and its values (v. 4). It is those values that have seduced the majority into seeking the society's approval, thus not God's.

The faithful must continue to seek the approval and name that God would give them (v. 5). That is, faithful overcomers will retain their name,

---

3. Wilson, "Revelation," 4:270.

as Jesus will himself vouch for them before God in his very throne room (he ever lives to make intercession for us, Heb 7:25).

So the issue is to care about God's evaluation, not people's. Beware the praise of the wider society.

1—He has spirits, stars. We do not learn of his having the seven spirits until Rev 5:6, where they are the horns and eyes of the slaughtered and standing Lamb, who boldly approaches the Enthroned One to claim the scroll. In having these spirits (explained in comment at 1:4 how these refer to the Holy Spirit), he has omnipotence (seven horns) and omniscience (seven eyes). There, these spirits are sent into all *ha'aretz,* the earth/land. He is the all-knowing ruler with all power to enforce his will. Having the seven stars brings special attention to his primary concern that the churches respect his rule.

2–3—They are spiritually groggy; they need to arouse, wake up, or else! Then they need to strengthen, remember, obey, repent. The call to wake up implies inattentiveness, lack of appropriate, needed vigilance, but also not yet final deadness (2).

2—Even what has not died is on that verge. Immediate obedience is required; delay is disobedience. Their works are unfinished and thus lifeless. These must get pushed across a finish line in order to qualify as good in the Lord's eyes.

3—They received by hearing, so it was a word. It is that previously learned message they must obey anew. Thief-like surprise will overtake all who are not watchful, alert, who continue drowsy, unprepared. (See discussion at 16:15.) The only effectual preparation is faith. Unless they comply, his coming to them will be a coming against (ESV, NET) them. The Greek *epi* could also be translated *upon* (NKJV).

4—Not everyone in this church is deserving this rebuke; some are clean, worthy (complete works). Soiled garments = imperfect deeds, those performed for the approval of the unclean society, rather than for their Lord (cf. Matt 6:1).

Walk with the Lord in white speaks of his utter approval, his promise of justification in final judgment and welcome into all the fullness of eternal life, as in the next verse.

5—Overcomers will wear white, clean garments; their names will not be erased. "Greek cities in the ancient world maintained a list of citizens in a public register. When someone committed a criminal action and was condemned, he lost his citizenship and his name was then erased from the register."[4]

7–13—Philadelphia: Keys, open door, little power. The weak but faithful church. "When I am weak, then I am strong" (2 Cor 12:10).

7—David = king, royal authority, which is absolute. Key = control of access, both for salvation and condemnation: he opens to some and incarcerates others. "What he opens no one can shut and what he shuts no one can open" (NIV).

8—"I know your works," but he does not tell what those are until the end of the verse. Though relatively weak, they have exerted the force necessary to maintain their grip on the Lord's word, obeying him (also v. 10). Stated negatively, they have not denied his name, they have not renounced him publicly. Cf. Rev 2:13, "you [Pergamum] hold fast my name, and did not deny my faith." Cf. Luke 9:50; 11:21.

He indicates his approval in the middle of the verse: I am the only one that can shut the door that I have opened for you; [lucky for you,] that does not depend on your powers, as they are minuscule.

9—Someday that synagogue of Satan (cf. Rev 2:9) will bow in subjection. Cf. Ps 110:1, as the Father will compel Messiah's enemies to bow to him. Does this indicate that these faithful ones had been expelled, locked out from the synagogue? Had they been powerless, forced to bow?

10—Because they have kept his word (see v. 8), he will keep (same Greek word both times, *tēreō*) them from the world's hour of testing. That hour must refer to the coming judgments described in chapters 6–19. This seems to be more than a promise to preserve them through the trials and tribulations that are predicted in the rest of the book. To keep them out of (*ek*) seems very different from to keep them through. Further, the promise is to keep them out of the hour or season itself. This fits a pre-tribulation rapture. (Others he keeps through the season, Rev 7:4–8; still others he comforts when they have endured faithfully unto death, 2:10; 7:9–20.)

"The word of my perseverance" (NASB) is probably better rendered "my word about perseverance," meaning the Lord's command to endure. NET is surely right in rendering it "you have kept my admonition to endure steadfastly."

---

4. Wilson, "Revelation," 4:272.

This is the first of eleven occurrences of "the inhabitants of *ha'aretz*" (or a near equivalent). See discussion in part 1 above.

11—"Hold on/fast" translates a verb of strength (*kratei*, the same verb as is discussed at Rev 2:15): be strong, keep hanging in there. This he says to those with little power (v. 8). With the previous word of promise— "I am coming soon"—there is hope that relief is coming soon.

"So that no one will take away your crown": this crown is precious; we cherish and value it highly. So we are highly motivated to hold fast. This holding cannot be with the physical person, so it must be spiritual; thus it must be faith. This then corresponds to Rev 2:9, "Be faithful unto death." Faith is always faith in Jesus. Genuine faith endures, is strong. False faith is temporary; at some point it walks away and ceases to believe.

Crown, *stephanos*, does not refer to some reward or rank lower than a king. Even the victorious Laodiceans are promised enthronement (Rev 3:21). See discussions at 4:10; 14:14 regarding crowns.

How someone might take away that crown is not at all clear. The *you* is singular, addressed to the angel, and so speaks to the church collectively. John's point is especially the exhortation to hold on so tightly—*kratei* (see above)—that no one would ever be able to wrest it away. Johnson suggests "either Satan or men could rob them of their crown by diverting them from exclusive loyalty to Jesus."[5] Agreeing with Johnson, exclusive loyalty to Jesus is that to which they and we must hold tightly.

12—Pillar: A permanent fixture in the heavenly throne room, privileged to remain there forever. In Rev 13:6, the saints are the temple itself (as also in Eph 2:19–22; 1 Pet 2:5).

Names (my God, new Jerusalem [i.e., Messiah's bride, Rev 21:9–10], my new name): like parental/husband ownership.

14–22—Laodicea: No commendation, lukewarm, on the verge of being vomited by the Lord.

14—Amen occurs seven more times in Revelation. But this is the only time it is the Lord's self description. Every other time (Rev 1:6, 7; 5:14; 7:12 [2x]; 19:4; 22:20) it speaks of agreement, endorsement, approval, "strong affirmation of what is stated" (BDAG). BDAG explains this occurrence as "Christ as the ultimate affirmation." That is still cryptic but not opaque. So he does not stop there.

5. Johnson, "Revelation," 455.

He always bears true witness, but especially before Pilate when his life was on the line. He is the Messiah.

Finally, he is the beginning of God's creation. But here John uses the same word for beginning as he does in John 1:1, where he also writes about creation and the Lord's place in it. Thus it is highly probable he means to allude to that verse and that reality. The one dictating this letter to Laodicea is affirming ("Amen") that he was "in the beginning (archē) . . . [and] all things were made through him" (John 1:1, 3).

The church of Laodicea is reminded the Lord is telling the sworn truth that he was at creation and was and is the Creator himself. Your Creator who always speaks truth says:

15–16—I know the true facts.

On cold/hot water:

"Laodicea must have been notorious as a city which, for all its prosperity, could provide neither the refreshment of cold water for the weary, nor the healing properties of hot water for the sick; its lukewarm water would be useless for either purpose . . . . The church in Laodicea was providing neither refreshment for the spiritually weary, nor healing for the spiritually sick."[6]

The author repeats the pair cold/hot three times.

This church is, like others before, on the verge of being rejected, like tepid water out of the mouth of one expecting, demanding refreshment.

17—The sentence begins with "for" or "because" (hoti), providing the logical connection from the cold/hot criticism.

Their self-esteem was high, haughty; the Lord's esteem of them was low.

They smugly boasted of material wealth. In fact, he doubles the word rich/wealthy. First it is the predicate adjective, "I am rich," then the verb, "I have become rich." It is cocky boasting, confirmed by the next line: "I have no needs or wants."

The Lord charges to the contrary that they are not only impoverished but also blind and naked and, for good measure, wretched and pitiable.

Here too the descriptions are of spiritual condition; they must be looking at the things seen instead of unseen (2 Cor 4:16; 10:7).

18—Fortunately for them, the Lord has all they need: wealth, white clothes, cure for blindness (addressing the last three of v. 17). But they

6. Rudwick and Green, "Laodicean Lukewarmness."

must come to him. He promises to enrich them, to clothe them extravagantly, and to heal their blindness.

19—He offers this reproof and training because he loves them/us
(cf. Prov 3:12; Heb 12:5–11). Mythbusting alert: the verb is not *agapaō*, as
some might expect or hope, but *phileō*. The zealous thing to do is to turn
back to him or to repent earnestly (as Jas 4:9–10).

20—Even if the church as a whole does not repent, he reaches out to
every individual ("if anyone"; confirmed in the overcomer statement of v.
21) and will accept the invitation of any who welcome him, and certainly
provide all he promised in v. 18.

Sharing a meal signifies profound acceptance and mutuality
(fellowship).

21—Amazing hope for overcomers from all churches: reign with
him and the Father-King of heaven forever! This is our destiny. See Rev
5:10.

Overall impressions of the seven churches unit:

- The Lord is absolutely supreme, such that no deviation from submissive obedience and allegiance is tolerable. The vision of Rev 1:12–16
  (reinforced in the sender identity statements) should burn into our
  heart and psyche so that we fear and adore him deeply, constantly.

- He promises fabulously extravagant eternal blessings to his faithful
  followers.

- Churches are responsible to enforce internal conformity to purest
  devotion.

- Churches are commonly populated by true and false followers.
  (Evangelism begins there, with the goal of either converting the
  false professors or driving them away.)

Chapter 4

1—John is ushered into the presence of God in heaven, allowed to
see, and commanded to report.

"What must take place after these things" is almost word for word
identical to the ending of Rev 1:19, his original charge to write in this
book (*ha [mellei/dei] genesthai meta tauta*; there is no meaningful

difference between *mellei* and *dei* in these statements). Nowhere else does the author use this phrasing. So this verse marks the beginning of that final section of the book (aside from the epilogue, 22:6–21).

"The first voice that I had heard" is either that in Rev 1:8 or that in 1:10. Verse 8 is first, but it is not described as a voice that John heard. The first time John says he heard a voice was in 1:10, and that was the voice of the one he saw in that great vision, the glorious Lord Jesus himself, when he directed John to "write what you see" to the seven churches. That was also the only voice like a trumpet prior to this. As well, this speaker is the one showing John the scene, which fits with 1:1.

2—Spiritual realm: The throne room of the King of heaven!

This throne is in heaven (throne, 11x in ch, 4); thus he is King of heaven.

Introduced as a seated or sitting one (*kathēmenos*, anarthrous), that is, an Enthroned One. Heaven's throne has an occupant, which should interest us greatly. (Then in v. 3, he is *ho kathēmenos*, that Enthroned One.)

I am inclined to doubt the capital S on spirit (with NRS). I think the author is saying that his experience is spiritual.

For what it is worth—perhaps not much—this heavenly King is never described as crowned, neither with *diadēma* nor *stephanos*. But he is the Enthroned One thirteen times (see below).

This is the first person of the Trinity, God the Father, not God the Son. That one first appears in this scene in Rev 5:5–6 as the Lion-Lamb.

3a—The first thought of John's readers would be, "Tell us what he looked like." The King is described as resembling two stones, jasper and carnelian. (Two more stones are mentioned later: emerald, v. 3b, and crystal, v. 6.) But that is all the description of the King himself we get. Perhaps John's minimal description is meant to comply with the second Sinai prohibition against making any graven image of God (Exod 20:4–5). We must never forget, God is spirit; this vision is spiritual, and heaven is a spiritual domain. But we can describe such spiritual realities only in material likenesses.

3b–6—Everything is oriented in relation to the throne and thus to the King, the relational issue being indicated by prepositions:

–around (v. 3): surrounded (*kuklothen*, circle-like) by rainbow-like emerald

–around (v. 4): surrounded (*kuklothen*) by twenty-four thrones, elders seated, dressed in white, with gold crowns (*stephanos*); hence these are kings, loyal vassals

–out from (v. 5): thunder and lightning from the throne

–before (v. 5): seven burning lamps = divine Spirit(s) (see comment at Rev 1:4)

–before (v. 6): sea of glass (again in Rev 15:2)

–in middle . . . and around [i.e., inner circle] (v. 6, paraphrased translation): four living ones

3b—Rainbow: see Ezek 1:28 ("As the appearance of the rainbow in the clouds on a rainy day, so was the appearance of the surrounding radiance. Such was the appearance of the likeness of the glory of the LORD" [NASB]), the final descriptor there of the glory of God. This resembles emerald, without elaboration. It must suggest spectacular beauty, as if a rainbow is not beautiful enough.

4—Twenty-four elders crowned and enthroned. Elders are leaders of the people of God, common in the OT and NT. These must correspond to the twelve plus twelve of the tribes of Israel and apostles of the church, as in the new Jerusalem, Rev 21:12, 14. The crowns are *stephanous,* not *diadēmata*; but they are also golden, and these personages are enthroned and reigning with Jesus and the Father (3:21; 22:3; cf. 2 Tim 2:12). So the crowns are royal, not merely triumphal.

Their white robes indicate their perfect holiness, satisfactory to be in the presence of this holy King. In Rev 3:4–5, white garments are promised to the victorious in Sardis.

The faithful martyrs in the fifth seal are given white robes (Rev 6:11). The same faithful martyrs are seen clothed in those white robes in 7:9, 13–14. Finally, there is a blessing pronounced for all who shall have washed their robes (22:14), clearly the blessing of admission to and reigning in the glorious eternal kingdom.

See verse 10 for their only activity described in this scene.

5—This is the first of four lists of thunder and lightning (also Rev 8:5; 11:19; 16:18; see comment at 16:18).

Why burning lamps or torches? It is obvious John has Ezek 1:13 in mind: "In the midst of the living beings there was something that looked like burning coals of fire, like torches darting back and forth among the living beings. The fire was bright, and lightning was flashing from the fire" (NASB). These must be the same beings, lamps like burning coals, lightning. All must agree this is a mysterious image: spirit beings, the active presence of the Holy Spirit of God, depicted in (spiritual) fire and lightning.

In the next chapter (Rev 5:6) these spirits are the Lamb's seven eyes and horns which are sent on a mission into all *ha'aretz*.

6a—"Sea of glass like crystal." This image is biblically unprecedented. It seems an odd feature in the presence of the King. Glass and crystal suggest calmness of surface and purity of water. These traits stand in radical contrast to the popular ANE mythological concept of seas as being forboding, dangerous, the abode of sea monsters, the place from which ships too often do not return. In the presence of the King of heaven, even the sea is tame.

This is like (*hōs*) a sea, somehow not the same as what we know as sea. Again, this is heaven, hence a spiritual domain.

In Rev 15:2, this same sea is further described as fiery: "like (*hōs*) a sea of glass mixed with fire." On it, the tribulation martyrs seem to dance (stand). They neither sink nor are burned. In 22:1, we read of a river, not a sea, in the new Jerusalem whose water (living water or water of life) is clear as crystal, suggesting that it is perfectly pure, absent of any contaminants. See also 21:2 and comment on the absence of a sea in the new earth.

6b–8—The four living ones (one of the terms Ezekiel uses, the other being cherubim). They have many eyes front and back (full of, stated in both vv. 6 and 8), somewhat like the wheels of Ezekiel's vision chariots (Ezek 1:18). They look like the living ones in Ezekiel's vision (v. 7); they call out the words of the seraphim in Isaiah's vision (v. 8; Isa 6:2–3).

7—Like (all similes) lion, bull, human face, eagle (with wings spread as in flight; Ezek 1:10). The first three are earthbound; the eagle patrols the sky. All are kinglike masters of their domains: lions of the wild animals, oxen of the domestic animals, man of all earthly creatures, eagles of the bird domain.

–With six wings, eyes all around (as Ezek 1:18; 10:12).

–They call "holy, holy, holy" (as Isa 6:3).

–They give the King glory, honor, thanks.

8—Echoes Isa 6:3, Isaiah's vision of God enthroned; adds the eternality statement of Rev 1:4, 8.

Eyes inside and out, indicating God has created them to be fully aware of their situation. If "holy, holy, holy" is not just a praise declaration but also a warning, as I believe it is, these are constantly watchful that God's presence not be contaminated, broached by any defilement. They do not take a break or a day off (literally, they have no rest); they are constantly, eternally vigilant, guaranteeing the King will never have to bear with or deal with any unholy crasher.

These are most probably the seraphim of Isa 6 and the cherubim of Ezek 1, 10, etc., and the real beings which the gold covered sculptures of the mercy seat represent. They seem to be a special species of angel, perhaps a small population. (Cherubim are first seen in Gen 3:24 guarding against Adam and Eve and their descendants reentering the garden, where they might "take from the tree of life, and eat, and live forever" {Gen 3:22].)

9—These also give glory, honor, thanks. Is this different from the "holy" cries? Yes, if "holy, holy, holy" is a warning to would-be intruders.

10—The twenty-four elders fall prostrate in worship (repeated in Rev 19:4)—in acknowledgement of his holiness—and cast, offer, or present (*balousin*) their crowns, signifying they are not worthy to be regarded as kings in his presence. Only the King is worthy.

11—These elders cry, "Worthy are you . . . to receive glory, honor, power [royal ascriptions] . . . for you created."

Apart from his creative work, nothing would exist but him. It doesn't take much contemplation of our world to exclaim, "Amazing creation—amazing Creator!" The two great works of God must be judged creation and redemption, the respective praises of chapters 4 and 5 (vv. 9–10). One could then conclude that even redemption is creation, new creation. This King is the only reason any of us and our world exist. We owe him eternal praise.

Creator/creation figures prominently in Rev 3:14; 4:11; 5:13; 8:9; 10:6; 14:7; 21:1, 5.

Sit: 33x in Revelation, in the following uses:

- God on throne: 13x (7x in chs. 4–5; 3x in Rev 6:16—7:15; 3x in chs. 19, 20, 21)
- Elders on thrones: 2x (chs. 4, 11)
- Riders on colored horses: 4x (Rev 6:1–8)
- Riders on horses: 1x (Rev 9:17)
- Son of Man on cloud: 3x (Rev 14:14–16)
- Equals dwell on earth: 1x (Rev 14:6)

- Prostitute on waters, beast, heads/mountains/kings, as queen: 5x (chs. 17–18)
- Jesus and enemies on horses: 4x (ch. 19)

Throne: 47x:

- The throne of heaven, occupied always and only by God the Father: 37x (Rev 1:4; 3:21; 4:2, 2, 3, 4, 5 [2x], 6 [3x], 9, 10 [2x]; 5:1, 6, 7, 11, 13; 6:16; 7:9, 10, 11 [2x], 15 [2x], 17; 8:3; 12:5; 14:3; 16:17; 19:4, 5; 21:3, 5; 22:1, 3)
- The Son's throne: 1x (Rev 3:21)
- Satan's throne: 2x (Rev 2:13; 13:2)
- Twenty-four elders' thrones: 3x (Rev 4:4 [2x]; 11:16)
- Beast's throne: 1x (Rev 16:10)
- Martyred saints' millennial thrones: 1x (Rev 20:4)
- Great white throne: 2x (20:11, 12): this must be the same throne as God's in heaven.

Chapter 5

Same setting as chapter 4. Focus on the scroll/book (vv. 1, 2, 3, 4, 5, 7, 8, 9) and the Lamb (vv. 5, 6, 7, 8, 9, 10, 12, 13) who takes it.

1—Attention directed immediately to the scroll. Significantly, it is discovered to be in the King's right hand, which fact indicates this scroll is of extreme importance. (One might with a little liberty imagine this great King possesses a vast library. But this singular book he entrusts to no one; he holds it personally for this moment.)

Writing on both sides harkens to Exod 32:15. Like the law given to Moses, this is law concerning *ha'aretz* given to Messiah, the new and greater Moses.

2–5—Dramatic introduction to the Lamb, demonstrating that only he is qualified to claim the scroll, which also signals the extreme importance of the scroll.

2–4—If none can be found to open the scroll, John's reaction signals that would be the most catastrophic loss. The strong angel with his loud

voice can certainly be heard throughout heaven and earth and even under the earth by every sentient being. Of course every being that is not
the Creator is one created by him. Not even the most arrogant and asser-
tive, let alone the most pious and pure, of all humanity and angels dares
to approach the great King to claim this scroll. The seriousness of this
situation shuts down all pretentiousness and all chutzpah, which does
not often happen in the world we know.

4—The verb weep is in the imperfect tense, indicating ongoing un-
controllable sobbing, which itself indicates John's read of the situation: if
no one is qualified to take that scroll, in some sense, all is lost. The entire
creation program shall have failed. The eternal destiny of the universe
would be evil, not good.

5—John's fear is relieved with the assurance that a champion, no, the
Champion has been located.

He is Lion of Judah (Gen 49:9), Root of David (see Isa 11:10).

He has overcome/conquered.

His victory is what qualifies him to take and open the scroll. That
victory is specified in verses 9–10: by his death he redeemed humans
from every people group. In order for this scroll to be claimed and
opened, there had to be redemption, and only the Redeemer could do
the opening.

This reassuring word was delivered by one of the elders. Of the
twelve occurrences of the word elders (which is always plural), only here
and Rev 7:13 is the reference not to the entire group of twenty-four.

This is the only time in Revelation where our Lord is called Lion,
whereas references to him as Lamb abound.

6—He is between (literally, in the middle of A and in the middle of
B) the throne (with living ones, cherubim—A) and the elders (B, whose
thrones are around the central and highest throne). Thus the Lamb is
identifying with the elders, in a central and mediating place (as 2 Tim
2:5).

He is the Lamb, standing even though slaughtered (see v. 9).

He has seven horns and seven eyes (= omnipotence, omniscience).

This is the first of thirty times the Lord is called Lamb, and that does not include the several more references where pronouns stand for that noun (e.g., Rev 6:3, 5, 17).

Slaughtered yet standing speaks of death and resurrection. He hasn't cheated death by escaping danger (like Daniel and his friends) but has defeated (conquered, *nikaō*) it by experiencing it and coming back to life, immortal life—not back from the dead but alive on the other side of the door of death.

Elsewhere we are taught that he is seated on the throne at the right hand of the supreme majesty of heaven (Ps 110:1, cited several times in the NT: Matt 22:44; 26:64; Mark 12:36; 14:62; 16:19; Luke 20:42; 22:69; Acts 2:33–34; 5:31; Rom 8:34; Eph 1:20; Col 3:1; Heb 1:3, 13; 8:1; 10:12; 12:2; 1 Pet 3:22). The concept is that he is heaven's King's vassal to rule earth (also Ps 2:6–9). Here he is not seated but standing and approaching the great throne to claim the scroll.

Ideally, any judge-king needs to know as much as possible, all facts, all truth, and needs sufficient power to act on that knowledge in order to provide real justice and enforce perfect rule. The seven eyes and seven horns represent that omniscience and omnipotence required of the ideal Ruler.

By God's seven spirits (see comment at Rev 1:4) who are everywhere, he knows all the facts—all the obvious plus all the secrets—on *ha'aretz*. If the spirits have been sent, they were sent by the King to gather intel.

7—He claimed the scroll without any nervousness or hesitancy. It is rightfully his. The similarity to Dan 7:13–14 is so strong that the equivalency must be understood. This one is not called Son of Man—not here. But this reference and those in Rev 1:13 and 14:14 reinforce one another.

8—The four living ones and twenty-four elders prostrate themselves before the Lamb, acknowledging his greatness and submitting reflexively and voluntarily. In Rev 4:8, the living ones were calling out continuously the perfect holiness of the King, and in 4:10, the twenty-four elders fell before the King in worship, presenting their crowns.

Each of the elders (probably not the "living ones") has a harp and a bowl of incense prayers (as in Rev 8:3).

Harps are also found in Rev 14:2; 15:2; 18:22. Only the last reference is earthly. The other three speak of instrumental music performed by redeemed humans in the presence of the King of heaven. In all three cases, the next line begins "and they sang." Here the harpist-singers are the twenty-four elders. In 14:2, they are unidentified ones whose audience includes the King, the living ones, and the elders (and whose cantata is learned by the 144,000 on earth). In 15:2, the harpist-singers are tribulation martyrs in this same throne room.

Each of these harpist-singers also holds a bowl filled with saints' prayers converted into incense, which certainly pleases the Lamb and the King. The content of the prayers must be for salvation, salvation that this Lamb is completely competent and pleased to provide, as embedded in the next verses.

9–10—They sing a new song (a phrase appearing six times in Psalms; Isa 42:10; repeated in Rev 14:3), paraphrased and amplified, "Worthy are you (Lamb), for you purchased by your death a people for yourself out of all nations. You will make them your kingdom of priest-kings, as the elders are themselves kings [enthroned and crowned] and priests [in the presence of the King, presenting the incense of the saints' prayers]."

His worthiness to claim earth is consequent to his redemptive death (slaughtered lamb). By his sacrificial death, he redeems not just Israelites but gentiles of all sorts as well.

"Reign on earth" as Adam and Eve were originally intended (Gen 1:26, 28). This reign will include both the millennium (Rev 20:4–6) and eternity (22:5). See also 3:21; Luke 22:29–30.

11—Many (innumerable; cf. Dan 7:10; Heb 12:22) angels (different from the elders and the living beings). Those in Dan 7:10 insure there will be perfect order in this court.

As elsewhere (Rev 7:9), this must be a very crowded and/or a very large throne room and the decibel level deafening—in a good way.

"I saw and I heard" was commonly the experience of prophets by which they received messages from heaven they were to pass to inhabitants of ha'aretz.

12—"Worthy is the slaughtered Lamb to receive [the same kind of praise the King receives]"; cf. Rev 4:11. This litany of nouns suggests the many associated kinds of praises that should be attributed to a good and great King. See comment at 7:12.

13—Now every knee bows and every tongue confesses (Phil 2:10–11; Isa 45:23) that Jesus is Yahweh, Lord-King of everything. Long live the King and the Lamb!—the two dominant characters of chs 4 and 5 and of Pss. 2 and 110. The Lamb is acclaimed equally with the Enthroned One, for he is in every essential way his equal. There is no reason to see this praise as coming only from the redeemed. That is, even Satan and all the damned join in uttering this confession, though not necessarily at this time.

14—The four approve, their amens complementing their "holy, holy, holy"; the twenty-four bow in humble and grateful worship.

Chapter 6

First through sixth seals

1–8—First through fourth seals: complementary, colored horses.

9–11—Fifth seal: martyrs' cry for revenge, justice.

12–17—Sixth seal: unprecedented cosmic shaking, terror seizing all (unbelieving) mankind.

These six seals are not to be seen as successive but as a depiction of the program of the scroll. Further, while there are six seals, the first four, the four horses, are a collective statement rather than a sequence of different events.

In these seals, the program of the Lord's second coming is shown to entail first his invading and reclaiming the earth/land (first through fourth seals, colored horses), second his avenging (= justice) the wrongful deaths of his faithful servants (fifth seal), and third his use of cosmic cataclysms to strike terror in the hearts of all who have not yet bowed to him (sixth seal).

Together they build anticipation for the grand climactic seventh seal, which is the seven trumpets, the seventh of which is the culmination of the Lamb's second coming.

1–8—For a more complete discussion of these horses and riders, see part 1 above.

Briefly: White horse (vv. 1–2): victory; red horse (vv. 3–4): chaos, sword; black horse (vv. 5–6, destruction of grains but not grapes, olives): tactics of invading force; pale green horse (vv. 7–8, death by sword, famine, pestilence, beasts): expelling the tenants of Messiah's land (Jer 2:7) for the sin of defiling it (Ezek 36:17).

The four summonses are called by the four living ones (introduced in Rev 4:7).

1–2—White horse rider certainly but lopsidedly wins, which is the point of the curious expression "conquering and to conquer." This syntax represents the Hebrew idiom of certainty, imperfect (or another verb form) plus infinitive absolute of the same verb. This white horse with rider is matched in Rev 19:11, and the two are the same: King Jesus himself. (See appendix 1 of part 1 for an expanded discussion.) The author begins with the declaration that this one will certainly, finally triumph. Before the battle begins, any uncertainty of outcome is put to rest. (One might imagine the introduction to the contestants before a boxing match or the Super Bowl with the judges' announcement to all which one will soon be crowned the winner.) This will have a great comforting effect on his followers as they face deadly persecution. (Similarly, the reader is clued in advance in 12:7–12 to the loser, Satan, and in 14:1–5 to the winners, Jesus the Lamb and the 144,000.)

3–4—Red horse rider is Gideon-like, defeating invaders by inducing them to kill each other (see Judg 7:22). "Slay one another" is also seen in Hag 2:22; Zech 14:13; 1 Sam 14:20; 2 Chron 20:23; Ezek 38:21.

5–6—Black horse rider is Joshua-like, invading *ha'aretz* to drive out the inhabitants and assume occupancy of the land; preserving ("do not damage") durable olive trees and grapevines while destroying single season grain crops.

Grapes and olives appear together very often in OT, referring to highly valuable perennial crops (Josh 24:13).

See Deut 7:13; 11:14; 12;17; 14:23; 18:4; 28:51 for connection of grain, wine, oil.

7–8—Pale green horse rider is like the agents God used to drive Israel out in Nebucchadnezzar's day, as described especially in Ezek 14:12–21: sword, famine, pestilence, wild beasts. (That author set up his prophecy back in Ezek 5:2 and 17; reiterated in 6:11.) God's design in Ezek 14 is to cut off man and beast (vv. 13, 17, 19, 21) from *ha'aretz*, to drive the people of the remaining kingdom of Judah out of the land, specifically because of their disobedience to God's Sinaitic terms of relationship, in fulfillment of the threats of curse laid out in Deut 28.

Hades is mentioned four times in Rev (here and Rev 1:18; 20:13, 14), always coupled with death. It has the sense of the grave (NLT), the Greek mythological place of the dead.

8—For the one quarter factor, one should compare Ezek 4:2, 12, where the fatality factor was one third.

9–11—Fifth seal: this might be seen as not so much a judgment as a promise of justice. The program of the Lamb's coming includes the four horses and this. That is, in his coming to drive out the wicked tenants of the land, he will simultaneously be avenging his faithful servants killed unjustly by those inhabitants of the land (v. 10). In opposing the true Lord of the land, they sought to exterminate his faithful followers (cf. the parables at Matt 21:33–36; 22:1–14). Here, he promises to bring perfect justice.

We expect to find the blood of the sacrificial animals under the altar (Lev 4:7, 18, 25, 30 34; 5:9; 8:15; 9:9), thus a holy sacrifice, pleasing to God. These are martyrs who were slaughtered because of "the word of God and the testimony they maintained" (cf. Rev 1:2, 9; 20:4; very serious stuff), words and testimony about Jesus as the true King to whom all must bow. Jesus then is what the inhabitants of the land sought to silence by killing these.

The martyrs fully expect that the holy and true Lord will bring justice and avenge their wrongful deaths attributed to the inhabitants of *ha'aretz*. As soon as the last martyr has died and the company is complete, that judgment will come.

The opening verses of the seventh seal (Rev 8:3–5) seem to indicate the imminency of God's answer to these accumulated prayers.

This is a case of justice delayed (v. 10) but eventually fulfilled perfectly (v. 11).

9—Souls (*psychas*) speaks of incorporeal spirits (as 2 Cor 5:8).

Slaughtered (*esphagmenōn*) speaks of "the killing of a person by violence; . . . butcher or murder someone" (BDAG).

This is the first reference (of nine) to the altar. Later, the altar is golden, has hot coals, has an attending angel, and is the source of a verbal message. See more discussion at Rev 9:13.

10—See vengeance statements at Rev 16:7; 19:2. They address their cry to *despotēs*. This word occurs ten times in nine NT books. It is a synonym of *kurios*. BDAG defines it, "one who has legal control and authority over persons, such as subjects or slaves, *lord, master.*"

The day of God's vengeance is a day for rejoicing: Deut 32:43.

11—Receiving white robes constitutes immediate assurance that these are the approved ones and so implies their killers will be convicted and judged, though not immediately. This also anticipates that more will soon join their company through the events to be described later, especially Rev 11:7; 13:7, 15; 20:4–6.

The idea that the number of martyrs should be soon (literally, yet a little time) completed (literally, fulfilled, *plērōthōsin*) argues powerfully against the notion that the short time statements at Rev 1:1, 3 indicate that this book is about the history soon after John's day, i.e., the first century (contra preterism). Obviously, the number of faithful martyrs continues to mount to this day. So the little time (*eti chronon mikron*) these must wait for vengeance continues to our day and will continue to the end of the worst of times, the great tribulation (see 7:14).

12–17—Sixth seal: Natural calamity and men's fear of final judgment.

12–14—Earthly and astronomical cataclysms, fulfilling especially Isa 50:3 (black like sackcloth); Joel 2:31 (dark sun, blood red moon); Dan 8:10 (falling stars, though these are angels); Isa 13:10; Ezek 32:7; Joel 2:10; 3:15 (darkened stars); Isa 34:4 (sky roll like scroll); Isa 54:10; Jer 4:24; Nah 1:5 (quaking mountains).

"Oh, that you would tear heaven open and come down, that the mountains might quake at your presence" (Isa. 64:1 NASB).

The rhetorical effect is of terrifying, seemingly world-ending destruction of the universe. This is, after all, the sixth of seven seals, so the reader is to understand this is just before the end.

The first and last are earthly; between them, sun, moon, stars, sky.

15–17—Men high and low reverting to being cave dwellers, seeking to hide in anticipation of the imminent great judgment day. See Isa 2:10, 19–21; Hos 10:8.

Those who have not put their hope in the Almighty Sovereign of the universe can only fear the worst. God judges people's allegiance as committed either to him or against him: there is no neutrality or ambiguity.

An important question the reader should bring to scenes like this is how would sane, faithful people respond? How should these respond? The answer is simple and obvious: they should plead guilty and immediately cast themselves on the mercy of the court; they should bow in submission to the Judge-King before the day of his great mercy runs out. The theme of repentance will be reprised in scene after scene through the next many chapters up to the scenes of final judgment in Rev 11:18 and 20:11–15. Sadly, most of those scenes tell the story of eternally self-destructive, stubborn defiance against the Almighty.

16—The express object of fear is the central characters of chapters 4 and 5, the King of heaven and the Lamb-Lion King of earth. These would rather be buried alive by mountains collapsing on them than face the judicial wrath of the supreme sovereign of all. Such burial will not however provide escape from judgment.

Where these seek protection from God in the rocks, the psalmist seeks God as his rocky safe place: "You have given commandment to save me, for you are my rock and my fortress" (Ps. 71:3 NASB).

Neither of these scenarios needs be understood literally. But what they represent is eminently serious and real.

17—"The great day of their wrath" speaks of the day of the Lord. See also "the great day of God the Almighty" in Rev 16:14. These cannot be different days. That day begins with destruction of the Lamb-Lord's opponents and continues forever with his beneficent rule, first over this first, cursed creation (one thousand years), then over the new. That day has been predicted by God's faithful prophets for millennia, and it will come.

The last expression is the rhetorical question, "Who is able to stand?" (See Ps 76:7; Joel 2:11; Nah 1:6; Mal 3:2.) The sense here is that no one can escape the judgment, and no guilty ones shall have right standing, justification, after the verdict is pronounced, but all will certainly be condemned. However we soon see standing ones, Rev 7:9, who were martyred during the great tribulation (surely including those of the fifth seal), subsequently and forever after filled with joy, never again to weep.

Together these first six seal judgments present the program of the scroll. It is about the Lord evicting the wicked inhabitants of his land for defiling it, claiming it for himself (first through fourth seals); promising vengeance to the martyrs whom the same inhabitants of the land abused (fifth seal); and warning of impending deadly judgment on all those enemies (sixth seal).

As the seventh seal is the seven trumpets, it is in those trumpet judgments that the scroll program is accomplished.

Chapter 7

1–3—Pause ordered before seventh seal.

Mark the saints before releasing the winds and damaging earth, sea, trees. This must be recognized as a clue to the content of the seventh seal: harming earth, sea, trees.

John and readers expect number seven next. There must be very high excitement over the prospect of the opening of the climactic seal, due to the evident importance of the scroll (see discussion at Rev 5:1–5). So this pause heightens the suspense that has been building through the first to sixth seals.

These four angels correspond to the first four trumpets.

1—"After this I saw" echoes Rev 6:9, 12, the beginnings of the fifth and sixth seals respectively, confirming the expectation of the immediate opening of the seventh.

They have taken their stand, perfect tense, suggesting movement into assigned positions as actors following the director's stage blocking.

The verb for holding back the winds, *kratountas*, is a word indicating strenuous exertion of exceptional power. See comment at Rev 2:15. These are mighty, not wimpy angels, and they are restraining strong forces. There is no human power capable of restraining even light breezes.

2–3—The angels use a signet brand to mark indelibly and prominently, so that identity cannot be mistaken. The effect is the same as wearing a team uniform that is unmistakably distinctive from the opposing team's uniform.

2—The seal is God's distinctive mark of ownership.

3—After God has his saints marked (described in vv. 4–8), these angels are to release the winds, so that they may carry out divine punishment against the unmarked population by doing significant but not utter harm to earth and sea and trees.

The word for damage or wreck was used in the third seal's command, do not damage (*adikēsēs, adikēsēte*) the oil or wine (Rev 6:6).

On marking saints, God's servants, then slaughtering the unmarked, see Ezek 9:4–6.

4–8—Marking the saints, 12,000 from each of the twelve tribes of Israel.

These 144,000 are to be spared the injury or harm (*adikeō*) of the trumpets. They are also protected from the attacks of the beasts of chapter 13 against those who out of true loyalty to Messiah Jesus refused to bow to them, antimessiah and his false prophet. Thus they reappear at the beginning of chapter 14 standing triumphantly with the Lamb on Mount Zion.

Some see these as the church, all believers in the time of the tribulation, even comprising the army Messiah will use to defeat that of Satan and the beast. There is, however, no internal clue to that effect, nor is there anything nonsensical or impossible about the literal sense: Christian Jews from each of the tribes of Israel. As well, the next section (vv. 9–17) is obviously intended to represent the rest of the saints, as counterpart to these. So unless and until an alternative interpretation meets the burden of proof, that sense is to be preferred.

At the same time, surely the author intended some symbolic sense to both twelve and thousand while not feeling an obligation to spell that out. So while there is no good reason to reject the literality of the numbers, the symbolic value of them is undoubtedly the more important issue.

Elsewhere he speaks of every tribe, tongue, etc., referring inclusively to Jews and gentiles (Rev 5:9; 13:7; 14:6), whereas here the author says every tribe of Israel (v. 4). This must be understood in that context as referring to Israel, exclusive of gentiles.

What is the rhetorical effect of the monotonous repetition "from the tribe of [X] 12,000"? As suggested elsewhere in these comments, this ancient author, like every other ancient prophet author, assumed and expected that his book would be read aloud to the people of God in group settings. The author must have intended to reinforce unforgettably that all twelve tribes would be represented by 12,000, a full complement chosen by God to be spared and thus to survive the tribulation, to enter the millennium in their mortality.

The author shows these same 144,000 in Rev 14:1–5 having indeed survived the tribulation in their mortality and standing triumphantly with the Lamb in Jerusalem, despite the beast's (antimessiah's) maniacal attempts to wipe out all followers of the Lamb.

There is probably little to be gained by exploring why these twelve, exclusive of Dan, and why in this order, and why Joseph instead of Ephraim. Many standard commentaries explore the facts and possible explanations. The fact that the word sealed is used with the naming of the first and last of the tribes and not the middle ten seems to be the author's one concession to the reduction of the monotonous repetition.

9–17—Multitudes from nations clothed in white, standing in the heavenly throne room, praising the King and the Lamb.

Distinctions from the 144,000:

- Innumerable (v. 9).

- Nations, tribes, peoples, tongues (v. 9). Which is more likely: that these nouns are the same as the sons of Israel (v. 4) or that they are different? Surely the default interpretation must be that they are different, unless and until strong evidence is adduced to the contrary. If John was thinking in Hebrew, he was thinking *goyim*, commonly referring to non-Jews, i.e., gentiles. Thus they correspond to the 144,000 Israelites as counterparts. Those are specially protected to survive the deadly persecution against Christians; these are not so protected but are now seen in heaven, filled with joy.

- They are also before the throne and the Lamb (v. 9), i.e., in heaven, comforted (though not yet glorified, not yet in new creation bodies). The 144,000 need a seal, which means they are not in heaven; without this seal they would still be susceptible to injury and death. There they stand. (Recall Rev 6:17, "Who is able to stand [before the judicial wrath of God]?")

  They are clothed in white, they hold palm fronds. Does that speak of the Feast of Tabernacles, which was a kind of harvest festival? See Lev 23:33–40; Zech 14. Their appearance is coupled with rejoicing. Others robed in white are the overcomers of Sardis and Laodicea (Rev 3:3–4, 18), twenty-four elders (4:4), prior martyrs (6:11), and Messiah's heavenly armies (19:14).

- They come out of the great tribulation (v. 14), that is, from the specific narrow time frame that is the concern of chapters 6–19.

- *skēnōsei* (v. 15): The King of heaven himself will personally provide them all the shelter they could ever need or want.

- They are also shepherded (*poimanei*) by the Lamb (v. 17).

- They remain before the throne, where they serve and worship the King continuously forever (v. 15); they will never again hunger or thirst or suffer from the sun's heat (Isa 49:10; Ps 121:6) or know tears of sorrow (vv. 16–17).

These then are comforted (though not yet glorified), gentile and Jewish saints who died during the tribulation (presumably martyred). They joyfully praise and worship God for his salvation (vv. 9, 10, 15), so that even the angels also praise and worship him (vv. 11–12). While 144,000 Jews will be protected (vv. 4–8), other faithful ones—i.e., these—will die by the hands of antimessiah and his supporters. But here we do not see any resentment or complaint. The last thing the author says here is no more tears and one of the first is palm branches, bespeaking joy (cf. Lev 23:40). The Lord is here called the Lamb four times (vv. 9, 10, 14, 17), reminding all that he was the first and prototypical martyr (v. 14 speaks of his atoning blood).

9—Such a large congregation; this must be a very large throne room (cf. Rev 5:11).

10—It must also be very noisy, joyously noisy.

"Salvation to our God" may sound strange to us, like God receives salvation. Some translations include "belongs." There is a precedent for this in Ps 3:8, "Salvation belongs to Yahweh." There is no word meaning belong in the original of either the psalm nor this verse, but that is probably the best single word to capture the idea.

The idea is that God the King of heaven of chapter 4 and the Lamb of chapter 5 are together the only Savior. He has that power, and he exerts it toward his favored ones, the faithful, righteous, and not toward the wicked rebels. Salvation is the ultimate blessing, the highest and best composite of gifts, benefits he can bestow, and he freely and lavishly bestows it on the followers of the Lamb. He rescues them from ultimate harm, unto ultimate life. (John 10:10 is not about fullness of life in our mortality in this first creation world but the absolute best possible life in the new creation.)

See also Rev 19:1, "Salvation and glory and power belong to our God." The praise here is ascribed to the King and the Lamb.

11—Other angels in the throne room. (In Rev 5:11, we read of "myriads of myriads and thousands of thousands" of angels in the throne room.) They and all privileged to be present voluntarily acknowledge the supremacy of the King.

12—These praise God as "our God." They itemize seven qualities that belong to him, the ideal majesty. (For similar lists, see Rev 4:9, 11; 5:12, 13; also 1:6. The word appearing in all lists is glory.)

13—We need to know who these are and from where they come.

14—John prefers not to risk guessing wrong. He turns the question back to the elder who posed the question. John's answer "you know" means "you tell me."

The great tribulation must refer to chapters 6–19, from white horse to white horse. It is Daniel's seventieth week, and it is the tribulation of Matt. 24:21.

Washed robes, also Rev 22:14, are the same as the white robes, verses 9 and 13.

15—They worship a King. That's what worship is. On this verb of worshipful service (*latreuousin*), see comment at Rev 22:3.

Isaiah speaks of glorious shelter (Isa 4:5–6) in that day when God raises up branch-man (Isa 4:2).

17—Springs of living water, tears wiped away: these are already enjoying some of the blessings of new creation, new Jerusalem, Rev 21:4; 22:1. Compare to Luke 16:25.

Chapter 8

1–5—Seventh seal; introduction to the seven trumpets

1—Silence: as holding their breath, anticipating the big one, the seventh seal. But this cannot be the seventh seal, for the scroll of Rev 5:1–5 demands a stupendously consequential climax.

2—The first thing he saw upon the opening of the seventh seal is seven trumpeter angels. This adds support to the conclusion that the seal is not the silence but the trumpets, as the first, fifth, and sixth seals are all introduced as visions, *kai eidon*, "and I saw."

On trumpets, see Joel 2:1–2 and 2:15:

> Blow a trumpet in Zion,
>   And sound an alarm on my holy mountain!
> Let all the inhabitants of the land tremble,
>   For the day of the LORD is coming;
> Surely it is near,
>   A day of darkness and gloom,
>   A day of clouds and thick darkness.
> As the dawn is spread over the mountains,
>   So there is a great and mighty people;

> There has never been anything like it,
>> Nor will there be again after it
>> To the years of many generations. (Joel 2:1–2 NASB)

"Blow a trumpet in Zion . . ." (Joel 2:15, followed by humble repentance language in vv. 15–17).

Joel 2:1, day of Yahweh: trumpet warning of God's wrath coming against inhabitants of *ha'aretz*.

Joel 2:15, day of Yahweh: trumpet call to Israel to repent (vv. 15–17), followed by national salvation (vv. 18–20).

These themes are so close to the ideas of the scroll that we must conclude our author had Joel 2 in mind. The trumpets are simultaneously the announcement of doom to the inhabitants of the land, *ha'aretz*, and the call to Israel to repent. Those who repent will be saved. The tribulation inhabitants of *ha'aretz* are faithless Israel. They are seen suffering divine pressure to repent. Some do, some do not. Repentance is the big idea of the sixth trumpet, showing the contrast of those who do not and those who do repent (Rev 9:20–21; 11:13).

Elsewhere, trumpets signal war (day of Yahweh), announce festivals and seasons. See Num 10:9–10.

The priests in Josh 6:4–7 are equipped with ram's horns to signal battle alarm, destruction for Jericho, victory for Israel, seven days—all remarkably similar to themes of these trumpets as the seventh scroll or seal. John probably means to allude to these secondarily, and he refers primarily to Joel 2.

3–5—This scene must be the satisfying resolution of the fifth seal, the cries of martyrs for vengeance (Rev 6:9–11). It also fits with the seventh seal, the seven trumpets, indicating that the trumpets are the retributive punishment on those inhabitants of *ha'aretz* (6:13; 8:13; 11:10) alive at the time who persecuted God's saints (including many in 7:9–17).

The scene begins in heaven with prayers as incense that bring God immense pleasure. It finishes with that incense fire being flung to earth in retribution on the guilty. At the sixth trumpet, it will be seen that these expressions of divine wrath are also opportunities for the wicked to repent and submit to God.

3—The prayers of the saints are being stored up in heaven to be answered in vengeance on the day God designates. It appears that the prayers and the incense are to be mingled. This angel is performing this service of a priest right before the King on his throne (repeated in v. 4).

4—God finds these prayers very pleasing (implied). He has delayed acting in affirmative response to them until now.

5—The fact that the incense was thrown to earth—specifically *ha'aretz*, the promised land—says the prayers were about injustice, abuse; and the abusers were the inhabitants of *ha'aretz*.

This also says that the trumpet judgments to follow are God's answers to those martyr prayers. Graciously, God is still holding out the offer of forgiveness to any who would repent.

This is the second of the four lists of thunder and lightning (also Rev 4:5; 11:19; 16:18).

7–12—First to fourth trumpets: earth/land (*ha'aretz*), sea, fresh waters, sun-moon-stars (as also first to fourth bowls).

The angel of Rev 14:6–7 commands the worship of God as Creator of "heaven . . . earth and sea and springs of waters." God who created earth and its inhabitants also provides them all that is necessary for life, survival. These inhabitants have despised him, and so he will convert these from life supports to instruments of death.

All four involve a one third factor (cf. one quarter in fourth seal): sparing two thirds, giving warning, opportunity to repent.

The first three are fiery, fitting with the image of heavenly altar fire being flung to earth. The fourth ironically results in the partial darkening of the heavenly lights (perhaps thought to be fires).

Death is mentioned explicitly in the second trumpet (v. 9) and third trumpet (v. 11) and so is perhaps assumed in the first and fourth trumpets. One of the key differences between the fifth and sixth trumpets is that it is said no one would die from the fifth trumpet plague, whereas very large numbers of humanity would die in the sixth trumpet.

The effects of these catastrophes are probably more the point than the means (e.g., something like a mountain, v. 8). Still, the images are meant to strike terror in the readers of every generation.

7—First trumpet: burn land, trees, grass by fiery, bloody hail, which was flung to the earth, the same wording (only the voice of the verb was altered) as in verse 5.

8–9—Second trumpet: bloody seas killing sea creatures, sinking ships (by a factor of one third), by something like a fiery mountain.

10–11—Third trumpet: poison fresh water sources (one third), killing many men by fallen fiery star, wormwood.

12—Fourth trumpet: darkened (by one third) heavenly lights.

13—Announcement of three woes corresponding to last three trumpets, targeting the inhabitants of *ha'aretz*.

Midheaven is where birds fly. See Rev 14:6; 19:17, the only other occurrences of this word. And it is directly overhead (according to the BDAG comment).

The first woe announcement, at the end of the fifth trumpet (Rev 9:12), is superfluous, contributing nothing to the meaning of the story line, and the third is missing. Only the second serves a literary purpose. It indicates the actual end of the sixth trumpet. That is, the only purpose for the three woes feature is to guide the reader to include chapter 10 and 11:1–13 in the sixth trumpet, rather than deciding that it ends at 9:21.

Chapter 9

The fifth and sixth trumpets together bridge from the first four to the climactic seventh. They have important similarities to each other and marked differences from all the other trumpets. The escalation of punishment is obvious: bad as the fifth is, the sixth is dramatically worse. The white horse rider is ramping up the pressure on the wicked to repent while he holds that door of opportunity open just this little while longer.

1–12—Fifth trumpet: scorpion-locusts, five-month excruciating but non-lethal stings on the unsealed.

1—God gives (*edothē*, divine passive) a fallen angel authority to release these things. Like a jail break, but approved by the warden. (In Rom 10:6–7, abyss is opposite of heaven.) This angel is also the king of these creatures (v. 11).

2—The opened pit belches smoke as from a furnace. Without saying so, this is hell exposed.

3—Scorpion-locusts empowered by God (*edothē*).

4–6—Their power.

4—Unlike natural locusts, these do no damage to vegetation, only the unsealed men (referring to Rev 7:4–8). Remember 7:1–3, where the angels were clued that their delayed mission is to attack earth and sea and trees. That was then carried out in the first to fourth trumpets.

5—Their sting is non-lethal, yet tormenting (iterated three times) for five months.

6—The sting will be so painful, men will wish they would die, but death will elude them. This idea is repeated with synonymous wording, evidently for emphasis.

7–10—Their appearance: like war horses, crowned, human faces, women's hair, lion teeth, iron breastplates, noisy wings, scorpion tails. The rhetorical effect of this relatively lengthy description is much more important than a point by point explanation. The effect is simply to depict them as terrifying, terrorizing. They look and sound as scary as they are dangerous.

11—They obey a king called destroyer. Thus their mission is destruction, though they are denied deadly power by God.

12—This statement about the woes is completely superfluous. By itself, it contributes nothing. As stated elsewhere, the only reason for the woes is to define the ending of the sixth trumpet, the second woe.

13–21—Sixth trumpet (part one): two hundred million lion-headed, snake-tailed, fire-breathing horses, massacring one third of mankind. Thus this is a dramatic escalation from the fifth trumpet. The scene concludes with the sobering report that the survivors refused to soften under the pressure and repent.

This scene is not the entirety of the sixth trumpet, as argued elsewhere. The trumpet continues until the second woe announcement in Rev 11:14 and includes two or three more scenes.

13–15—Four angels have been pent up at the Euphrates for this day. What does that mean? We have no other clue and so cannot but take this at face value. At the Euphrates, they are poised for attack on Israel.

13—Upon the sounding of the sixth trumpet, a voice arises from the altar in the immediate presence of the King and issues the call to that sixth trumpeter angel: now! This seems to be the voice of God the King himself.

14—After he has sounded his trumpet, the angel is directed to release four destroyer angels who have been confined to carry out an assignment (v. 15) on cue. Euphrates appears only twice in Revelation, here in the sixth trumpet and again in the sixth bowl, both penultimate. John probably intended by that coincidence to show escalated warning to repent, for the end is very near.

15—Four angels kill one third of mankind by this angelic cavalry.

16—Two hundred million cavalry seem commanded by the four. As elsewhere, it may be best to translate the number strictly, as ESV, NIV: "twice ten thousand times ten thousand." It seems that ancient Greek did not have words for the numbers million or billion, etc. The point here is not a literal or exact number but an inconceivably massive army, larger by far than anyone could imagine could be amassed in that day. This is shock and awe in the extreme. Compare the number at Rev 5:11, "myriads of myriads [or] ten thousand times ten thousand, and thousands of thousands."

17—The appearance of the two hundred million riders: breastplates of red (fire), blue (sapphire or hyacinth), and yellow (sulfur or brimstone). This is the only description of the riders, which is curious in that they are never described as armed, nor are they the effective cause of the deaths of the victims.

The appearance of the two hundred million horses: lion-like heads, breathing out fire, smoke, and brimstone or sulfur. Verse 19 adds information about their dangerous tails.

Besides these two verses (vv. 17–18), fire and sulfur occur together four more times, in Rev 14:10; 19:20; 20:10; 21:8, every time of the eternal punishment of the damned. The idea here then is that hell itself overtakes and consumes these victims. They are burned alive by the fires of hell.

18–19—The fire, smoke, and brimstone/sulfur are now called plagues, and they will be the cause of death of one third of mankind (none of whom were sealed in Rev 7:4–8).

19—Not only is there lethality in their mouths, now it is learned there is also at least wounding power in their snake-like tails.

20–21—Attention to survivors: despite all their crimes (fourteen accusations listed here), they stubbornly refuse to repent. This will be contrasted in Rev 11:13. (See the discussion of repentance in the sixth trumpet in part 1 above.)

On litany of traits of idol worship, see Dan 5:23.

On survivors, see 2 Chron 30:6–9; Luke 13:1–5; on catastrophes intended to lead to repentance, see Amos 4.

No woe here; instead, that comes in Rev 11:14.

Chapter 10

There is a stand-alone completeness about this chapter with a clear disconnection from both the preceding and the following. Yet it is contained within the local unit, the sixth trumpet, that includes the latter half of chapter 9 and the first half of chapter 11. More on that in the introductory comments to chapter 11.

Main events or features of this chapter:

- The angel brings an open booklet, that is, not sealed (vv. 1–2).
- The angel calls, and thunders respond articulately, verbally, yet John is forbidden to record the content (vv. 3–4).
- The angel swears by God: time is running out; the seventh trumpet is the end, and it is coming soon (vv. 5–7).
- John is told to eat the booklet, told it will be sweet then bitter, told he is to prophesy one last time (*palin*) to or concerning all peoples (vv. 8–11).

Voices in this chapter:

- Strong angel: verses 3, 5–7, 9, 11
- Seven thunders: verse 3
- A voice from heaven: verses 4, 8, 11

There is also anticipation of the seventh trumpeting angel in verse 7.

1—As with so many other visions and oracles, this begins with "and I saw," *kai eidon.*

"Cloud": see Rev 1:7; 11:12; 14:14, 15, 16. Those references, respectively, speak of Jesus Son of Man in the second coming, the two witnesses resurrected and withdrawn to heaven, and the Son of Man swinging a sickle, harvesting the faithful of *ha'aretz.*

This strong angel is remarkably like Jesus in chapter 1. He is coming down out of heaven wrapped in a cloud. Wow! That sounds a lot like the second coming. But this is just an angel. It is like God means to shoot some adrenalin in those who understand: this is not he, but for a moment you thought it was. This is just slightly premature. We haven't yet finished the sixth trumpet or heard the seventh.

In this vision, John and the angel with the book are on earth.

2—Feet on sea and land (earth): solid position of authority. Sea and land, since unexplained, symbolize both the whole planet and the peoples (territories) of gentiles and Israel respectively. It is also mimicked by the dragon's station in Rev 13:1.

3–4—First, the angel roars like a lion. That is followed by an echo reply of thunder, reverberating seven times.

Seven thunders: think Ps 29. The idea there is that thunder is the voice of God, or that God's voice is like thunder. When God speaks, it is awesome and terrifying. The idea here is that God (by the angel) is speaking an awesome and terrifying word. This word should send shivers down our spines.

John's instinctive reaction is to write what he heard with understanding from the thunders (yet curiously, he was not inclined to write the angel's message). The fact that John is told not to write the specific verbal message (cf. 2 Cor 12:4) suggests that God wanted John to know more than he permitted him to say. He needed to tell us that. The voice delivering this message is unidentified. The same speaker speaks again in verse 8 and probably in verse 11.

5–6—He swears as on a stack of Bibles: this is truth.

6—A most solemn oath, sworn by the eternal one, the one and only Maker of all.

"No more time" (*chronos ouketi estai*) = last chance, confirming that the sixth trumpet is about repentance (cf. Rev 2:21), last chance for those who have survived the first to sixth seals and the first to sixth trumpets yet have to this point stubbornly refused to repent. One common use of *chronos* is "occasion for some event or activity" (BDAG), time as opportunity. BDAG also says it can mean delay, as here. Those two senses seem to overlap in this case. There shall be no more delay, so the day of opportunity to repent is almost at its end. The time of final reckoning has come.

Ezek 12:28 seems especially pertinent: "None of my words will be delayed any longer." (Cf. 2 Cor 6:2; Heb 4:1–11.) Where faithless Judah-Jerusalem had been saying that prophecies of judgment either would not be fulfilled or not in their lifetime (vv. 22–23, 27), Ezekiel then prophesied that the disasters would come soon.

7—Seventh trumpet is imminent, and it is the end (*etelesthē*), the fulfillment of prophecies. It is about the gospel (preached, NASB, but gospelized, *euēngelisen,* in Greek) God revealed to the prophets. The gospel is about God's supreme kingship.

9–10—Eat the scroll: think Ezek 2:8–10; 3:1–3. ("Written on it were lamentations, mourning and woe," Ezek 2:10; cf. Ps 19:10; 119:103; Jer 15:16.)

Bitter in belly after being sweet in mouth. His commission is bittersweet. It is a great privilege to be filled with God's message to speak, yet that message, in this case, is ominous.

11—They (said) = the two speakers of verses 8, 9. See listing above of voices in this chapter. See also Rev 11:1.

John's next prophecy concerns the entire human race.

Chapter 11

Chapter 10 served as a hinge or separator of the sixth trumpet, parts one (Rev 9:13–21) and two (11:1–13).

1–13—The last part of the sixth trumpet, set entirely in Jerusalem during the latter half of the great tribulation, Daniel's seventieth week.

Jerusalem is largely overrun by the wicked, including but not limited to gentiles—Jerusalem, whose destiny is to be the capital of David's son's kingdom and home of faithful and godly ones only. Antichrist is there. The two witnesses—one Moses-like, the other Elijah-like—are powerfully testifying, prophesying, and exhibiting divine powers in judgment. They will be hated but not silenced, thanks entirely to supernatural protection.

Moses demanded Pharaoh acknowledge Yahweh and release his people. Elijah demanded the people and the king acknowledge Yahweh and reject Baal and his prophets.

God is jealous for Jerusalem. He chose that city, that it should be the capital of his Vassal's kingdom, thus the place of his earthly throne, and that it should express his and his Vassal's glory, which is holy.

These three and a half years are the last days of that city's uncleanness, her prostitution. God is counting down the days until he rises and fulfills his promise of Zech 1:16–17:

Therefore thus says the LORD, "I will return to Jerusalem with compassion; my house will be built in it," declares the LORD of hosts, "and a measuring line will be stretched over Jerusalem." Again, proclaim, saying, "Thus says the LORD of hosts, 'My cities will again overflow with prosperity, and the LORD will again comfort Zion and again choose Jerusalem.'" (NASB)

There is no mention of any repentance during the three and a half years, not till the very end (v. 13). Nor is there a statement of the prophets' message. But the reader knows that anyway. The implication is that all residents of the holy city will be exposed to the message and the undeniable evidence of divine approval, and virtually all shall persist in hateful opposition. Nevertheless, the prophets never tire, and they never deviate from their conviction and commission. The only serious threat is against their opponents, as God perfectly protects them from deadly intentions and instead empowers them to turn the tables and call down consuming fire on their tormentors.

God is, as always, fully in control. When he decides they have preached long enough, he will withdraw his protection, allowing their enemies to kill them, as he has allowed his saints throughout history to suffer martyrdom. For three and a half days, their dead bodies are left in public view for all to gawk, for all to satisfy themselves they are truly dead: finally, that torment is ended, their prophesying is ended. But that is not the end. With the whole world watching, God grants resurrection life to the two, not so that they may resume their preaching but so that they may be miraculously delivered, triumphantly raised to a heroes' welcome and comfort in God's throne room.

While the onlookers are still stunned, God causes a deadly earthquake (think Luke 13:1–5.) The storyteller turns our attention immediately to the survivors, and describes how they fear and glorify God, meaning, they repent. The reader is to remember that these shall have heard the prophetic testimony of the two for the entire three and a half years, and they shall have witnessed and survived all the prior disasters (seals, trumpets, and bowls) and steadfastly maintained their refusal to bow to Jesus as Messiah-King. Further, the reader is to realize how near to the end this is: final judgment comes in the person of Messiah Jesus almost immediately after this. So these shall have repented and converted at the last possible moment and opportunity but not too late.

1–2—Measuring the temple, altar, worshipers, but not the outer court in the holy city, which God will give to the wicked to trample for those three and a half years. Whatever else may be intended, it speaks to the unideal situation of coexisting: the holy city will be occupied by the holy people but also trampled by the wicked. "The Lord knows who are his" (2 Tim 2:19).

The speaker is at first unidentified. But the opening of Rev 11:3, "I will give," seems to settle the question: God gave John the measuring rod and directed him. It also seems possible God spoke through an angel—perhaps one of the voices in chapter 10—as so many other times in Revelation.

Verse 1 may appear to speak of the heavenly setting. But verse 2 makes that impossible. If the enemies of God are in control of any part of God's temple, this is earthly and first creation. What are we to make of this temple? Are we to understand there is to be a material architectural structure? Without meaning to speak to that, I think we should rather ask whether that is the author's point. I think the author knowingly led us in verse 1 to think of the spiritual rather than the material viewpoint. So while the setting is earthly, the view or vision is of the spiritual realities in that place at that time. The enemies of God and of his people dominate the holy city, Jerusalem, for those three and a half years, though God does not allow them to dominate that which is truly his—his spiritual temple, i.e., his people, true believers—as indicated by the language of measuring.

The main point is that the holy city, earthly Jerusalem (v. 9, etc.), will be dominated by the godless for three and a half years. Gentiles (perhaps Palestinians and other Muslims) will run freely (*patēsousin*, same word as in Luke 21:24; Rev 14:20; 19:15, with the sense of trampling) throughout earthly Jerusalem. By their wickedness—an inevitable result of defying God, the Creator and true, righteous King of all—they will defile the city.

Cf. Luke 21:23–24: "Woe to those who are pregnant and to those who are nursing babies in those days; for there will be great distress upon the land and wrath to this people; and they will fall by the edge of the sword, and will be led captive into all the nations; and Jerusalem will be trampled under foot by the Gentiles until the times of the Gentiles are fulfilled" (NASB).

Yet in the midst of this, God will have his own people, Christian Jews (like John and the believers in Acts 2), worshiping him as he is in his true temple, his people, and he will faithfully own (measure) them. Two prominent leaders are spotlighted in verses 3–12.

1—"Rise," a common Hebrew idiom (*qûm*) of preparation to act (more evidence that John is thinking in Hebrew).

Is this a literal physical temple? By the time John writes this, the Jewish church had long since given up on participation in the Jerusalem temple. They had been converted to thinking of the spiritual, heavenly temple of Heb 8–9 and the redeemed people of Messiah as the new earthly temple (1 Cor 3:16; Eph. 2:20–22; 1 Pet 2:5). This seems to be confirmed in Rev 13:6. This measuring is not just the building (temple, as Ezek 40) but also the altar and the faithful worshipers. Somehow the three objects of measurement must go together. The measuring seems to speak of God's ownership—this much is still holy, despite all that is going on around them—and the connection of the people with the temple must speak of the people's faithfulness, especially when contrasted with the nations (v. 2). It also suggests God's reciprocal faithfulness to them ("They are my people").

2—By contrast, John is commanded not to measure the outer court, the area faithless gentiles will be permitted to trample.

This is the first of five references to three and a half years (also Rev 11:3; 12:6, 14; 13:5, three different expressions). These are obvious allusions to Daniel's seventieth week, which is divided in two (Dan 9:27, as well as Dan 7:25; 12:7). These references in Revelation must be to the latter three and a half years when antimessiah, the first beast (Rev 13:1–10), shall have broken his covenant of peace with Jerusalem, turning good times to bad (see Dan 9:26–27).

3–12—The career of the two witnesses. The Jerusalem setting during the latter half of the tribulation continues.

This section culminates in repentance in Jerusalem (v. 13), just before the second coming (seventh trumpet), though the author does not describe or deny any evangelistic success prior to the very end.

3—God's chosen witness/prophets. (They are called prophets in v. 10.) "Prophesy" speaks of receiving God's message and delivering it to men. "Witness" speaks of solemn truthful testimony, respecting only the judge. Their prophecies (v. 6) are called testimony, *marturia*, from the same root as witness, *martus*, in verse 7. (See comment there concerning the content of the prophecy/testimony.)

This is the same three and a half years as in verse 2.

"I will give" likely represents the Hebrew idiomatic use of *nathan*, give, best represented in the NIV "I will appoint" rather than the more prevalent "I will give authority," though that is implied.

Sackcloth speaks of rejecting common human values in favor of repentance, extraordinary humility before God, pleading for mercy. See Matt 11:21; Luke 10:13; Gen 37:34; 1 Kgs 21:27; Joel 1:8; Esth 4:1–4; Isa 37:1–2; Dan 9:3. More specifically in this context, these two are modeling for Jerusalem what fearing and glorifying God (see v. 13 and comment at Rev 15:4) should look like.

4—Olive trees represent oil as fuel for lamps; lamps represent light of heavenly truth. The olive trees/lampstands (menorahs) can only be from Zech 3–4. The divine Spirit of Messiah, the Priest-King, fuels the light of the gospel these witnesses shine in Jerusalem, the truth to which they testify.

"Stand before the Lord of the whole earth" also comes from Zech 4:14. A key issue there is in Zech 3:2: God has chosen Jerusalem (which was also central to Zechariah's first, second, and third visions). Here (Rev 11:5, 7–10), Jerusalem hates God's faithful prophets. But they will nevertheless prevail in their mission, not because of their excellencies but God's powerful protection (cf. Zech 4:6, "not by might, nor by power, but by my Spirit").

That there are two witnesses may allude to the legal minimum for an accusation to stand (Deut 17:6; 19:5; cf. John 5:31–39).

Their proximity to the Lord of *ha'aretz* indicates his authorization and approval, as he has sent them, and they will faithfully proclaim his message. They stand for and speak for the Priest-King Messiah, who is coming soon, as Zerubbabel and Joshua together were the living prophecy of the coming Priest-King. They are the John the Baptist of the second coming.

5—Some will hate them and attempt to attack them, but God has empowered them to protect themselves and even to kill their would-be killers. The fire devouring the enemies recalls Elijah (2 Kgs 1:10–14).

Why the repetition of the protasis ("if anyone wants to harm them"), first in the present indicative, then the aorist subjunctive? As well, the second apodosis ("he must be killed in this way") seems superfluous, a mere abbreviated repetition of the first. These seem to indicate this certainly will happen, perhaps multiple times.

6—Plagues of drought, turning water to blood (etc.) recall Elijah, Moses, respectively. See Mal 4:4–5. These they are empowered to do at will, "as often as they desire," throughout the entire three and a half years. Elijah's drought was also three and a half years (Luke 4:25; Jas 5:17). Both Moses and Elijah and their plagues were about people knowing that Yahweh is God (Exod 7:17; 1 Kgs 18:36–39). In both cases, some believed, while others hardened their hearts in unbelief.

These replicate divine judgments against faithless Israel (Elijah) and Israel's enemy, Egypt (Moses). In this day, Jerusalem is more like Moses's Egypt and Elijah's (Ahab's) Israel than Messiah's bride.

There is no reason to think God will bring back these ancient men for this mission. If he could prepare a Moses for that mission and an Elijah for that, he certainly can prepare a couple more in this penultimate day.

7—God has a particular mission for these. When they complete it, he will remove their protection, leaving them exposed to the murderous wrath of the beast, antimessiah.

That beast won't be formally introduced until chapter 13. By the time we get there, we already know this about the situation in Jerusalem in his heyday.

"Comes up out of the abyss": he is so described in Rev 17:8, but in 13:1 as coming out of the sea. Abyss means the sea many times in the OT (Gen 1:2; Ps 32:7; plus many others). The bottomless pit (Greek *abussos*, Rev 9:1; 20:1) may suggest a dark, evil, confining place even beneath the sea. Of course, the idea is not meaningfully different from hell.

There is no specific summary statement of the content of the prophecy/testimony. But surely it must be the gospel: "Jesus is the true King. All must repent and bow to him. This beast character (v. 7) is an evil imposter. If you align with him, you will suffer his fate of eternal damnation. But if you align with Jesus, he will reward you with eternal life in his glorious kingdom."

This is the first of two statements (also Rev 13:7) of minor victory by this beast. That is, he triumphs over some of Messiah's faithful ones in that he kills them. These victories are of course not final, as Messiah will raise his faithful martyrs (vv. 12; 14:1; 15:2–4; 20:4–6; answering the prayers of 6:9–11) and send the beast to the lake of fire (19:20).

8–10—In their death, they will be treated with utter contempt.

8—Why is Jerusalem called Sodom and Egypt? She is in this day as wicked as those at their worst, as wicked as ever. As God has chosen

Jerusalem for his capital and for his Son's bride, he holds nothing back from his insulting and derogatory name-calling of what she has become; she is, after all, the place of the most heinous crime of all history, the crucifixion of their Lord. I think John expected readers would readily connect this to the name-calling in Rev 17:5 and recognize that both speak of Jerusalem in the penultimate day before the Lord's coming.

Ezekiel associates Jerusalem with Sodom and Egypt in Ezek 16: Sodom six times in verses 46–56, Egypt in verse 26. See also Isa 1:9–10.

As simple, clear, and obvious as this identification is, some refuse to let John speak so simply. To Beale, it is "the ungodly world system" and "the evil world system."[7] John has provided no evidence for such a view.

9–10—These three and a half days will be given to celebration and taunting, as if to say, "Finally, we are rid of them; we win, they lose. Finally, they get what they deserve."

9—Such disrespect of dead human bodies is a trait not of civilized but the most uncivilized society. (Cf. the crime of Moab in Amos 2:1, "Thus says the LORD, 'For three transgressions of Moab and for four I will not revoke its punishment, because he burned the bones of the king of Edom to lime'" [NASB].)

10—These will be for them the happiest days since those two emerged in Jerusalem.

In conclusion, the victims of their torment are identified as "those who dwell in/on *ha'aretz*," inhabitants of Jerusalem and Israel who routinely, defiantly violated the Lord's terms of tenancy, whom he would eventually expel from his land (*ha'aretz*; see v. 15). They shall have tormented these people by proclaiming the grace message of God's forgiveness through the voluntary sacrificial death of their Messiah-King, which of course carries with it the demand of repentance—turning in humble submission to the Judge-King and voluntarily entering a plea of guilty, coupled with supplication for forgiveness—and submissive allegiance.

11–12—The days of their celebration come to a terrifying end. With the entire world's attention (v. 9), the resurrection and heavenly ascension of the two shall be undeniable. Talk about celebrity! Cf. Ps 16:10.

Antimessiah will have his way in the city for those three and a half years, except that these two will be thorns in his side. They will preach the name of the true Messiah, while counterfeit messiah (antichrist) will seek to suppress that message. They will be light (truth), empowered by God's

---

7. Beale, *Revelation*, 843 (see also 591, 755).

Spirit (v. 4). Their greatest evangelistic fruit will come after their death and resurrection (see v. 13).

11—They will all fear, but not yet glorify (cf. v. 13).

12—Heavenly ascent, just like their Lord's. All their enemies could do was stand by and watch.

13—Immediately, mere moments after the two rise off the planet, an earthquake shall strike Jerusalem, causing the deaths of 7000. The repentance of the survivors of Israel stands in contrast to the unrepentance of the survivors of non-Israel, as described in Rev 9:20–21, at essentially the same time. These converts shall have heard and rejected the preaching of the two for the entire three and a half years. But now at the last opportunity, their eyes will be opened, they will come to their senses spiritually and bow in repentance and loyal faith.

This earthquake surely must be the same as that in Rev 16:18–19, the seventh bowl (though this is the sixth trumpet). Both devastate Jerusalem shortly before Messiah's glorious return.

On "fear and give glory," see especially Rev 15:4 and comment; see also 14:7 and the antithesis in 16:9; see also Matt 9:8; Luke 5:26; 7:16.

Later, in Rev 16:11, followers of the beast will curse the God of heaven following the fifth bowl judgment.

This is the cumulative national repentance of Israel anticipated in Zech 13:8–9; Matt 10:23; Rom 11:15, 23, 26.

On Israel's long-standing stubborn refusal to repent, see Neh 9:29; on Israel's occasional ancient repentance, see Neh 9:2; on Israel's eventual repentance and restoration, see Zech 12–14.

Now the continuation of the sixth trumpet past the end of chapter 9 makes sense. Now the insertion of chapter 10 makes sense. The sixth trumpet—from Rev 9:13 to 11:13—is the last chance to repent. Some refuse, while some, specifically Jerusalemites, finally, at long last, almost but not quite too late, repent, believe, bow, and glorify God, as the two witnesses proclaimed. They had consistently rejected the evangelistic appeal of the two for the three and a half years (though these also heeded the angel's warning not to accept the mark of the beast, an irreversible, eternally fatal commitment; 14:9–11).

14—Not until now is the sixth trumpet finished.

This is the only reason for the statement in Rev 8:13 about the three woes. It is entirely unnecessary in 9:12 and completely absent following the seventh trumpet. John used the woes for the singular purpose of preventing readers from making the otherwise understandable mistake of thinking the sixth trumpet ends at 9:21.

15–18—Ultimacy. At long last, the rightful Lord's eternal reign begins. This is what we have been waiting for, this is what the scroll is about, this is what messiahship is about. Hence, this is what the gospel is about. This is the good news. (To be precise, this marks the beginning of his millennial reign. But that will flow without interruption into eternity.) His loyal and royal elders rejoice in praise over this and that justice is finally brought both to the saints (as a reward) and to the wicked.

Allusions to Ps 2:1–2, 5, 12 in verses 15, 18 must not be missed or minimized. This is the day prophesied in that psalm.

15—The kingdom here is of the *kosmos*, not of the *gē*. *Kosmos* occurs only two more times in Revelation, both times in the expression "foundation [*katabolē*, i.e., creation] of the world" (Rev 13:8; 17:8). *Gē* (pronounced "gay") occurs a total of eighty-two times in eighteen chapters. *Gē* refers to both the promised land and the whole planet, depending on context, while *kosmos* refers to the whole planet. But *kosmos* is also John's word in his Gospel for the corporate population of humankind that opposes God and Messiah (see esp. John 15:18–25; 1 John 5:19). From this day forward and forever, the *kosmos* will bow to her Creator and rightful Sovereign.

16—"Worship," *proskuneō*, has a connotation of the posture of being prostrate, so its pairing with "fell on their faces" is somewhat redundant: "they prostrated themselves facedown in worship/allegiance." Their acknowledgment is of his supremacy and righteousness in judgment. He does what he wants (Ps 115:3), and what he wants is that which is right. Here, the right is the long-awaited righting of all past and existing evils.

17—"Who is and who was." Perhaps it is curious that John does not add "and who is to come," as in Rev 1:4, 8; 4:8 (compare 17:8, 11, where the beast falls short of God's eternality). But the eternal future is the big idea in the rest of the verse, as it was in verse 15.

He is the Almighty, so, of course, his power is great. In fact, one might call that an understatement. But then, words can never capture the magnitude of the infinite. Because his power is infinite, it is inevitable that he should reign. The only curiosity is that he waits this long to do so.

The explanation is that he is also longsuffering, giving opportunity after opportunity for rebels to repent. The point here is that he will delay for only a limited time. See also verse 18.

"Begun to reign," as in most translations, renders the simple aorist (participle), *ebasileusas*; that is, the author did not include a verb "begun" in the Greek. But virtually all agree this must be the ingressive usage.[8] Otherwise, this would be translated as the NKJV "you have taken your great power and reigned."

18—References to Ps 2 are deep and strong, especially after those in verse 15: "the nations raged" (cf. Ps 2:1); "your wrath came" (cf. Ps 2:5, 12).

The wicked are here called "the destroyers of *ha'aretz*." We should wonder why they are so described. One might expect instead to read that the reason was that they did not accept Jesus into their heart, or that they refused to bow to Jesus as King. But this wraps up the scroll of seven seals, which has been about reclaiming *ha'aretz* from the wicked, contaminating tenants, as wicked and defiling as the Canaanites Joshua encountered (cf. Rev 6:5–6) and as the Jerusalemites Nebuchadnezzar defeated (cf. 6:7–8). When God promised the Land (*ha'aretz*) to Abraham, he spoke of the not yet complete iniquity of the Amorite, the inhabitants of the land of that day (Gen 15:16). Of course, these are also those who refused to bow to Jesus, declined to invite him into their hearts. (Side note: no matter how zealous one may be for environmentalist causes, if one refuses to bow to the true and rightful King of earth, Messiah Jesus, one will be judged as having been a destroyer of earth. The enemies of earth's King are not true friends of the earth.)

19—Transition, buffer: God is erupting in judgment.

The ark is in the holy of holies and is the repository of God's copy of the covenant document, which includes the standards by which people are to be judged or blessed. What follows in chapters 12 to 20 is attention to his enemies and their crimes. They will soon get the justice spelled out in the covenant, the justice they deserve.

The scene is heaven but the effects are to be felt on earth.

This is the third of the four lists of thunder and lightning (Rev 4:5; 8:5; 16:18). It is like an explosion of divine activity arising from the

---

8. Wallace, *Grammar*, 559.

throne, or in this case the ark of the covenant (in the presence of the Enthroned One) which is in his temple, his throne room.

Chapters 12–20

The scroll unit (chs. 6–11) is now finished. Chapter 12 marks the beginning of the second of two major sections from white horse to white horse. This unit is dominated by the leading antagonists, Satan (the dragon), antichrist (first beast), false prophet (second beast), and the great prostitute Babylon. The final paragraphs of the unit describe the victorious second coming of the hero, Jesus, and the eternal execution of the antagonists and their followers, all whose names are not written in the book of life.

Chapter 12

The chapter is a single literary unit consisting of three sections—verses 1–6, 7–12, and 13–17—with primary attention to four characters: the woman Israel, her newborn son Messiah, the dragon Satan, and other children of the woman.

Big idea: this is the formal literary introduction to the chief antagonist, the villain leader, Satan. His character is established by a few select images. He is defined by his most consuming passion, which is to kill God's chosen Savior of Israel and of the world, Messiah Jesus, and thus to thwart God's great program of blessed dominion over creation. Where he once had free access to God's throne, the domain of heaven, he and his minions were forcibly evicted by the superior powers of God's angel armies. Now on earth, he stalks first Messiah's mother, Israel (introduced in vv. 1–2), then her other children. Despite minor victories, he is ultimately thwarted at every turn as God protects all his chosen ones, though we will soon see again how God's protection of some does not include safety in the days of their mortality.

Satan is the biggest villain, but he will be thwarted and defeated. He correctly recognizes God's intentions, his grand program for history, and seeks to scuttle those. Ferocious as he is and despicable as his intentions are, he will be frustrated. He loses the battle with heaven's bouncers, a portent of his ultimate defeat and eternal judgment described in chapter 20.

The chapter implicitly forewarns all humanity against following him. He is doomed; he is the biggest loser. He does not win, because he cannot win. So then all who would follow him are likewise doomed.

Verses 1–12 are suprahistorical (perhaps pre-history, except v. 6 and the beginning of v. 5); verses 13–17 are prediction of a specific time and specific events (v. 14, three and a half years).

Israel is a major element in God's plans of redeeming the world. Messiah is the seed of Abraham and the Son of David, the King of Israel (representing the two enduring covenants from the OT); he is also the seed of the woman (Gen 3:15). Satan knows this and seeks to exterminate believing Israelites. That helps explain why God ordered that 12,000 from each tribe be specially sealed, protected (Rev 7:4–8).

1–6—Two great signs (vv. 1, 3): the woman in labor and the dragon waiting to devour the child. This vision of two signs throbs with echoes of OT images.

1–2—Sun, moon, twelve stars suggest Joseph's second dream (Gen 37:9). But where the eleven stars and sun and moon bowed to him in Genesis, here the twelve stars are collected. So this is not about one tribe ruling the others, but it is about the family, Israel. This is the pregnant woman who gives birth to Messiah (v. 5), confirming she is Israel (not Mary and certainly not the church).

2—She is in labor; delivery is imminent (so the dragon is salivating, ready to devour the newborn, v. 4).

3–4—Dragon is enormous, red, with seven heads, ten horns, seven crowns (diadems). He casts one third of the stars (= angels, vv. 7, 9) down from heaven to earth and sets himself to devour the woman's newborn son.

The image of dragon suggests enormity and power coupled with beastly viciousness. It is also akin to the serpent (cf. v. 9), especially from Gen 3:1–5, 13–15, who was known for being wickedly intelligent, conniving, and malevolent.

3—Seven heads, ten horns: mimicked by the first beast (Rev 13:1; 17:3, 9, 12). The crowns are on heads (whereas the beast's ten crowns are on his horns, 13:1). Satan is a king; in fact, he is a king of kings. See chapter 17 comments for discussion of the horns. Daniel's fourth beast also had ten horns (Dan 7:7–8; Daniel's beasts will be important background also in the next character, the beast from the sea, Rev 13:2).

4—As he fell from heaven to earth (see vv. 9, 12) he dragged with him one third of the star-angels. The verb swept away (NASB, *surei*) is used four other times (John 21:8; Acts 8:3; 17:6; 14:19), all meaning to drag forcibly, even against one's will. The point here is probably not that this was in violation of their will, but rather that this powerful dragon initiated and exerted considerable coercive force in this action. These must be his angels who fight with him against Michael et al., as this fall must be the aftereffect of the battle in verses 7–9.

5—This Son is the king promised in Ps 2:7. The idea in Ps 2 is that this is the one chosen by God the King of heaven to rule from Zion (v. 6), so he is King of Israel. He is authorized by the King of heaven to enforce obedience by all peoples and all nations (v. 8) and to execute capital punishment as he may judge necessary (v. 9), so he is King of earth.

He is snatched away to heaven and God's throne. The King of Revelation 4–5 is most pleased to protect, receive, and honor this one.

On this word snatch (*harpazō*), see Acts 8:39; 1 Thess 4:17; 2 Cor 12:2, 4 of saints being supernaturally, instantly removed by God from one place to another. A thief nabs sheep (John 10:12), but no one can nab a saint from God's hand (John 10:28, 29). So are we to rescue some, as it were, from hell's fires (Jude 23).

6—The woman, the mother of Messiah (Israel, but especially the remnant of faithful, Christian Jews, those who refuse to submit to the beast) flees (from her home, Israel, Jerusalem) to a wild place prepared by God, where she finds refuge for three and a half years (also v. 14). This flight is that described in Matt 24:15–21.

This three and a half years is when the two witnesses are preaching in Jerusalem (Rev 11:3; as are also the three and a half years in v. 14; 13:5).

The Israel focus is confirmed by the role of Michael (v. 7), Israel's special angel (see below).

7–12—War in heaven; Satan defeated, expelled, cast down to earth. How were we ever going to learn this apart from divine revelation? God decided the saints need to know this.

7–9—Summary of the war and its outcome.

7—The scene is heaven, which is where the two signs (vv. 1, 3) were set.

The combatants are Michael (and his angels) vs. the dragon (and his angels). Satan's hatred is not ultimately toward Michael and the other righteous angels, but against God the King of heaven and his Son the

Messiah, the King of earth. But Satan cannot get past God's first line of defense. Of course, the King of heaven does not actually need defenders; he is entirely capable of destroying any and all opposition.

Michael (= "who is like God," meaning, no one is like God) is prince of Daniel's people, Israel (Dan 10:13, 21; 12:1). He is called great prince (Dan 12:1) and archangel (Jude 9; the archangel in 1 Thess 4:16 is unnamed). He was opposed by the prince of Persia (Dan 10:13) and fought against him (v. 20) and anticipated similar opposition from the prince of Greece (Dan 10:20). Those seem to be the evil spiritual forces (demons) supporting the overruling empire of Daniel's day (Persia, Dan 11:2) and the next one (Greece, Dan 11:2). So Michael must be the faithful angel assigned by God to support Israel. This is another factor supporting the interpretation that these chapters are centered on Israel, rather than the whole world indiscriminately.

8—The dragon had been mighty to fling star-angels down from heaven to earth (v. 4), but here is himself overpowered, forced out of heaven.

9—Being forced out of heaven, he was cast (*eblēthē*; it may be a minor point, but there is no downward direction language until v. 12, "he came down," *katebē*) to earth. The author redundantly repeats the sound "thrown down" three times in this sentence and again in verses 10 and 13, obviously for effect. So when a translation like NET simplifies to only one occurrence of the verb, it unfortunately buries part of an authorial point.

The identity of the leader of the defeated army (Satan) is emphasized by five substantives (the first two of which have extreme adjectives; cf. Rev 20:2): the great dragon (from v. 3, where he was also described as red); the ancient snake (alluding to Gen 3); the one called *Diabolos* (a Greek word meaning accuser, a near synonym to *katēgōr*, v. 10); the *Satan* (a Hebrew word meaning adversary); and the deceiver, described as one who deceives or seeks to deceive all mankind. While the real Satan disguises himself (2 Cor 11:14), the author does not allow this or other characters to wear literary masks; he requires they appear in the costume that fits their actual character. (This is an important argument for the identity of the rider of the first white horse in Rev 6:1–2.)

One of the most regular descriptions of the devil is as liar and deceiver (Gen 3:4–5; John 8:44; Acts 5:3; 2 Cor 11:3). Deception is a regular trait and stratagem of the evil ones in Revelation: the verb *planaō* (deceive) occurs in Rev 2:20; 13:14; 18:23; 19:20; 20:3, 8, 10. Not only is

Satan banned, but all liars are specifically excluded from the new Jerusalem (21:8; 22:15).

When the author wants to indicate that an event involves more than just Israel, one of the ways he does so is by the expression *oikoumenēn holēn*, the whole world, also in Rev 3:10; 16:14. In other places, he speaks of every tribe, tongue, etc. See 5:9; 13:7; 14:6. See also comment on 7:4, where the author speaks explicitly of every tribe of Israel.

An obvious point the author intends is that Satan is a loser—defeated and expelled from heaven—though this will not be fully realized until the end (Rev 20:10).

10–12—Heavenly pronouncement in three statements: God is supreme (and so his salvation prevails) over the dragon, expelling him from heaven (v. 10); the martyrs triumph in the end over the dragon (v. 11); and heaven celebrates, whereas earth has terrible days ahead, though not many (v. 12).

The speaker is identified only as a loud voice in heaven, presumably an angel.

10—Satan's expulsion means God's kingdom's victory. That victory is assigned specifically to the main characters of chapters 4–5, the King of heaven and the Lamb, here called his Messiah-Christ (the same wording as Ps. 2:2).

The paratactic connection of salvation, power, and kingdom is typical of John in Revelation (see Rev 1:9 and comment). The idea here is that God's kingdom is one of absolute power and ultimate salvation.

The words kingdom and authority are complementary and mutually defining: both Father and Son (to use traditional Trinitarian terms) are legitimate kings, and both have royal authority.

Satan accuses the faithful (v. 10) and deceives the faithless (v. 9). (The faithless are always gullible. Satan cannot deceive the faithful, but he can deceive the faithless. See Matt 24:24; 2 Thess 2:9–12.)

11—The saints, the ones accused by this accuser, triumph over the dragon (after being defeated by him in their martyrdom) through the Lamb's blood and theirs: final victory through non-final death. They maintained (the word of) their testimony of commitment to Jesus's supreme royal authority with the correlative denial of Satan's and the beast's lordship. They paid with their lives for their faithful witness. They feared "him who is able to destroy both soul and body in hell" (Matt 10:28) more than they feared death. These will be fabulously compensated by their Lord. See Rev 7:17; 21:4; Rom 8:18; 2 Cor 4:17; 1 Pet 1:6–7; 4:13.

12—This is a day of exuberant joy in heaven but of terror for earth. It won't be much longer until this whole history is finished.

Earth and sea are warned of his soon but short-term reign of terror, previewing chapter 13 and the two beasts.

That he has little time argues against the amillennial-postmillennial position that he was bound (Matt 12:29) and incarcerated (Rev 20:1–3) by the Lord during and ever since his earthly days.

13–17—Satan's desperation and the woman's deliverance from his dragon rage. This scene was anticipated in verses 6, 12.

If Satan cannot kill Jesus (v. 5), he will attempt to exterminate his mother, Israel. Satan's plan B strategy is to defeat Jesus's kingdom plan by genocidal elimination of Israel, his would-be kingdom people. But God will not allow that to happen either. All of verses 14–17 are predictive of Israel during the latter three and a half years of the great tribulation.

13—The word persecuted (NASB, NKJ) or pursued (ESV, NET, NIV) is *diōkō*. Its primary sense is pursue (as in Rom 9:30, 31), but it is the usual word for persecution (as in Matt 5:10–12; John 15:20). The idea is often very close to the word hunted (e.g. Acts 26:11). Here the dragon will pursue them with the intent of persecuting them unto death.

14—After God rescued the son by snatching him to the heavenly throne (v. 5), he rescues his mother by giving her not just any eagle wings but *the* eagle wings and a prepared refuge in the desert ("her place"). There he will provide for her for the three and a half years. (See comment on Rev 11:2.)

In verse 6, she fled into the wilderness to escape the dragon; here, she flies by means of the wings of a larger than average eagle. These eagle wings must be metaphorical of an otherwise undefined but effectual means of escape. This recalls Exod 19:4 (perhaps also Isa 40:31), where God through Moses takes credit for enabling Israel to escape from Egypt: "You yourselves have seen what I did to the Egyptians, and how I bore you on eagles' wings, and brought you to myself" (NASB).

15—The dragon spewed water to flush her out, to sweep her away by a torrent. This seems to be his last trick in his attempt to eradicate her. What this will be in the actual event is probably unknowable before it happens. But when it happens, we will be able to say, "Sure, John's description (a flood from the dragon's mouth) was exactly right."

16—But the land (*ha'aretz*) saved her. This is, of course, God's doing once again. The dragon spewed water from his mouth; the land opened its own mouth, consuming the flood, saving the woman. Perhaps we are to understand these saved ones to be identical to the 144,000 sealed ones.

This is a kind of reversal from the destruction of Korah, when God caused *ha'aretz* to open up and consume him and his family (Num 16:30–32).

17—When his designs on exterminating Israel are frustrated (by special divine protection), he turns his rage toward the unprotected Israelite saints, followers of Messiah Jesus (which is what ch. 13 describes).

"Keep God's commandments" means they fearfully respect him as King. "Hold the testimony of Jesus" means they refuse to renounce publicly their devotion to him as King.

(The Greek has a v. 18, which English translations have as the beginning of Rev 13:1.)

Chapter 13

Two beasts: the first beast (commonly known as the antichrist), verses 1–10; the second beast (a.k.a. the false prophet), verses 11–18. Both are counterfeit Messiah: the first rose from the dead (v. 3); the second is lamb-like (v. 11).

These two beasts must be real people for various reasons. First, they are both eventually thrown alive into the lake of fire (Rev 19:20). Second, the first is from Daniel's fourth beast/kingdom; and Daniel's kingdoms were also their kings (see Dan 2:37–38, as well as the obvious references to Alexander the Great, 8:5–8, and Antiochus IV, 8:9–12; 11:21–35).

Jesus predicted the proliferation of false messiahs and false prophets in the penultimate days (Matt 24:5, 24; Mark 13:21–22). Here we are introduced to the preeminent one of each class.

The second beast arises out of *ha'aretz,* and he mandates to those who dwell in *ha'aretz.* Where the first beast is a gentile world ruler (arising out of the sea, v. 1), the final phase of the fourth empire of Dan 2 and 7, the second beast is a leader of Israel. According to Dan 9:27, antichrist ("the prince who is to come," the first beast of Rev 13) makes a covenant with Israel, bringing peace and prosperity (Rev 17–18). The second beast, the leader of Israel in that day, enforces Israel's cooperation.

1–10—First beast

Satan has only a short time, and he knows it (Rev 12:12). Frustrated that he could not touch Messiah, nor flush out the woman represented in the 144,000, he comes next after the the rest of her children (12:17). This chapter is then the description of his fury against the woman (believing Israelites) and her faithful but unprotected children.

1—(This first sentence of v. 1 is the eighteenth verse of ch. 12 in the Greek.)

The dragon stands where sea meets land. So there is continuity from chapter 12. Surely there is symbolism in this place. The angel of chapter 10 likewise stood with one foot on sea and one on land (Rev 10:2). Here, sea and land are not so specifically identified. But at this place, the dragon sponsors his two beast goons, one from the sea and the other from *ha'aretz*.

The first beast emerges from the sea. Surely this reference to the sea is symbolic. Given the evident connection back to Dan 7, with its gentile kings (kingdoms) dominating Israel, land represents Israel (*ha'aretz*) and sea thus represents non-Israel, the gentile world (Dan 7:2–3).

The first beast has ten horns, seven heads, ten diadems (on his horns), and blasphemous names (on his heads). He is thus a counterfeit king of kings.

2—He is like a leopard, bear, lion, Daniel's first three of four beasts in reverse order (cf. Dan 7:4–6). He is some kind of composite of Daniel's beasts, while he is specifically the fourth.

He received power/throne/authority from the dragon. (But he was given authority by God in v. 5.) Sounds like Ps 2, the dragon mimicking the King of heaven appointing his Son King of earth (*ha'aretz*). This beast is counterfeit (anti-) messiah. As messiah was given great authority, even to carry out capital punishment (Ps 2:9), so this one is authorized by his lord Satan to kill those who resist his and their rule.

3—One of his heads appeared killed (*hōs esphragmenē*, like it was killed) and the wound healed. This is counterfeit resurrection of the counterfeit messiah. Not Satan nor either of these beasts has the power to give life to the dead. This feature is reiterated in Rev 13:12, 14 (mortal wound, sword wound); 17:8 (he was and is not and will come). See also in 17:6–8 the explanation for the separate identities of the heads.

All *ha'aretz* (Israel) was mesmerized and followed him (= worship, believe in). Amazed often indicates witnessing the supernatural, a miracle. See the amazement (same Greek word and cognate) in Rev 17:6–8 and that discussion.

4—They worshiped the dragon and the beast:

–the dragon because he empowered the beast;

–the beast because he appeared indomitable.

Worship is giving allegiance to a king; both the dragon and the beast are kings. See also Rev 16:10.

Just as true worship of God the Father entails submissive faith and worship of the Son (e.g., 1 John 2:22–23; 2 John 9; John 8:19), so this dragon and beast have a corresponding affiliation.

"Who is like the beast? And who can go up against him and conquer him?" obviously implies they believe him or at least acclaim him to be indomitable. Compare Rev 18:18: "Who is like the great city?"; Exod 15:11: "Who is like you, Yahweh?"; and Deut 9:2: "Who can stand before the sons of Anak?"

5—The beast is arrogant (boastful, immodest, hubristic; Dan 7:8, 20) and blasphemous (slandering God and his people; cf. v. 6; Jude 8–10), gifts seemingly from God. *Edothē*, divine passive, occurs twice in verse 5, twice in verse 7, once each in verses 14 and 15. These beasts are never off God's chain. Their powers are limited to God's specific permission.

God also gives him a forty-two-month career. This is the same three-and-a-half-year period as in chapters 11–12.

Why would God raise up and authorize someone like this into his program? See Rom 9:22–23.

6—He proceeded to blaspheme God and his dwelling, i.e., his heavenly subjects. God dwells among his people; we his saints are his temple/throne room. The overcomers (from Philadelphia) shall be pillars in God's temple (Rev 3:12).

Cf. 2 Pet 2:10; Jude 8: arrogant false teachers who brazenly "blaspheme the glorious ones" (ESV). Blasphemy is connected with unrepentance (refusal to bow voluntarily) in Rev 16:9, 11.

7—God also grants him permission to fight and kill saints (Dan 7:21, same beast, same time frame)—not including the 144,000 or the two witnesses—and rule over all kinds of people.

8—Many non-saints in *ha'aretz* will loyally follow him. Why do we not translate many as all, when that is the Greek word? First, they are described here as not written in the Lamb's book, thus excluding any elect but not yet saved ones; second, some will repent in the end, Rev 11:13, and so will have refused his mark; cf. 14:9–11.

Technical translation discussion: the phrase "from the foundation [i.e., creation] of the world" is closest in Greek word order to "Lamb slain," but could semantically go with "written." NIV, NKJ interpret the former; NAU, ESV, NET, NRS the latter. In the Greek, the phrase ends the verse and immediately follows "slain"; it is separated from "written" by twelve words. For this reason, "Lamb slain from the creation of the world" might seem more defensible. However, the statement in Rev 17:8—"whose name has not been written in the book of life from the foundation of the world"—is so similar as to tip the scales. These people's names were not written in the slaughtered Lamb's book of life before creation; so it is that they chose to throw in with the beast.

"The foundation of the world" is also found in Matt 13:35; 25:34; Luke 11:50; John 17:24; Eph 1:4; Heb 4:3; 9:26; 1 Pet 1:20, following either before (*pro*) or from/since (*apo*). The idea is the beginning, like the construction of a building. In these, it must refer to the very beginning of God's creation project. It is most explicitly connected to the creation account in Heb 4:3–4.

9—Those who can hear are urged to pay attention: "a word to the wise" (cf. Rev 2:7, etc). Only the deaf, the fool, would not take notice. This expression is slightly different from that which occurs at or near the end of all seven church letters (where the wording is always exactly the same), and this is the only place where this wording occurs. Here the implied word to the wise is: do not ever accede to this beast's demand of loyalty.

10—Some are destined (cf. Heb 12:1, "the race that is set before us") to captivity, others to sword. After all, it was God who granted the power the beast exerts. Saints are exhorted to endure in faith.

Textual critical comment: The first verb of the second clause is active in some translations (NAS, NKJ, NRS), passive in others (ESV, NET, NIV). If passive, this is parallel to the first; if active, this is poetic justice: he who kills with a sword shall be killed with a sword. (Actually, there are a dozen variants, testifying to the difficulty of the original, according to NET notes.) But the similarity to Jer 15:2 settles the question for me in favor of the active voice, since this author loves to echo OT prophets: "And it shall be that when they say to you, 'Where should we go?' then you are to tell them, 'Thus says the LORD: "Those destined for death, to death; and those destined for the sword, to the sword; and those destined for famine, to famine; and those destined for captivity, to captivity"'"

(NASB). There, the point is that the wicked of Israel will not escape divine punishment. Thus this is a word of consolation and encouragement to the faithful in days when it seems they are the ones on the brink of extermination.

11–18—Second beast

He is the false prophet in Rev 16:13; 19:20; 20:10. After chapter 13, he is never again referred to as the beast. In the places where he is called the false prophet, he is always subordinate to the first beast.

11—Emerges out of *ha'aretz* (= Israel).

Two lamb-like horns, dragon voice: masquerades as (the true) Lamb, but is betrayed by his voice.

12—Closely related to the first beast: his authority, which he exercises before him or in his presence, by the authority of (repeated two verses later and again in Rev 19:20).

He requires *ha'aretz* and its inhabitants to pay allegiance to (= worship, *proskunēsousin*) the first beast, the one whose mortal wound was healed.

Like Jason and Menelaus in the days precipitating the Maccabean revolt, this one throws in with the gentile despot and seeks to force all Israel to submit to him. (See Dan 8; 1 Macc 1:11–15; 2 Macc 4–5.)

13—He performs great signs, makes fire come from heaven to *ha'aretz* (Elijah-like). These signs are still in view in verse 14, where we learn this power was given to him, a fact which seems so obvious it almost goes without saying.

So we have competing miracle workers in Jerusalem: see Rev 11:5–6 (cf. Exod 7).

14—He deceives, tricks earth's (Israel's) inhabitants by the signs (cf. Rev 19:20, those who received the mark had been deceived). But then, being the enemies of God's people and of God, these have been rejecting the truth for their whole lives (cf. Rom 1:18, 25: these suppress the truth and exchange the truth for a lie; also 2 Thess 2:10–12), rendering themselves gullible dupes, defenseless against deception.

He requires them to make an image "to the beast . . . who had the sword wound yet lived."

15—God gives him the power to give breath and speech to the image. No ordinary illusionist could do this. (This makes me wonder if even he will be surprised by his powers. But being so blinded by hate, he won't be able to think straight and give God the credit he deserves for those powers.)

He requires all (Israel) to bow to the image, on pain of death. This sounds like Dan 3. These victims are seen singing in heaven's throne room in Rev 15:3–4 and reigning with Messiah in 20:4.

16—He requires all (Israel) to receive a mark on right hand or forehead. Those who comply seal their doom by so doing (Rev 14:9, 11; 19:20), whereas those who refuse this mark shall reign with Messiah (20:4).

Merism: small + great = all; rich + poor = all; free + slave = all.

17—Only those who have the mark may buy or sell.

The mark consists of the first beast's number or name (or perhaps the number of his name).

18—The number is 666 (not 616), "the number of man."

The wise are urged to calculate the number. It seems most likely the calculation will remain elusive until that day in history. The faithful— wise, insightful (cf. Dan 11:33; 12:3)—will in that day be granted insight to connect this prophecy with what they see happening around them.

Chapter 14

This follows the scenes introducing the dragon (ch. 12) and beasts (ch. 13), in which saints were persecuted and killed (Rev 13:7, 15) and pressured to accept the 666 mark on pain of economic ruin (13:16–17). The impression coming out of chapter 13 is that the dragon and beasts hold all the cards; no one can withstand their power. Their final victory seems inevitable. But we have already seen in 12:7–12 that Satan is the loser and in 6:1–2 that Jesus is the winner. We have also seen that some—the 144,000 and the two witnesses—will be supernaturally protected.

This chapter separating and linking chapters 13 and 15–16, both about the beast, provides a sneak peak to reassure readers that that beast will not win in the end (vv. 1–5). The chapter ends with a description of the final judgment of the righteous and the wicked, with the Lord harvesting his faithful ones before releasing angels to harvest the wicked (vv. 14–20). In between are three angelic messages issuing solemn warnings to the inhabitants of *ha'aretz* in the days of the beast that they need to repent and worship the Creator. Simultaneously, they need to withdraw from the wicked city, Babylon, and refuse the beast's and false prophet's required brand, 666 (vv. 6–13).

The three paragraphs are three visions: verses 1, 6, and 14 all begin with "and I saw" (*kai eidon*), typical prophetic language (see comment at Rev 8:2).

1–5—144,000 with Lamb on Mount Zion

Once the dust settles, we see who finally stands on Mount Zion: not the dragon or beasts, but the Lamb, plus his protected 144,000. This is a fast-forward preview of that which immediately follows the beast's reign. This is at the second coming and the beginning of the millennium.

God's seal on these (Rev 7:3–8) guarantees there will be a nation of Israel—pure, faithful, holy; a truly new generation of Israel (cf. Matt 24:34)—when Messiah comes to rule for the millennium.

Chapter 15 begins with a complementary company of saints (anticipated in Rev 14:12–13): those are in heaven, having fallen victim to the beast's deadly wrath, and triumph over him in resurrection. These in chapter 14 are singing the same song as those.

1—While the section is about the 144,000, it begins not with their standing, but the Lamb's. The 144,000 are with him, not the other way around. (See Luke 21:36: "Keep on the alert at all times, praying that you may have strength to escape all these things that are about to take place, and to stand before the Son of Man" at his coming [NASB].)

They rejected the beast's mark (cf. Rev 13:16; as did many others who suffered martyrdom, 14:13; 20:4), having instead the Lamb's and heavenly King's names on their foreheads. Is this the seal of 7:3? In NT times, a master might tattoo his own name on a slave's forehead.[9]

"Standing" speaks of possession, victory, rule, and most importantly, life (cf. Rev 6:17; 7:9). But the parallel to 15:2–4 may be more directly relevant. There the saints stand on heaven's glassy and flaming sea and are also victorious over the beast by having refused to bow to him. Where these 144,000 survived the great tribulation, thanks to the special seal mentioned in 7:4, those in chapter 15 were faithful unto death.

9. Osborne, *Revelation*, 310.

In this whole section, it is noteworthy that there is no sign or whiff of either beast or the dragon.

2–3—Having just seen the Lamb and his followers on earth, next he hears music from heaven: harps (v. 2), unique choir (v. 3). Are those the 144,000? No, they are heavenly musicians in the throne room. Their oratorio reaches earth, which these 144,000 but none else are able to learn (v. 3b). This heavenly music is probably to be identified with the scene described in Rev 15:2–4.

Before the sound (*phonē*, which in other places must be translated voice) is described as harp music, beautiful beyond description, it is like many waters and like great thunder: very loud. Other loud voices and sounds follow in verses 6, 9, 15, 18. Other harps appear in Rev 5:8 and 15:2, both of which are heavenly scenes where faithful saints sing God's praises.

A heavenly oratorio from the throne room, music fit for the great King, far superior to anything composed by earth's greatest musical geniuses. Now that heavenly music has been learned by an earthly choir, these 144,000. The two choirs are identical in every way except that one group was protected so as to survive the wrath of the beast and the other was not.

The 144,000 are the redeemed of *haʾaretz*.

4–5—The 144,000 are perfectly pure as the purest of virgins, devoted to the Lamb, God's first fruits (cf. Jer 2:3: "Israel was holy to the LORD, the first of his harvest. All who ate of it became guilty; evil came upon them, declares the LORD" [NASB]), utterly truthful. Pure, undefiled virgins recalls the Sinaitic defilement—requiring sacrifices—of even proper monogamous intimacy (cf. Lev 15:16, 18; 1 Sam 21:4).

For the second time (vv. 3, 4), they are described as purchased (*agorazō*), indicating Someone did the redeeming.

In verse 3, they are purchased (perfect passive participle) from *haʾaretz*. Being 144,000 from the tribes of Israel (Rev 7:4), this supports the interpretation that *haʾaretz* means Israel. In verse 4, they are purchased (aorist passive indicative) from men as firstfruits to God and the Lamb.

The scene is thus complete. It follows the scenes of the dragon and beasts and precedes those of the seven bowls of judgment. It is followed more immediately by two scenes: of three angel announcements (Rev 14:6–13) and two harvests of *haʾaretz* (14:14–20). It assures us readers of the outcome: the Lamb wins. He proudly owns these as his kingdom subjects. But for the seal God placed on them (7:3–8), these would have been martyred like so many others (7:9–17; 14:13; 15:2). Being sealed, however, they survive the great tribulation and the beasts' wrath to enter the Lamb's earthly kingdom in their mortality, the seed population (along with the last-minute converts of 11:13) of the millennial nation of Israel. Also, just as a talented choir fit for heaven's King sings his praises, so the Lamb has an equally fitting choir and oratorio. The harmony of heaven and earth is repaired, as "the kingdom of this world has become the kingdom of our Lord and of his Messiah" (11:15).

6–13—Three angel messages

The first is two verses (vv. 6–7), the second is one verse (v. 8), the third is three verses (vv. 9–11). The last two verses are encouragement to the faithful (vv. 12–13; not a fourth angelic message). The first message is good news, the gospel; the second and third are dire warnings.

6–7—First angel "gospelizes the eternal gospel" (literally, having an eternal gospel to gospelize) to those who dwell (sit) in *ha'aretz* (Jews) and to everyone else (gentiles). The content is the demand "fear and give glory," meaning repent (see notes at Rev 11:13; 15:4), worship; that is, bow to the King.

The juxtaposition of two groups of hearers (v. 6) confirms again that *ha'aretz* (Greek, *gē*) sometimes means Israel, the land promised to Abraham. In the very next verse, the same word means the planet, defined by its pairing with heaven.

6—Though lacking the definite article, this eternal gospel must be definite (NIV, NKJ), since there cannot be multiple eternal gospels. So it must also be the true gospel. That is, how likely is it that God would send out an angel with a gospel message, people would do exactly what he demanded, and then they would still suffer God's eternal judgment? That is simply impossible.

7—Judgment day is drawing near. Judgment has been deserved every day since the fall in Eden. So every day is merciful longsuffering, which must not be mistaken for divine resignation, giving up on ultimate judgment.

The list of macroelements of creation (heaven, earth, sea, springs) anticipates the first four bowls. God as Creator is a major theme of the book, seen especially in Rev 4:11; 21:1, 5. Here, the four objects of the first four trumpets and first four bowls are explicitly connected to the Creator (creation) theme. (Also 3:14; 5:13; 8:9; 10:6, all using the *ktis-* root.)

8—Second angel: fall of Babylon (which fall is again announced in the seventh bowl at the end of ch. 16) foreshadows chapters 17–18. Babylon has been exceptionally influential for evil. This brief description highlights primary traits: fornication and intoxication of gentiles, *ethnē* (think *goyim*). She could have been influential for good, but alas! She has made others around her drunk on self-destructive, twisted, self-indulgent (spiritual) immorality (*porneia*), devoting herself to false gods, lovers.

While explicitly announcing the impending demise of this city, it implicitly warns any who have ears that they should separate themselves from her. She is doomed, and all who refuse to detach themselves from her will suffer her fate (cf. Rev 18:4 and comment).

This angel is echoing Isa 21:9 (which he does again in Rev 18:2), where the doom of Babylon is good news for redeemed Israel. John will soon clarify that this Babylon is Jerusalem of the great tribulation, which, like the Jerusalem of Jesus's day, opposes the God who chose her. So the doom of that Jerusalem is good news to all saints, including especially faithful Jews, who with the coming Messiah will eventually stand on the reclaimed and cleansed Mount Zion (14:1)!

From where does this Babylon the great come? This is the first of six occurrences of this name in Revelation. The author has not prepared his reader for it, so the careful reader might think this intrusion abrupt, almost random. On the other hand, perhaps the author did prepare the reader for a wicked city back in Rev 11:8, "the great city," the city where the Lord was crucified, unmistakably wicked Jerusalem.

9–11—Third angel: beast worshipers are doomed to hell. So they are warned to escape from his clutches before it is too late and not to take the beast's mark. The doom of those who do is certain.

9—Bowing to the image and/or taking the mark amounts to beast worship, an irrevocable promise of loyalty. Loyalty to the beast antiking is enmity against the true King, Jesus.

10–11—This description of the eternal suffering of the wicked comports with those elsewhere: torment, fire, and brimstone, forever and ever, smoke, no rest. (Side note: it is hard to imagine that an author who subscribes to annihilationism would express his theology this way.)

The statement about the presence of angels and the Lamb is unique in the entire Bible. Elsewhere, the wicked are judged eternally "away from the presence of the Lord" (2 Thess 1:9). Perhaps the idea is similar to Rev 13:12, 14 where "before" or "in the presence of" (*enōpion*, likely the Greek equivalent of the Hebrew *liphnei*) has the sense of being approved and authorized by the one; in this case, approved by the holy angels and authorized by the Lamb.

10—The image of God's wrath as drinking of wine comes from Ps 75:8; Isa 51:17. In Jer 25:15–17, the drinking is forced on the wicked nations. The future tense here, shall drink, may also have that connotation.

There is a word play on the words rendered "wine of anger." Where in verse 8 Babylon made nations to drink the "wine of passion [*thumos*] of immorality," here God makes the beast worshipers to drink the "wine of anger [*thumos*]," the same Greek word.

The wine is literally "mixed unmixed [*kekerasmenou akratou*]." Where wine was commonly diluted (mixed) in that day, the mix of God's wrath is undiluted, mixed (verb) unmixed (adjective).

12–13—Encouragement to the faithful.

12—"Faith of Jesus" (Greek genitive) = faith in Jesus (as most translations, including NET, which champions the subjective genitive of the same expression in, for instance, Gal 2:16). Maintaining this faith, including obedience, requires endurance, especially under such extremely trying circumstances. True saving faith is obedient faith, because it believes *that* he is King and believes *in* him as King. Those who truly respect him as King will respect his every word, his every command. Not to obey the King is not to respect him; it is defiance, rebellion.

13—Write it down: this is truth. Death by persecution is a gateway to blessing. This is a reversal of the common assumption: the dead are the cursed ones, the living are blessed. Their mortal life shall have been toil and faithful works. These shall not be forgotten; they shall be honored and rewarded with rest. They shall have resisted and opposed the beast and the culture of the city (much like the *kosmos* of the Gospel of John) out of steadfast loyalty to Messiah. This shall have been exhausting, yet they did not finally flag, even when faced with the ultimatum to deny him or die. Not till they have died will they know rest. But that rest is worth the price paid (cf. Rom 8:18). Just a few verses later, in Rev 15:2–4, we meet that company, and indeed they are blessed and enjoying their blessings to the fullest.

6–13—To review the three: bow to the Creator, escape the clutches of Babylon, and resist the beast, or you will go down with them.

This one-two-three punch of angelic announcements from midheaven to all inhabitants of *ha'aretz* (most especially in Israel) shall have been complemented by the preaching of the two witnesses and countless other faithful ones, many of whom testify faithfully to their deaths (v. 13).

This is a gospel not of invitation but of demand to bow to the true King of earth, Messiah Jesus: bow or die. This is a real opportunity to change one's allegiance, and though the text does not mention it, it seems likely some, even many, will. It is the only right and sane thing to do. Yet most will wickedly refuse. This gospel preaching, as that of the two witnesses, will fall on mostly deaf ears: see refusal to repent in Rev 16:9, 11.

14–20—Two harvests: the separation of righteous and unrighteous. As the opening paragraph of the chapter projects to the second coming, this too projects to the separating judgment. This corresponds to the second and seventh parables of Matt 13 (vv. 18–23, 36–43, 47–50).

The commands and response statements of verses 15–16, 18–19 are nearly identical.

14–16—First harvest: "Son of Man," no judgment (grain).

17–20—Second harvest: an angel, very bloody (vintage).

14—"One like a son of man" = the Son of Man. (See comment at Rev 1:13.)

"White cloud" recalls the transfiguration when whiteness and cloud were both prominent. So this seems to be the second coming, which marks the beginning of Messiah's millennial reign.

Gold *stephanon* on the Son of Man. We are sometimes told that a *stephanon* is not a royal crown but a winner's laurel wreath. But being golden, this one cannot be in any meaningful way different from a diadem, a king's crown. Compare to John 19:2, 5 where the crown of thorns is *stephanon*, but was intended as a mock royal crown. Note also John's propensity in the Gospel to use synonyms indifferently. Of course, Son of Man is the supreme earthly King (Dan 7:13–14).

Sharp sickle in his hand: compare sharp sword in the mouth of the Lord in Rev 19:15, double-edged sword in 1:16.

15—This angel is not commanding the Son of Man; he is calling out in obedience to the heavenly King's command. The Son of Man waits for the Father's timing. This cry is how the Father declares this is the time. This cry corresponds to that of the first "living one" in Rev 6:1.

16—He harvests *ha'aretz*. While the Lord will certainly be in charge of the harvest of the whole earth and all mankind, Jews and gentiles, it is still possible the author means to speak in this place of the harvest of a part of the earth, namely, the promised land.

The verb *etheristhē* (it was harvested), coupled with *exēranthē* (ripe, dried) in verse 15, speaks especially of a grain harvest by waiting until a certain degree of drying has occurred.

17—"Another angel . . . also had a sharp sickle" is a different harvester, though with identical harvest implement. This one too is acting on orders from the King, having just emerged from heaven's throne room sanctuary.

18–19—This harvest is unmistakably of grapes, indicated in four nouns (*tous botruas tēs ampelou* . . *staphulai* . . . *lēnon*, the clusters from the vine . . . grapes . . . winepress). This metaphor lends itself to the image of blood in verse 20.

18—This angel is responsible for the fire of the altar. For sacrificial worship to proceed, the tending of altar fire must not be allowed to fail. (See Lev 1:7; 6:9, 12–13; Mal 1:10.) This angel's main job calls for constant vigilant attention. He is a partner in the sacrifices, though his role is rarely appreciated; he rarely gets praise. He has proven himself responsible and can be trusted to carry out this assignment.

19—This harvest is also of *haaretz*. It is also unmistakably one of judgment, expressing the wrath of God.

20—The image of treading the winepress of God's wrath was first expressed in Isa 63:1–6.

Blood to horses' bridles for two hundred miles: it seems strained to insist on strict literality, especially since we have only two dimensions. How wide is this, one angstrom or ten thousand miles? It certainly is intended to speak of unprecedented, copious gore.

The harvest blood flows outside the city. We need to wonder why the author used the definite article for city. The chapter began with a scene on Mount Zion, which is the city of Jerusalem. How is it unlikely that Jerusalem would once again be central to eschatological events? Our prima facie interpretation must be that this is indeed located at Jerusalem, and that the earth (vv. 15, 16, 18, 19) refers primarily to Israel.

What is missing is an unambiguous statement of the qualities of the two harvests, i.e., the righteous, the wicked. There is entire consensus that the latter harvest is of the wicked and that the blood is the result of divine judgment. The fact that the Son of Man harvests first and an angel follows with divinely ordered slaughter may correlate with the judgment in Matt 25:31–46, where Son of Man (accompanied by all the angels) first confers blessing of kingdom admittance on the sheep—faithful gentiles who survived the tribulation (and expressed their devotion to King Jesus by supporting persecuted Christian Jews)—and then pronounces judgment of kingdom exclusion on the goats—the unfaithful gentiles. That judgment is probably meant to include the kind of destruction described in Matt 24:51; 25:30—judgment of faithless Jews. As well, this judgment of separation likely correlates directly with that in Rev 11:18. See comment there.

Messiah claims his own (vv. 14–16; see Matt 24:31; Mark 13:27; Luke 21:28) and then assigns the slaughter of the wicked to angels (vv. 17–20; cf. Matt 13:49–50). See 2 Pet 2:9.

Chapters 15–16: Seven Bowl Judgments

Chapter 15

This chapter is the introduction to the final group of seven judgments, those called bowls. It describes a glorious worship scene (vv. 1–4), followed by a solemn scene of the entrustment of the bowls to seven angels attired for extraordinary solemn ceremony, processing with great pomp and circumstance (vv. 5–8).

1—"Great and marvelous sign" (see also v. 3, great and marvelous works): far beyond the ordinary, eliciting wonder and amazement. Deut 28:59 (LXX) speaks of great and amazing plagues, referring to the curses that God would bring upon Israel for defecting from the Sinai covenant, the climactic outpouring of which was the destruction of 586 BC. That wording supports the interpretation that these plagues are likewise centered on the people and land of Israel.

The outpouring of God's judgment, of these seven bowls, has not been witnessed; it will be a marvel to behold.

"Last . . . finished": yet, this is not final judgment. Rather, this is punishment—perhaps like torture (think plagues, beatings)—reminiscent of the ten plagues on Egypt, directed against the beast followers, proving their refusal to repent, not unlike Pharaoh. Thus these bowls are essentially the same as the sixth trumpet: last chance to repent. (See additional comment at v. 7.)

This verse is a summary of the scene, as the angels are not given the bowls until verse 7.

2–4—These are victors from the day of the beast. They, not he, have the last laugh, so to speak, the ultimate victory. He had conquered (*nikaō*) them (Rev 13:7), yet now we see they have conquered (*nikaō*) him. (See comment on overcoming at the introduction to ch. 2.) They now comprise a throne room praise band.

This scene is heavenly, and so spiritual, not physical. Redeemed saints, including these, will not receive glorified bodies until the second coming (1 Cor 15:52; 1 Thess 4:16).

It is appropriate that we see this scene before proceeding to the outpouring of the bowls, because these are those victimized by those being afflicted in chapter 16.

2—These are the counterparts to the 144,000 of Rev 14:1–5. Those stand on Mount Zion (earth), these in the throne room (heaven), beside or on (*epi*) the glassy sea (4:6), now enflamed. (There also is fire in the presence of God the King-Judge in Dan 7:9–10.)

In God's throne room, even the sea is placid (Rev 4:6), safe for the saints. Even when 15:2 adds that the glass is fiery, the saints safely stand on that sea.

Whereas the 144,000 had been sealed, protected from the beast, these were unprotected, vulnerable. Both sing the same heavenly music; the music in both places includes harps. The defeated enemy in view is explicitly the beast of chapter 13.

3–4—Before the ceremony of the giving of the bowls and their outpouring is the victors' song extolling God for his works and ways, which the context requires be specifically the impending bowl plagues: they are great and marvelous, just like the sign (v. 1), righteous and true, and they rightly elicit fear-and-glory worship.

3—Lamb's song is a recapitulation of Moses's (Exod 15; see also Deut 32:4): God poured out judging wrath on Egypt in his act of delivering his people. So now again here the salvation of God's people is coupled with judgment on their (and his) enemies.

In Egypt, he warned ten times, "Let my people go," as if then asking after each plague, "Do you give up yet?" Each time, Pharaoh had an opportunity to repent, which he stubbornly refused to do to the end.

The Lamb of chapter 5 was waiting for heaven's King to signal the time for him the Lamb to go claim his kingdom, *ha'aretz*. These singers sing his song, praising the King for general qualities soon to be expressed in particular judgments. Psalm 86 also captures the idea. (See quote at v. 4.)

These great and marvelous works of justice (righteous, *dikaiai*) are ultimately about exhibiting God's glory.

While normally thought of as King (God) of Israel, this statement somewhat surprisingly speaks of him as King of the nations (Hebrew, *goyim,* i.e., gentiles, non-Israel), recalling Jer 10:7, the only other time this expression occurs in the Bible. There, the context was the temple speech (chs. 7–10) and the warning to repent of emulating the nations and their idolatry and hateful wickedness. Even the gentiles must bow to Israel's God-King; how much more should Israel! Here, Israel has been listening to the false prophet, the second beast, in aligning themselves with the gentile antichrist in his godlessness (idolatry) and murder.

Lord God Almighty (*pantakratōr*) is probably John's rendering of Yahweh Elohim (or Adonai Yahweh) Tsevaoth.

4—All must and will bow and worship: the elect lovingly, joyfully; the wicked coercively, defiant to the end. The rhetorical question ("Who will not . . . ?") implies blindness, folly of refusal. It is almost unthinkable, and yet . . .

So we see in the bowls that the committed beast followers continue in their stubborn refusal to repent, continue to blaspheme, i.e., curse God (Rev 16:9, 11, 21; fourth, fifth, and seventh bowls). John is about to show us who will not fear and glorify.

This is the ultimate fulfillment of the prayer of Ps 86:9–10: "All nations whom you have made shall come and worship before you, O Lord, and they shall glorify your name. For you are great and do wondrous deeds; you alone are God" (NASB). They will never worship in the sense we commonly mean, but they will bow. All shall worship, because he is supreme majesty over all nations; because of his deeds, which are great, amazing, righteous (just), true; because he is uniquely holy. Implied: how much more should Israel bow willingly!

Given that John uses the verb repent (*metanoeō*) twelve times (eight of which are in chs. 2–3), we should ask why he chooses here and Rev 11:13 and 14:6–7 instead to say "fear and give glory." The idea of repent is from the OT, *shuv,* turn or turn back. It is especially directed toward Israelites who are wrong with God, the opposite of being right with God. They are wickedly moving away from rather than toward God. (Remember, he made the world and all people, he owns the world, he rules it. All are eternally obliged to submit and acclaim him as the King that he is.) So what is required is reversal. The paired verbs fear and glorify do not imply as exclusively that one is wrong with God. Rather, these are the proper reverential response of the faithful as they see God as he is in truth. Fearing and glorifying is forever the right response of the most devoted of servant worshipers, as here in 15:3–4; it is faithful worship. For that matter, of course it is always the right response of all of creation. Hence, toward those who have not voluntarily bent the knee to their Creator, fearing and glorifying would constitute a radical change, an utter turning from defiance to submission. So fearing and glorifying includes but is not limited to repentance, which is in a sense a one-time, once-for-all conversion.

The two ideas also occur together in Ps 22:23; Matt 9:8; Luke (5:26); 7:16.

5–8—This is a most solemn ceremony.

Emerging—processing—from the holiest place, the heavenly throne room of the Holiest One, the same as Rev 4, Isa 6.

5—Is the sanctuary normally closed? It is closed to anything and anyone that is not holy. The doors now open so that these special angels might proceed. They are open only for these angels to walk out, not for anyone to enter (v. 8).

This is the *ohel moed*, the tent of meeting. What is the use of the genitive—"the sanctuary, that is, the tent of meeting" or "the sanctuary of the tent of meeting"? Whether genitive of place (the special sanctuary of the tent) or of apposition (the sanctuary is the tent), the point of the sanctuary is that the Suzerain of heaven and earth, the Creator-Judge of humankind is enthroned there. He now pours out judgment on the villains of chapter 13 and their followers.

6—Great ceremony attached to this next act: angels process from the sanctuary in the finest ceremonial garb, spotless shining linen with golden sashes, reserved for the most special occasions. This suggests the highest holiness of their mission. One might think these outfits would be reserved for the Lamb's wedding. It is hard to imagine how John might describe attire for a greater event. The punishment of the beast and his followers is a holy and God-honoring occasion.

7—Each is presented with a bowl. The bowls are golden, signifying special ceremonial usage. The presenter is one of the four cherubim (the living beings). Each bowl contains God's wrath. The potions in the bowls are all unique. We shall soon learn this is wrath against the beast and his followers. This is final (v. 1) in the same sense that the ten plagues against

Pharaoh were final: the last chance to repent but not the final judgment of the great white throne (Rev 20:11–15).

The wrath is once for all, whereas God lives and reigns supreme forever.

8—Temple filled with smoke in Exod 40:34–35; 1 Kgs 8:10–11; 2 Chron 5:12; Isa 6:4. In the Exodus, 1 Kings, and 2 Chronicles passages, entry into the temple was prohibited as long as the cloud/smoke persisted.

This outpouring of punitive power (the bowls) is one of the great exhibitions of God's holiness. It signals that what follows is not an uncontrolled outburst but a studied, purposeful, and sober warning from the final Judge: "This is your last chance to do the right thing. If you think this string of plagues is rough, you need to know they are tiny by comparison to the ultimate judgment that will come on all who persist in defiance of the Almighty, the righteous Judge of all." Isaiah says, "When your judgments are in *ha'aretz*, the inhabitants of the world learn righteousness" (Isa 26:9).

Chapter 16

The objects of this wrath are identified in the first and fifth bowls (vv. 2, 10) as the beast and his followers.

A primary theme is their stubborn refusal to repent (fourth and fifth bowls, vv. 9, 11) coupled with blasphemy, cursing God (fourth, fifth, and seventh bowls, vv. 9, 11, 21). These bowls are the last opportunity to repent, but they work out effectively to be the final proof that the beast and his followers will never repent. Nothing short of external coercion will bring them to their knees (Phil 2:10–11).

Their choice to follow the beast is simultaneously the corresponding choice to defy and oppose God. (Whether the choice is active or passive makes no difference.) That must change. They must repent and bow to their Creator or suffer extreme consequences. Not to bow is abject defiance. As they pressured the Lamb's followers to renounce their loyalty to him and transfer it to the beast, these bowls are effectively the same from God in the reverse direction: pressure on beast followers to convert to Lamb followers. They are a kind of divine persecution of beast followers.

1—All seven are to be poured out on *ha'aretz*. Yet the first is uniquely poured onto *ha'aretz* (in distinction from the second, third, and fourth). The reference in verse 1 is to earth as the counterpart of heaven, especially the Holy Land, *ha'aretz*; that in the first bowl (v. 2) is land as the counterpart of seas, rivers, heavenly bodies.

The first to fourth bowls follow the same pattern as the first to fourth trumpets: land, seas (bodies of salt water), sources of fresh drinking water, heavenly bodies. See comments at Rev 14:7 on the connection of these four to God's creation.

2—First bowl
Summary: On earth/land (think *ha'aretz*), sores (abscesses, ulcers, *helkos*), those who took the beast's mark and worshiped his image.

These are not two groups but one; there is one-to-one correspondence.

This certainly could be the narrower *ha'aretz*, the land of Israel, especially considering the attention in the sixth bowl to the Euphrates River (v. 12).

3—Second bowl
Summary: On the sea (the Mediterranean, to the author and earliest readers), bloody death, kills sea creatures.

It would be bad enough if the blood were freshly let. But the description seems to suggest that it is congealed blood, like that of a man or animal that has been dead for a while, which, of course, decomposes quickly, giving off repulsive stench and breeding flies.

Surely it is unnecessary to read all/every literally (though many commentators assume it). To be sure, most of the times that John uses the word *pas* (all, every), it does or could conceivably be all. In Rev 8:7, "all green grass" could conceivably be literal, and grass would reappear next year. But here it is "all sea creatures" (*pasa psuchē zōē*), referring to animal, not plant life; and we know that species once extinguished do not reappear. Will the Lord repeat Gen 1:20–22 at the beginning of his millennial reign? Would it be permissible for our author to use this expression to represent the reality of the massive depletion of the sea creatures' population? See other instances of a figurative (hyperbolic) all: Rev 11:6; 18:2, 12, 17; also Acts 2:5; 7:22; 1 Cor 1:5; Eph 1:8 could be "great wisdom," Phil 1:9 "great discernment." Hyperbolically, the idea is many or much, perhaps even most.

4–7—Third bowl: punishment (v. 4) plus three verses of comment (vv. 5–7).

4—Summary: On the rivers and springs, bloody.

The natural sources of drinking water become bloody. This certainly recalls the first plague on Egypt, the water of the Nile being turned to blood (Exod 7:14–25).

5–7—The author inserts here remarks from two heavenly voices: the angel and the altar.

5–6—This angel of the waters must be the third angel of the seven, the angel who just poured out his assigned bowl onto the fresh drinking water supplies.

His remark is one of approval of the poetic justice of this judgment: "You, God, are just; what you are doing in this particular judgment is equitable."

6—"They deserve it," literally, they are worthy (as the King and Lamb are worthy of glory, etc.; Rev 4:11; 5:12) of drinking this cup of blood, a cup of death. The punishment fits the crime. They poured out the blood of God's innocent ones; God in turn converted their drinking water to blood.

7—John has mentioned altars in five previous chapters. See comments at Rev 6:9 and 9:13. Never were we led to suspect this altar might have something to say. It seems to be entirely sympathetic to the cries of the martyrs it shelters. Here, the altar recognizes all seven bowls as God's answer to the prayers of the martyrs in 6:9–11 from under the altar.

In Rev 15:3, God's ways were praised as true and righteous, evidently anticipating these bowl judgments. The altar now affirms these judgments from God are true and righteous.

8–9—Fourth bowl

Summary: On the sun (but not moon and stars, as the fourth trumpet, Rev 8:12), to sunburn men, they blasphemed/slandered God's name and did not do the normal and right thing: repent and give God the glory he is due.

Besides being equitable judgment, these first four bowls are yet another opportunity to repent: they are the patience of God (2 Pet 3:10) toward the many he has let live through them. The anticipation is building that they will soon suffer ultimate judgment, despite having been granted opportunity after opportunity to bow and worship. Should they do so, this God and final Judge would grant them forgiveness, grace, salvation, full participation in his glorious kingdom.

10–11—Fifth bowl

Summary: On the beast's throne, darkening it; subjects (same as those of the first bowl) chewed their own tongues, blasphemed (= cursed, slandered) God, the absolute opposite of repentance.

Curious juxtaposition with fourth bowl, shifting from burning sun to enduring darkness.

Similar to the fifth trumpet being excruciating but non-lethal pain. Similar to the sixth trumpet, part one (Rev 9:13–21), in that they only grew more hateful, more hardened, like Pharaoh. But that could also be said of every successive judgment plague.

10—This throne must refer to the beast's domain; kingdom, that which is spiritual but earthly. "They" is the subject population.

The penultimate (ninth) plague on Egypt was also darkness (Exod 10:21–29). That marked the last time Moses and Pharaoh faced one another. The next plague, the death angel and Passover, the most severe punishment of Pharaoh and his nation, resulted in Israel's exodus from Egypt.

Our author draws a connection between darkness and tongue-gnawing pain. The best explanation seems to be to connect this experience with that of hell as described by the Lord in Matt 25:30, outer darkness and gnashing of teeth (in agreement with Osborne).[10] This is not that eternal judgment, but it is probably to be regarded as a foretaste of it.

11—Pains (*ponōn*) from verse 10, sores (*helkōn*) from verse 2.

Here and Rev 11:13 are the only occurrences in Revelation of "the God of heaven." Where these cursed the God of heaven, those in 11:13 feared and glorified him at the end of the sixth trumpet. That revival was precipitated by a deadly earthquake, which seems likely the same as that in the seventh bowl (16:18–19), also a catastrophic earthquake in Jerusalem and surrounding cities.

The works of which they should have repented must be essentially the same as that list in Rev 9:20–21, as well as their guilty part in abusing and killing the innocent saints (v. 6; also perpetrated by the beast's faux bride and gun moll, Babylon, 17:6).

12–16—Sixth bowl

Summary: On the Euphrates, clearing the way for kings of the East, three frog spirits, Har-magedon.

10. Osborne, *Revelation*, 588.

12–14:

- Bowl dries Euphrates, facilitating movement of kings of the East toward Israel. The kings from the East (v. 12) seems to be a subset of the kings from the whole world (v. 14).

- Frog-like demon spirits (from the evil three) employ hellish miracle-tricks to lure kings from all over the world (v. 14) to the war of God's great day.

15–16:

- The kings assemble at Har-magedon. (See my brief comment below and more complete discussion in appendix 3 above why this has nothing to do with Megiddo and what it is actually about.)

- (v. 15) For all their preparations, plans, they will be unprepared, caught with their pants down, in their jammies. No amount of scheming will prepare them for what they will face. The only way to be prepared is to repent, which is the one requirement this chapter shows they refuse to do.

12—The dried-up river is advance preparation for the marching of kings to join the anticipated battle or rather to gather as kings for allied battle plans. It is curious to learn that a bowl of (liquid) potion poured into liquid river makes that liquid dry up.

14—The frog spirits lure kings, no mention of their armies. Actually, the verb is gather, which is repeated at the beginning of verse 16. But coupled with the demonic signs, this gathering is by luring.

The great day of God the Almighty must be, like Rev 6:17, the same as the day of the Lord. It is not mere coincidence that both these references are in the sixth of their respective sets of judgments: penultimate reminders and warnings that the ultimate is coming soon.

15—Parenthesis (agreeing with NAS, ESV, NET, NRS).

"I am coming when they don't expect": words of the Lord Jesus (as Rev 2:5, 16; 3:11; 22:7, 12, 20). That is, when I come, despite their war preparations (v. 16), they still won't be ready. Here, they are preparing for the ultimate war, but they are not doing the one thing it takes to be truly prepared: repenting, surrendering to King Jesus. (This sounds similar to Jeremiah's urgings that Zedekiah lead Jerusalem in surrendering to Babylon's armies, Jer 21:8–9; 27:12, 17; 38:2–3, 17–23. It also sounds similar to Isa 22:8–11. See Isa 27:5, where God urges his enemies, "Let them lay hold of my protection, let them make peace with me, let them make peace with me" [ESV].) Those who do not properly prepare will be caught by the moment as a soldier in his pajamas and slippers instead of battle gear when he hears the battle alarm. Of course, God does not need additional advantages. The point is that he has all advantages, even surprise timing.

The simile of coming like a thief is first found in 1 Thess 5:2 ("the day of the Lord will come like a thief in the night"), then 2 Pet 3:10 ("the day of the Lord will come like a thief"), and again in Rev 3:3 ("I will come like a thief"). The idea is that only those alert to the Lord himself will not be caught off guard; with all others, he will have the advantage of surprise. In the 1 Thessalonians and 2 Peter statements, it is the day that comes with surprise; here, it is the Lord himself (as also Rev 3:3), though the immediately preceding phrase is about the great day. Similar language and thought are also found in Matt 24:43 and Luke 12:39.

Cf. Neh 4:23, where the wall builders never changed out of their work and battle clothes.

16—"They gathered them": the subject of gather in verse 14 was the frog spirits and so also here. (In v. 13, the verb is singular, because the subject is neuter plural, *pneumata*; as the verb to go out, v. 14, is also singular, for the same idiomatic reason). "Them" is the kings of the whole world (v. 14, not just the kings of the East). These kings get tricked (by the false miracles of the frog spirits) into joining the doomed alliance. Of course, this is entirely God's plan, so the outcome is precisely what he purposed to accomplish.

There are no armies in these verses, only kings (though NET translation note says armies are implied, so they supply that in their translation, as does NLT—with which I disagree). They gather at the mountain of assembly (*har mo'ed*, not Megiddo; cf. Isa 14:13), Satan's throne. This is war council, not war or battle. The war for which they are gathering and preparing is that in Rev 19:11–21.

None of these—dragon, beast, false prophet, kings—has yet chosen to repent, submit, glorify God, so the day will certainly catch them off guard. They will all certainly be defeated, utterly destroyed.

17–21—Seventh bowl

Summary: Into the air; "it is done"; lightning-thunder-earthquake-hail (vv. 18, 21); great city, cities of gentiles damaged by earthquake; Babylon the great remembered for payback wrath (v. 19); providing transition to chapters 17–18.

The sixth trumpet was the last chance to repent, and the seventh trumpet was the second coming. This is the last of seven bowls, the completion of the wrath of God (Rev 15:1) against the beast and his followers (16:2, 10).

17—Where the sixth bowl was poured onto a river (and made it dry), this one is poured into the air, which may suggest two connections. The fact that everyone must breathe suggests no one can escape this. But it seems likely John was also referring to the idea expressed in Paul and surely shared by the other apostles that Satan is the prince of the air (Eph 2:2), and so this plague is a direct blow to his domain.

"It is done" or literally "it has come to pass" (*gegonen*, perfect active indicative third person singular of *ginomai*). From context, the idea seems to be, "That's it. That was their last chance to repent."

The voice comes from the throne. The speaker is God, the King himself.

18—This is the greatest earthquake ever (with lightning and thunder): "I warned you I would shake earth (*ha'aretz*)" (cf. Hag 2:6, 21). Is this the same earthquake as Rev 11:13? It must be. If so, while the survivors in Jerusalem repent (11:13), many others persist in cursing God (16:21). As that one shakes Jerusalem and surrounding gentile cities, this one shakes *ha'aretz*, the promised land. This must also then be contemporaneous with the first scene of the sixth trumpet, 9:13–21, which also culminated with unrepentance. This earthquake is likely also the same as 6:12 and Ezek 38:19.

This is the fourth of four lists of thunder and lightning (Rev 4:5; 8:5; 11:19; here), the last three of which also include earthquake and the last two of which also include hail (added to this list soon in 16:21).

19—Catastrophe on three-plus cities: the great city, the cities of the gentiles, and Babylon the great. In Rev 17:18, the author will equate Babylon with the great city.

The great city and the cities of the *ethnē*, *goyim* seem complementary: if the latter is gentile cities, the former should be the great city of

Israel, the same as it was in Rev 11:8, Jerusalem. This great judgment is not as much against the gentile cities as against Jerusalem; that is, this author is much more concerned to prophesy about Israel and Jerusalem than gentile lands and cities.

20—Major geographic and topographic changes; cf. Zech 14:4. But more important, the islands and mountains are personified: "they fled." You might say they had the good sense to draw back so as not to get caught up in the fallout of her judgment. It is probably best to regard the two clauses as something like synonymous parallelism, so that both subjects go with both verbs: every island and mountain fled, so that they were not found.

21—Unprecedented, unimaginable hailstorm and still more blaspheming, cursing God, instead of repenting. These beast worshipers are incorrigible.

Chapters 17–18

This section is about the great prostitute, a designation used only in Rev 17:1 and 19:2. This whole section seems to be an expansion of the seventh bowl of 16:17–21. It turns out that character was previously seen, introduced as Babylon the great (14:8; 16:19; cf. 17:5) and as the great city (11:8; 16:19; cf. 17:18). Those are brought together, though not explicitly equated, in 16:19. This prostitute and the great city are equated in 17:18. It is Jerusalem, in her wicked defiance against God and her true King-Messiah Jesus. This wicked Jerusalem will flourish for a time, because of her willing association with the beast, antimessiah, but must ultimately suffer judgment from which she can never recover (17:16; 18:21–23). She is also intimately associated with the kings and inhabitants of *ha'aretz* (17:2).

Classic OT passages depicting Israel-Judah-Jerusalem as prostitute include Jer 3, Ezek 16 and 23 (Oholah, Oholibah), and the book of Hosea. One of the earliest predictions of Israel as prostitute is in Deut 31:16, and an even earlier warning is in Exod 34:16.

Ezekiel describes Jerusalem as a prostitute whom God would judge by gentiles (Ezek 16:35–42). There, the prophet also uses derogatory nation and city associations (Hittites, Amorites, Samaria, Sodom; vv. 45–46), not significantly different from the code names of Rev 11:8 (Sodom and Egypt) and 17:5 (Babylon). See also Jer 3:1.

The dragon of chapter 12 is finally destroyed in Rev 20:10. The beasts of chapter 13 are finally destroyed in 19:20. This prostitute is the other great villain of Rev 12–20, the last one introduced and the first one judged. She is intimate with counterfeit messiah, the first beast, as the counterfeit bride. She is briefly triumphant, even falsely glorious, but finally destroyed. The beast's associates, the kings of the earth, carry out against her God's death sentence.

The code name Babylon suggests this is an ancient, wicked, godless city and chronic enemy of God's people. Prostitute suggests the city has deliberately chosen to reject normal, honorable monogamy—potentially to an honorable husband—choosing instead to associate intimately with unloving, disrespectful, lawless lowlifes. (They are lowlifes in God's eyes, not necessarily humanity's, because they oppose him.) She has participated in the murders (including perhaps honor killings) by her lover, those like John the Baptist sent as best man to urge prophetically to choose instead the glorious groom to which she was born (by arranged marriage).

Forms of the word group *porn-* (prostitute, fornication) occur thirteen times in relation to Babylon. Only three other books of the Bible use it that many times (Ezekiel, Hosea, 1 Corinthians).

On the idea of city, see comment below at Rev 21:9.

Isaiah anticipates the purging and redeeming of Jerusalem in Isa 4:4–5.

Chapter 17

This angelic message is an announcement of her judgment, verse 1, carried out in verse 16. Cf. Rev 14:8; 16:19; 19:2–3.

1—The parallel between this verse and Rev 21:9 is striking: same kind of angel, same invitation, opposite woman-cities. The parallel continues between 17:3 and 21:10.

> Then one of the seven angels who had the seven bowls full of the seven last plagues came and spoke with me, saying, "Come here, I will show you the bride, the wife of the Lamb." And he carried me away in the spirit to a great and high mountain, and showed me the holy city, Jerusalem, coming down out of heaven from God, having the glory of God." (Rev 21:9–11 NASB)

Messiah's pure bride is new Jerusalem; antimessiah's very impure domestic partner and gun moll is Jerusalem today (cf. Gal 4:25). The balance is remarkable—but only if this prostitute is Jerusalem, not if, as many interpreters claim, she is Rome or some other. The most glaring reason she cannot be Rome is that the beast is Rome (Dan 2; 7).

1–6—Descriptors (ten):

- great prostitute (*pornē*; later, mother of prostitutes, *pornōn*)
- sits on many waters
- kings of earth/land (*ha'aretz*) committed fornication (*porneuō*) with her (she has given herself freely to many kings, reciprocally providing something the other values)
- inhabitants of *ha'aretz* got drunk on her *porneia* (fornication)
- in a spiritual wilderness (uncivilized, ironically anti-city)
- mounted (seated) on red beast, with blasphemous names tattooed, seven heads, ten horns (no crowns here, though the seven heads are seven kings, v. 10; recalls beast, dragon)
- dressed in purple and scarlet, adorned (gilded, v. 4) with jewelry (gold, stones, pearls; see the mournful memory of these lost, Rev 18:16)
- swilling from gold mug cocktail of abominations and uncleannesses (filthy, nasty abominations) of her prostitution (*porneia*)
- named (code): Babylon the great, mother of prostitutes (*pornōn*) and of abominations (of *ha'aretz*)
- drunk with blood of saints/witnesses (cf. Luke 13:33–34): she has shed (and consumed) much blood

2—The kings and inhabitants of *ha'aretz* habitually fornicated with her (but eventually turn on her, v. 16), consensually. This prostitute corrupted kings and peasants. Undoubtedly, many individuals will, in the days referenced here, engage in illicit, immoral physical-sexual relations. But the prophet's meaning here is spiritual. This city shall have cozied up to the end-time Canaanites. She shall have fully embraced their ways, and she shall have led them into even greater wicked indulgences, so that it can be said she made them drunk—rather than the reverse—on her wicked ways.

It will soon be seen that she also embraced a faux messiah-savior. She shall have sold herself as ancient Israel did, as described and decried by the OT prophets. OT Israel had a husband—not just an ordinary one, not just a good one, but the very best possible. Yet she walked away from him and gave herself to others in exchange for promises of fertility and security, which of course they could not and did not deliver. See Hos 1.

If prostitution wasn't bad enough, she also intoxicated herself and her lovers with potions described in verses 4, 6.

3—Wilderness is the most uncivilized place, yet she boasts the name of the sophisticated city Babylon. This adds to the irony.

She consorts not with a noble stallion but a monster beast (*thērion*; it might be helpful for movie and comic book aficionados to recall images conjured by the creators of modern fantasies).

This beast with blasphemous names recalls the little horn of the fourth beast of Dan 7:25, which in fact this beast is.

4—She is arrogantly ostentatious, dressed as a queen, since that is how she sees herself (Rev 18:7, 16), and she is a conspicuous consumer of a most vile potion, recalling Jeremiah's prophecy: "Babylon has been a golden cup in the hand of the LORD, intoxicating all the earth. The nations have drunk of her wine; therefore the nations are going mad" (Jer 51:7 NASB). She indulges in filthy abominations.

5—Not till here does the author identify this prostitute with the previous warnings about Babylon (Rev 14:8; 16:19). As bad as prostitution is, she is the worst, the mother of all prostitutes. (Let us not forget that though there are some today who seek to destigmatize prostitution, there was no such impetus in John's orbit of influence.)

6a—She is drunk, already a repulsive sight. She is drunk from copious consumption of blood. Since the saints and the witnesses of Jesus must be not two groups but one, the reader must ask why the redundancy. Her victims are holy (saints) in God's eyes and incur her wrath because of their steadfast testimony (witness) to Jesus's kingship. Her mount, the beast, is bent on absolute dominion, and she dutifully and cheerfully participates in punishing all opposition.

6b–7a—"I marveled a great marvel. The angel asked, 'Why do you marvel?'"

John is shocked by this great wonder.

John: "No, it can't be! Say it ain't so! This is what 'the great city' has become?"

Angel: "You really should not be so shocked."

Yet it turns out the inhabitants of *ha'aretz* will be amazed (same word, v. 8) at the falsely resurrected beast.

7b—The revealing angel promises to interpret the woman and the beast, but what we get next is interpretation of the beast, whose heads and horns are mentioned but not his crowns.

8–14, 16–17—Interpretation of the beast (heads in vv. 12–14; horns in vv. 16–17).

15—Waters (on which the woman sits)

18—The woman herself

The amount of attention given to the beast and the kings is an indirect but necessary way of describing the woman.

Identifying the beast: seven heads, ten horns.

8–11—The seven heads: a great riddle.

The author speaks of the beast in reference to two distinct though related entities. One is a composite of successive empires from ancient times to the end times. That one has seven heads. The second is the end-time manifestation of that transhistorical one, the antichrist. He is the last of the heads. The first beast is the transhistorical beast, and the second beast, the seventh head of that one, is the antimessiah of the great tribulation.

My suggestion for the identities of the seven heads is to begin with Daniel's four empires and extrapolate from there: Babylon, Medo-Persia, Greece, Rome, end-time Rome (whose king is antimessiah); then backward historically to Assyria and Egypt. Perhaps.

8—The first beast shall disappear into the abyss and then re-emerge (cf. Rev 11:7), only to be destroyed ultimately (reiterated in v. 11).

He will dazzle ("amazed"; cf. Rev 13:3; 17:6–7) the inhabitants of *ha'aretz* (whose names do not appear in the book of life) when they see him seemingly, falsely resurrected.

The first beast was and is not and (literally) will be (*parestai*, future tense of *pareimi*). This sounds quite similar to what is said of God, "Who is and was and is to come" (Rev 1:4, 8; 4:8). Here, instead, John avoids the verb come, because that is reserved for Jesus, the coming one.

9–10—The seven heads of the first beast are mountains, that is, kings, of which five are past, one present, one future, but short-term.

Again, his heads are seven mountains/kings (OT kingdoms are sometimes described as mountains; e.g., Ezek 35:2; 36:1) "on which the woman sits." She also sits on the second beast (v. 3) and on many waters (v. 1), which are gentile nations (v. 15).

We are talking about a city known by seven hills, with a history of (biblically notable) kings, five past, one present in John's day, one yet to come at the end of this age (see Matt 13:39). "Cities on seven hills" include Rome, Athens, Jerusalem, and many others around the world. That is, this is not a unique identifier.

11—The second beast, introduced in Rev 13:1–10, is also one of the heads of the first beast; he is one of the seven, and he is number eight; he is not numbers one to seven. Perhaps this reflects his death and resurrection.

The seven heads of the first beast seem to correspond to successive empires through history—five past, one present in John's day (Rome), one future (Rome again), yet there is some real solidarity about all seven, as with the statue in Dan 2.

8–11—The upshot: The first beast is a series of gentile nations that God has allowed and will allow to punish and rule over Israel-Jerusalem. The final iteration of that is the second beast, "out of the sea," the antichrist. He will arrive on the stage of history in the last days (v. 12) to become the leader of some form of the Roman empire *redivivus*.

He will allow Jerusalem to ride him (v. 3) in exchange for her cooperation in his quest to rule the world. He will at some point suffer an apparent mortal wound from which he will miraculously rise.

12–17—The ten horns of the first beast.

The origin of the ten horns is the fourth beast in Dan 7:7. The fourth beast is the final gentile power to dominate Israel before the advent of God's glorious kingdom (Dan 2:44; 7:13–14). But like the iron of the statue in Dan 2 and the fourth beast in Dan 7, that fourth empire is in two phases, the latter of which is directly confronted by the stone mountain and the son of man at what we know to be the second coming. In Daniel's dream, an eleventh horn arises later than the original ten (Dan 7:8) and turns out to be what we know to be the antichrist, setting up the clash that settles the question of the rule of *ha'aretz*, earth/land: antimessiah meets Messiah (cf. Rev 19:11–20).

In Revelation, this is the second beast. This beast has ten horns, which are the kings of *ha'aretz* (vv. 12, 18; cf. Ps 2:2, 10).

12—The ten horns = kings of the future day of the second beast. Thus both the second beast (i.e., the eighth head) and these kings are future to John (and us).

13—They share a common purpose (*gnōmen*), and all give their full support to the second beast.

14—Never has there been a fearsome alliance like this, bent on world conquest with the near certainty of success, seemingly holding all the cards (the impression created by ch. 13).

They will wage war against the Lamb (Rev 19:19), but the Lamb will destroy them (19:21); the Lamb cannot lose. He is and always has been and always will be King and Lord of all. At Calvary, the dragon and the first beast, represented in that day by Rome, the sixth head, destroyed him, but only temporarily. This is a statement of the ultimate outcome, which actually occurs after the fighting of verse 16.

On his side are the called/chosen/faithful, not that he needs their fighting power. They line up behind him.

15—This prostitute reigns (sits virtually, not literally, on a throne) over all kinds of gentiles.

She sits on waters (peoples, vv. 1, 15), on the second beast (v. 3), and on seven mountains, which are the second beast's heads (v. 9). She also reigns over or has dominion over (*echousa basileian*) the ten kings (v. 18).

If this is Jerusalem—and it is—when could this be? This has to be in those last days. See Rev 17:1–6; 18:12–13, 16, 22–23. All the biggest action in this book is set in the last three and a half years. The second beast and the whore take care of each other through those years. But this is an uneasy alliance, destined to break down.

16—The second beast and ten kings eventually change their tune: they turn on the whore, eat her flesh, and burn her (city). Mourning over her demise is the burden of chapter 18.

Is this not what Zech 14:2 is about? Then Zech 14:3–4 anticipates Rev 19:11–16, and Zech 14:5–21 anticipates Rev 20:4–6 and chapters 21–22.

17—This is God's purpose (*gnōmen*, as also in v. 13) for raising them up, as God is the one who inspired in them their common objective (*gnōmen*). They are God's agent for fulfilling his judgment against her. (These kings will get what they deserve in Rev 19:21.)

18—She is the great city; she (literally) "has a kingdom over" the kings of *ha'aretz*.

Here at last the author removes all mystery as to her identity. The only authorial possibility is Jerusalem, per Rev 11:8. No other identity for the woman can be supported from John's text.

Chapter 18

Setting: "After these things" (v. 1), i.e., after the second beast and the ten kings destroy her (Rev 17:16). The genre of chapter 18 is dramatically different from that of chapter 17.

This chapter is largely the reaction of observers of her fall. That is, they are recalling her glory days and marveling and mourning that that degree of glory should have faded so utterly, suddenly, and finally.

Suddenness of her demise: verses 8, 10, 17 (one day, one hour).

Weeping and wailing: verses 9, 11, 15, 19.

Finality: verses 14, 21–23.

The next chapter (19) begins with the reaction of the faithful: hallelujah! (Rev 18:20 is also a call for the faithful to rejoice.) By these her demise is regarded as justice served at last. Her extreme wickedness for all those years has not gone unnoticed, unpunished.

1–3—Very powerful angel whose radiance illuminates earth.

2–3—His message: Babylon is fallen, judged by God for great wickedness.

Fallen: from spectacular city to ghost town, now occupied only by demons and wild beasts; haunted.

Wickedness: she corrupted everyone she touched (except the faithful).

2—Delivered with powerful voice (remember: they did not have amplification, radio transmission, or recording devices): not just fallen, but fallen, fallen is Babylon the great. Literally, "she fell, she fell"; previously at Rev 14:8, originally at Isa 21:9.

"She has become a lair of demons, a haunt of every kind of foul spirit and every unclean bird and every unclean and hated beast." Cf. Isa 13:19–22.

The idea is that a once glorious and sophisticated city has died and become a ghost town; it has been taken over by the wild beasts and demons. (Still, at her heyday, she was a floozy, only pretending to be glorious.) That is the simple message of this entire chapter. That thought is extended and elaborated to simulate long-lasting wailing by those who mourn her demise.

(There are several textual critical problems in this verse. I do not regard them as consequential enough to delve into. I simply refer the interested reader to the NET Bible notes.)

3—She had seduced "all the nations" (perhaps consensually); the liaisons were immoral and materially profitable. The introductory causal conjunction (for, *hoti*) indicates that her demise is the just consequence for her *porneia*. Verses 4–7 confirm. There is an untranslatable wordplay between "fornicated" and "merchants," *eporneusan* and *emporoi*, separated by two short, minor words: "The kings of the land with her fornicated and the merchants." Those words are etymologically unrelated, but coincidentally they share their second syllables, -*por*.

The kings got rich when she insisted on sensually indulging (*strenos*; the corresponding verb occurs in vv. 7, 9, and these are the only three occurrences of these words in the NT) herself.

4–8—Angelic warning.

This speech by an unspecified heavenly messenger, simply called another voice from heaven, continues either through verse 8 (ESV, NRS, NET) or verse 20 (NAS, NIV, NKJ). Verses 4–8 are the announcement she will fall; verses 9–19 are simulated descriptions of the grief of her onetime allies and trading partners (perhaps lovers).

4—Call to the saints to distance themselves from her. Recalls the demands that Lot depart from Sodom (Gen 19:15) and that the Israelites distance themselves from Korah (Num 16:24–27). See also Jer 51:6, 9, 45; Eph 5:7. The idea is that physical separation represents the more important spiritual distance. They are commanded not to join her in her criminal sins nor in the judgment for those sins.

5—The figure of sins heaped high as heaven is not uncommon in the OT (Jer 51:9; Ezra 9:6; Ps 38:4). The second line is the explanation:

though judgment has been delayed, the crimes have not gone unnoticed. The time of reckoning has come at last.

6—Retributive justice will be so great, she deserves so much punishment, it is described as double (literally, "double the doubles") what she deserves (which is also common in the OT: Isa 40:2; Jer 16:18; 50:29). The second line is something of an echo of Rev 14:10.

7—Now the payback is described as equivalent. Repay her with torment and grief matching the degree of her onetime self-glorification and sensual living. It is poetic reversal: she had prided herself that her glory would never end. John is clearly paraphrasing Isa 47:7–8 ("Yet you said, 'I will be a queen forever.' These things you did not consider nor remember the outcome of them. Now, then, hear this, you sensual one, who dwells securely, who says in your heart, 'I am, and there is no one besides me. I will not sit as a widow, nor know loss of children'" [NASB]). Again, the irony is that Isaiah wrote of the Babylon that would just a century later crush Jerusalem and then forty-seven years later would be overthrown by Medo-Persia.

8—All her glory will end, not gradually, but suddenly and utterly. It will be gruesome: death, grief, starvation, fire. God is the judge who will pronounce the sentence, and his might is unequaled and unlimited.

9–19—Description of her old friends' mourning.

9–10—Kings of *ha'aretz.*

9—"Weep and lament": no single verb is strong enough; this is extreme sadness, grief (also in v. 15). They realize how much they have lost forever. These had reveled indulgently with her.

10—"Standing at a distance . . . torment" repeated in verses 15, 17. "In one hour," suddenly.

Aren't these the same ones who destroyed her (Rev 17:16)? Perhaps they only regret that the good times are over forever.

11–19—Merchants.

11—Commerce has completely dried up: the worst and most sudden, unexpected stock market crash.

12–13—Catalog of twenty-nine products they once marketed in her. They are especially luxury items, bespeaking widespread affluence. While the ESV and others read better by leaving out "and" (*kai*), keeping it where the author put it—twenty-eight times!—enhances the extensiveness intended by the author (see NAS). Read aloud slowly. If necessary, reinsert "and" before every item after the first, to feel the intended rhetorical effect.

14—All those gaudy things are gone, up in smoke. Again, John's actual wording gets watered down in translation. Here it is, more or less literally: "And the fruit of your soul's lust has gone from you and all the luxuries and the splendors [or luxurious things and splendid things] have perished from you, and no one shall ever find them again."

15–17—Those who had been so intimate will step back, helpless to rescue her, fearful of getting caught in her destruction.

15—Two verbs ("weeping and mourning") are required to express the depth of grief, response to their loss. (The grief is even greater in v. 19, these two verbs plus a third.)

16—The former glory (cf. Rev 17:4)

17–19—These verses begin and end with "laid waste in one hour."

On *erēmoō* (literally, make into a wilderness) see also Rev 17:16. Our days of extreme profits are over; we will never see a market like that again. In fact, it seems this may represent a financial collapse surpassing in degree and suddenness, unexpectedness—it catches everyone by surprise—all that has ever happened.

18—There will never be another like her. We witnessed the greatest ever. They said much the same of the beast (Rev 13:4). We followers of King Jesus know there will be one much better. But these cannot imagine outside their materialistic categories.

19—Three verbs of mourning. See verse 15.

20—Command to rejoice over her demise (fulfilled in Rev 19:1–5).

21–24—An angel throws a millstone into the sea, announces the absolute end of Babylon with all its attractions and the cause: sorcery and blood of saints. See Jer 51:59–64, where Jeremiah's prophecy against Babylon (Jer 50–51) was to be read to the royal court of Babylon. Then the scroll was to be weighted with stone and thrown into the Euphrates, symbolizing the certain and final demise of Babylon.

Never again will this Jerusalem be inhabited and dominated by the wicked. That is cause for rejoicing.

21—A great stone would quickly sink to the bottom of the sea, where it would remain forever.

22–23—She had been a place of perpetual partying and production. That had the effect of mesmerizing, as if by black magic (*pharmakeia*, the last word of v. 23), deceiving the revelers into believing those good times would never end.

24—Before leaving this story, readers need to be reminded she was also stained with the blood of innocent martyrs in *ha'aretz*.

Chapter 19

1–10—Out of the ashes of Babylon arises the long prophesied perfect bride, fit for her royal Groom, Messiah.

Four hallelujahs (vv. 1, 3, 4, 6; these are the only occurrences of hallelujah in the NT): God is to be praised for preparing all for the wedding of Messiah and bride, as he is to be praised for judging antimessiah's anti-bride.

1, 6—"I heard what sounded like (*ēkousa hōs*) the voice of a great multitude in heaven." Is this the same group as Rev 7:9; 15:2–4?—the tribulation martyrs? There is no nearer contextual option.

1–5—Cheers for the prostitute's demise.

This judgment surely relates to the fifth seal, avenging and vindicating the martyrs (Rev 6:9–11). On rejoicing at the judgment of the wicked, see Ps 58:10 ("the righteous will rejoice when he sees the vengeance; he will wash his feet in the blood of the wicked" [NASB]) in context.

1–2—First hallelujah. By judging finally the prostitute Jerusalem, God delivers glorious and mighty salvation to his people, who had been the victims of her wickedness.

1—Cf. Ps 3:8: "Salvation belongs to Yahweh; your blessing be upon your people," where the specific occasion was David's deliverance from Absalom, which was by the death of Absalom.

God's salvation is powerfully glorious, gloriously powerful.

2—Quotes from Ps 19:9 (also adapted in Rev 16:7) and Deut 32:43. According to his true and righteous judgments, he has avenged the martyrdom of his servants that the prostitute caused. Like the inhabitants of *ha'aretz*, she corrupted the land, particularly by putting the faithful to death, but also by the fornication of selling out to antimessiah, instead of holding herself pure and faithful for her true Messiah.

3—Second hallelujah, same voices. Quote from Isa 34:10. Justice demands she suffer death by fire forever, and that is also cause for celebration.

4—Third hallelujah. The entire company of the elders with the four living ones, the cherubim, endorse what the multitude has shouted and add their own hallelujah. Here, they reprise their worship from Rev 4:10–11, where the stated basis of praise was the King's work of creation. This time, it is his work of judging her who opposed his people and rejected her true Lord in favor of the hideous monster beast, the antimessiah.

5—"Voice . . . from the throne" occurs now for the third of four times (see also Rev 4:5 [*phōnē* translated there as sounds], 16:17; 21:3). It directs all the King's servants to praise him. If any did not participate in the praises of verses 2–4, here is their cue.

6–9—Cheers for the bride's preparedness for the wedding of the century—or, rather, of eternity. The bride is new Jerusalem; the whore is old Jerusalem (cf. Gal 4:25–26).

6—Fourth hallelujah. Once again, a great chorus crying at fortissimo, loud as Niagara, loud as thunder. Yes, it is a supremely good thing that God Almighty reigns supreme. See Rev 11:17.

7—The present occasion is the announcement of the impending wedding of Lamb and his bride. She is now ready, now that old Jerusalem is gone forever. The image of wedding suggests the Lamb has been eagerly yet patiently waiting for that special day. For this, God deserves great praise, rendered in the redundancy of two synonymous verbs, *chairō* and *agalliaō*, both in the subjunctive with imperative force, and further magnified by the expression "give [also the subjunctive] him glory."

8—God has granted her (divine passive) spectacular wedding attire: the saints' righteous deeds. Many of those righteous deeds shall have been seen and known by very few or even only God himself. See Matt 6:4, 6, 18; Luke 12:3. See also John 15:1–6, where it is up to the vinedresser, not the branches, to evaluate fruitfulness.

9–10—Who is the one speaking to John? It seems to be the angel identified in Rev 22:6, 16; perhaps the voice in verse 5.

9—Truer words have not been spoken (cf. Rev 21:5, 6; 22:6). What is so important as to warrant that affirmation? The first statement: it will be ultimate blessing to attend the Lamb's wedding.

10—Here and in Rev 22:8–9, John is impelled to bow to this angel. There (22:6) as here, the spirit of prophecy is at issue. True prophecy is essentially spiritual. (Cf. 1 John 4:1–6, where both true and false prophets are interchangeable with spirits.)

Why does John reflexively react this way? Perhaps he is overcome with the realization of the truth of verse 9. This angel has spoken for God a message of heavenly truth, the essence of which is Jesus himself. God is the source of the message, and Jesus is the content. One might also compare Rev 7:13–14, where John calls one of the twenty-four elders "my lord." Surely part of the idea is his profound, genuine humility, completely absent of any hubris that might be expected of such a celebrity as John, the disciple whom Jesus loved.

Overview of the continuous literary flow from here to the end:

19:11–21 (plus 20:1–3)—White horse rider (vv. 11–16), anticipation of victory (vv. 17–18), enemy forces prepared for battle (v. 19), immediate disposition of enemies: beasts (v. 20), kings, warriors (v. 21), dragon (20:1–3).

20:1–6—One thousand years.

20:1–3—Disposition of dragon is different from that of his associates—one thousand years (i.e., temporary, not eternal) imprisonment.

20:4–6—During that thousand years, Messiah reigns with his faithful resurrected martyrs.

20:7–10—"After the thousand years," Satan the dragon is released. He is still defiant (unrepentant, like so many others earlier), mounts yet another rebellion, his last. It is unsuccessful, as heavenly fire destroys his army before his forces get off a shot. Think 2 Kgs 1:10, 12. He is dispatched to hell ("lake of fire and brimstone"), joining the beasts.

20:11–15—Great white throne.

All non-saints are finally judged and sentenced to join Satan and beasts in hell's lake of fire and brimstone. Recall Matt 25:41.

21–22—New heaven and earth.

The natural flow fits premillennialism, not amillennialism or postmillennialism. Certainly the burden of proof must be on those positions.

Resuming chapter 19 comments:

11—This second white horse marks the closing of the large unit begun at Rev 6:1. But verse 11 cannot be the end of the unit. The unit must instead continue to include what verse 11 introduces, namely, at least through the end of chapter 19, probably through the end of chapter 20. See "continuous literary flow" discussion above.

11–16—His names: faithful and true (v. 11), Word of God (v. 13), King, Lord (v. 16); "he has a name written which no one knows except himself" (v. 12).

The first three are not really names, though the author uses the word *onoma* in verses 12, 13, 16 (in v. 11, "he is called").

What is the point of a name that no one knows (v. 12; cf. Rev 2:17)? He is all these other articulated truths which are knowable, yet he is so wonderful and glorious as to be beyond knowing completely. He cannot be reduced to verbal expressions, true and superlative as these are. The idea of naming is far more profound than any of us can fully appreciate. Perhaps its commonness belies or masks its profundity. The point is not a specifying label but an expression of the essence of the thing or person named. His new name is one none of us has ever heard. There is much more to him than we have yet learned. If that is true of the Pergamum overcomers, much more must it be true of this glorious Warrior-Savior. But when the naming is of a king, it also has majestic overtones.

11—"He judges and wages war" is hendiadys: the battle he initiates is the enforcing of the sentence of heaven's King. Justice comes to the villains of chapters 12–13 and to those who aligned with them. This is the stone mountain of Dan 2:34–35, 45, the end of the penultimate and the beginning of the Uutimate.

On heaven being opened, see Rev 4:1; 11:19; 15:5.

12—Eyes on fire seems to depict perfect knowledge, penetrating focus, determined purpose, purifying judgment. If he is King of kings, why should he not have numerous crowns? (On the unknown name, see discussion above.)

13—His voluntary self-sacrifice is never far from focused attention. That he goes to war wearing a robe dipped in blood is a vivid statement to both his armies and the enemy that he is out for vengeance, justified, righteous vengeance. He is bent on paying back those who put him on the cross. He is the slaughtered lamb standing (Rev 5:6). He is also the Word of John 1:1, he who was with God and was God in the beginning at creation. God created by a word (Heb 11:3).

14—He leads his army in the ultimate, genuinely holy war. What they are about is carrying out the decreed sentence of the holy King of heaven. See comment at verse 11.

His warriors are angelic, not human.

15—Armed for war. He attacks the enemy with his word; with a word he overrules and destroys even his enemies. The slaughter is extensive (wine press of divine wrath; see also vv. 18, 21; Rev 14:18–20). Here are echoes of Ps 2:9 (iron scepter); Isa 11:4 ("He will strike the earth with the rod of his mouth, and with the breath of his lips he will slay the wicked" [NASB]); Isa 63:3 (tread the winepress)—all bold, messianic eschatological prophecies.

16—Like a supreme commander, prominently displaying his four stars. He announces boldly that he intends to bring any and all rulers to their knees before himself. Even those who call themselves king must pay submissive homage to this one. One cannot miss the connection of thought to Phil 2:10 (Isa 45:23): "Every knee shall bow and every tongue shall confess that [this one] is Lord [of all]." But there is also Ps 2:7–9, 11–12. The best news is that this one wins and rules: the eternal future of the universe is good to the highest degree. But what is good news to some is terrifying news to the rest.

17–21—Victory (in fulfillment of Rev 6:2, "conquering and to conquer")!

17–18—Advance invitation to carrion birds: a feast will soon be yours. The repetition of "flesh" with ten qualifiers has the rhetorical effect of forcing the reader to survey a battlefield following a great slaughter, with no survivors of the enemy forces.

19—The opposing forces are arrayed. This is what they prepared for (Rev 16:12–16), yet they are pathetically and fatally ill-prepared (see comment at 16:15).

20–21—The enemy forces are destroyed: 100 percent casualties on their side, none on ours.

20—The villain leaders of chapter 13 are cast directly into hell. Their case was already tried in heaven before this battle. Again, see comment at verse 11.

21—The armies are utterly destroyed, providing the feast promised to the birds.

The disposition of the remaining villain supreme leader, Satan, is described in the next verses. The chapter break is an unfortunate interruption of an unbroken storyline.

Chapter 20

If there were no chapter break—and there wasn't in John's writing—it would be much clearer that this next section is a continuation of the ending of chapter 19. That ended with the final disposition of the beast and false prophet. But were we not introduced in chapters 12–13 to three villain leaders? What about the third, the devil himself, their supreme commander? That is how Rev 20:1 follows directly from chapter 19.

1–6—One thousand years, followed by "after the thousand years" (vv. 7–10).

The default interpretation must be literal. Ps 105:8 speaks of a thousand generations, rather hyperbolically. But where that verse describes that covenant (Abrahamic) as enduring to a thousand generations, verse 10 calls it everlasting (*olam*). Here, however, there are no contextual clues driving the reader to conclude this cannot be literal. That does not rule out some particular figurative sense; or, to turn it around, a figurative sense does not rule out a literal thousand years (contra Johnson).[11]

1–3—Dragon's thousand-year incarceration. This seems the logical next issue from chapter 20: having dealt with the beasts and the armies, what about the dragon?

This angel coming from heaven is under orders from heaven's King: arrest that dragon, throw him in the dungeon, lock it, guard it for one thousand years! We previously saw that Satan could not hold his own against Michael and his forces and was thrown out of heaven (Rev 12:7–12).

1—Chain symbolizes restraint, like handcuffs; enormous chain indicates it is unbreakable, inescapable.

2—The verb *krateō* (lay hold, seize) is synonym to *piazō* (seize, Rev 19:20), but implies a degree of strength greater than *piazō*.

The fourfold identification of the prisoner eliminates any doubt. He cannot masquerade or disguise himself. See discussion at Rev 12:9.

One thousand years is a long but temporary sentence (vv. 3, 7 speak of release after that). The contrast in verse 10, forever and ever, is just as it appears, the difference between the finite and the infinite.

3—Abyss is perhaps a bottomless pit; dungeon, later called prison (*phulakēs*, in v. 7). The prison door is overhead. It is sealed over (*epanō*)

---

11. Johnson, "Revelation," 481.

him. Together with "shut and sealed" and "key" (v. 1), it indicates escape-proof confinement. There will be no jailbreak.

Thus he is incapable of engaging in his typical activities, especially deceiving the nations (cf. v. 8, his first activity upon release from this incarceration).

4–15—Dominant words in verses 4–6, 11–15: death/dead (vv. 5, 6, 12, 12, 13, 13, 13, 14, 14) and life (vv. 4, 5, 12, 15).

4–6—Martyrs' thousand-year reign.

Continuity is in the thousand years (twice in vv. 1–3, three times in vv. 4–6). The only other occurrence of thousand years is in verse 7, which implies that the thousand years of verses 4–6 coincide exactly with Satan's prison sentence.

4—The first thing John says he sees is thrones, similar to Rev 4:2; then they sat, also echoing 4:2. God the King is so pleased with these that he allows this similarity of description of their reign to that of his own reign.

"They judge" means they rule, reign. "Was given" is the divine passive.

Faithful martyrs: beheaded; plus indicators of faithfulness: sat (enthroned), worshiped, received, lived, reigned—all constative aorists, placing stress on the fact of the occurrences.

There is no statement of exclusion of other saints martyred in some other way, nor for that matter other saints who were not martyred at all. These must include those described in Rev 13:15. It probably also includes all saints from all time (cf. Matt 8:11; 19:28; Luke 13:28–29; 22:29–30; 1 Cor 6:2).

The timing is post-beast. Messiah has just returned and now reigns during the thousand years of Satan's incarceration, after the beast has been finally dispatched.

Their testimony of Jesus was according to the word of God, which was undoubtedly given them by revelation (cf. Matt 16:17).

5–6—Not all the dead were resurrected at this time; only the blessed and holy ones. The wicked were excluded. These shall not be touched by the second death.

There is no mention of second resurrection. Instead, the notion of ordinals is introduced in verse 5, "first resurrection." Soon thereafter the author speaks of "second," but there it is in reference to death. I wonder if "second death" is a resurrection (as John 5:29) but unto damnation. Thus this author chose not to use the word resurrection for that, though John 5:29 does use the same word for both the righteous and the wicked.

Priest and king are linked, here of the saints, for this same thousand years.

Amillennialists' assignment of this thousand years to the church age, calling this section (vv. 1–6) recapitulation, is arbitrary; it lacks evidence. It asserts a discontinuity from chapter 19 that does not exist. That interpretation arises not from this text but from outside; it amounts to eisegesis, not exegesis. The only reason not to see a premillennial millennium here is that such does not fit one's system. The natural flow of these chapters is inexorable progression from climax (Rev 19:11ff) to happily ever after (chs. 21–22). A premillennial millennium fits in that flow perfectly.

Interestingly, there is no mention of the mortal millennial saints and so no mention of their resurrection. For the teaching about mortal millennial saints, we are tacitly referred to prior revelation, such as Matt 19:28.

What is the purpose or idea of the millennium? Satan shall have occupied the throne of earth for at least several millennia, since the fall. (Of course, God is and has been limiting the amount of damage he can wreak on the land and the people.) By the end of his day, the world will be at the brink of utter destruction. Such is the legacy of Satan's day. Then the true and rightful King of earth shall take over. In one millennium, he will make of this world the kind of paradise that should theoretically have developed under the rule of the first Adam (male and female). This he will do even with the curse of the fall still afflicting the world and the mortal population. (That does not get eradicated until the end of the first creation and the beginning of the new creation.) He will suppress and subdue the natural evil in the ground, overruling its unruly impulses to convulse destructively. He will also build a society and construct social systems that reward the impulses of the new nature, the redeemed inner man, and suppress the contrary impulses of the unredeemed outer man. God must win not only eternity, important as that is; he must and will win history as well.

7–10—Beast's liberty and demise.

7—Continuity is emphatic: "when [*hotan*, whenever] the thousand years are completed" (aorist passive subjunctive).

As promised (v. 2), Satan is released; he shall have served out his sentence (no early release).

8—Immediately he engages in deceiving the nations (gentiles, heathen; cf. Rev 18:23; 20:3; 12:9; 13:14; 19:20).

He is the best the world has ever known at deceiving. The only antidote is fidelity to him who is the truth itself. Refusal to avail oneself of that antidote is to guarantee being deceived. They are helpless to resist his deceptive seduction. See 2 Thess 2:10.

Gog and Magog suggests ancient wicked races of man.

It is questionable whether this or Rev 19:18 more closely mirrors the prophecies of Ezek 38–39. Revelation 19:18 is prior to the millennium; Rev 20:8 is after. Ezekiel 38–39 seems more pre- than post-, inasmuch as Ezek 37–39 describe crucial events marking the end of the tribulation and the beginning of the millennium, while chapters 40–48 speak of faithful Israel in the millennium under Messiah.

Innumerable, i.e., humanly unstoppable. Think shock and awe; overwhelming disparity of military might coupled with the will to exert all necessary force.

9—The object of his planned attack is focused and completely expected: Jerusalem. The situation is very threatening to God's city and people.

There is nothing sporting about Satan's intentions or strategy. Likewise, there is nothing sporting about God's action. Before Satan's armies can get off a shot, God simply consumes those armies with fire from heaven.

10—The end of Satan, like that of the beasts before and all nonsaints soon after. Remember Matt 25:41: this place was "prepared [not for humans, but] for the devil and his angels."

These are not terms of annihilation, cessation of existence—"shall be tormented," "day and night," "forever and ever"—but of conscious sensing.

11–15—Great white throne. Throne means the King is seated for judgment; white means the judgment is absolutely right and true; great means this is final. There is no appeal of this highest court's verdict (v. 12) and sentence (v. 15).

11—Earth and heaven fled; no place found for them: he is so awesome, terrifying.

As in Rev 4:1, John sees first a throne, then the Enthroned One.

12—The accused are not alive but dead. Judged according to their deeds (repeated in v. 13): all will be held to give account for their mortal lives. The verdict is guilty. Cf. Rev 3:2: "I find that your actions do not meet the requirements of my God" (NLT), as well as all seven church letters.

13—Regardless of what had become of their dead bodies, all will stand trial at this court. None will escape the summons to appear.

14—Death's death. See 1 Cor 15:27: "The last enemy that will be abolished is death."

Lake of fire seems to be the same as Gehenna in Matt 23:33.

15—One-to-one correspondence with names not included in the book of life.

Chapter 21

John is here tasked with describing the infinitely glorious new creation, which of course defies description in human language. Nevertheless, the divine Author has never let such limitation impair his communication, from Genesis to this point. We must seek somehow to balance exegetical discipline with liberated, sanctified, and biblically informed imagination.

1–8—New heaven and earth (= new creation).

The timing makes sense. The old with all its imperfections has been done away.

1—The first creation was incurably infected by the fall (Gen 3). Its destruction is described in 2 Pet 3:7–14, especially verses 7, 10, 12.

The language of new heaven and earth comes originally from Isa 65:17; 66:22; new Jerusalem from Isa 65:18.

No more sea: the entire surface of the planet is suitable for human habitation. (*Thalassa*, sea, occurs twenty-six times in Revelation, but most of those juxtapose sea with land, and several statements are about God as Creator of all.) In ANE mythology, the sea is typically the abode of sea monsters, a turbulent and dangerous place for men to challenge. This statement seems to say that there will be no sea on the new earth, whereas Rev 4:6 and 15:2 speak of a glassy sea in the heavenly throne room. See comments at 15:2.

2—Next: new Jerusalem, beautiful as a bride. See Rev 19:6–9.

She has been in heaven in preparation for the wedding on the new earth. Her adornment must be commensurate with the glory of her Groom. Verses 10–27 describe this city/bride.

3—Tabernacle, dwelling (*skēnē*): God's place is heaven, yet he now dwells (*skēnōsei*) among his redeemed on earth. The ancient tabernacle being earthly suggests it was his remote throne room. "The word became flesh and *eskēnōsen* among us" (John 1:14). The point there is not temporariness but residency. He no longer has to separate himself from his people by establishing and maintaining distance. They are now holy as he is; they are a new creation, as are heaven and earth.

This statement indicates the fulfillment at last of the idea of God and his people belonging mutually to each other, which is very common in the OT. "I/He will be your/their God and you/they will be my/his people" is found in Exod 6:7; Lev 26:12; Deut 29:13; 2 Sam 7:24; Jer 7:23; 11:4; 24:7; 30:22; 31:33; 32:38; Ezek 11:20; 14:11; 36:28; 37:23; Hos 1:9; 2:23; Zech 8:8; 13:9, plus numerous other references that lack the precise wording, but nevertheless indicate the same idea. It is also found below in verse 7.

4—He fully relieves his people of all the negatives of the first world. All those "have passed/gone away," same verb as verb 1. See also Rev 22:3.

Cf. Matthew 24:51; 25:30. Who is weeping now? Isaiah spoke of the end of death and tears in Isa 25:8.

5—He made the entire first creation by himself. When he was first introduced, he was on this throne (Rev 4:2) and he was praised as the Creator of all (4:11). Now he makes new. Paul speaks of the new creation as incorruptible (1 Cor 15:50).

"Faithful and true words" also in Rev 22:6.

6—"Done" (*gegonan*, perfect active indicative third person singular). This is plural, whereas that in Rev 16:17 was singular; otherwise, the two are the same. The idea may be "they have come to be," "let it begin," "finally."

He is uniquely the eternal one; none other can claim to be alpha or omega. So he and he alone can confer life everlasting as he possesses.

"Spring of living water." Think Fountain of Youth. Something as infinitely valuable as this might have a great cost attached. But it is free.

7—All this and sonship are for all conquerors. Think again of the overcomer statements in chs 2–3.

Son has important royal connotations in Heb 1, because it has those connotations in the OT references cited there. Man was created to be king of earth (Gen 1:26, 28). So he shall be, thanks entirely to the Creator, who became flesh to redeem the lost creation and its ruler, man, *adam*, male and female.

Paul develops our sonship in Rom 8:14–23 (not only in the word son, but also children, adoption, and the heart's cry of *abba*). It is who we are already (1 John 3:1–2), but the great unveiling awaits our glorification (Rom 8:19, 23).

8—Universalism is emphatically denied; exclusion is emphatically affirmed. It is a very good thing. See again in verse 27.

Cowardly is another description of the unbelieving in Matt 8:26; Mark 4:40, the only other NT occurrences of this word, *deilos*.

9–27—New Jerusalem (including Rev 22:1–5).

Jerusalem is the King's earthly capital city, and so is not precisely equivalent to heaven or earth. City is the place of civility, civilization, in contrast to wilderness (cf. Rev 17:3). City is where human rule has fully flourished; wilderness is where beasts prowl and rule. City is where law is respected and enforced, where people live in close proximity in harmony, love. All are like extended family. The King Jesus is said to marry this city, and so the city is the people of the city, though not without reference to place.

9–11—Introduction to the new Jerusalem.

9–10—Review parallel to Rev 17:1, 3.

9—Lamb's bride.

Why is this announced by one of the seven angels of chapter 16? Because one of them was the announcer of the antibride in Rev 17:1.

10—A spiritual (in spirit, not necessarily in the Spirit; see comment at Rev 1:10) vision of this city of heavenly origin. The city descends from heaven—like a fair princess down the grand stairway at a ball? The city seems to be created in heaven to be the crown jewel of earthly cities.

11—As glorious as God can make her, radiant (*phōstēr*), dazzling, like precious stone; literally, crystallized (crystal clear?) jasper. Jasper is one of the precious stones the heavenly King is said to be like (Rev 4:3).

12–21—Walls, gates, foundation stones.

Walls and gates speak of security; foundation stones speak of stability. Like the incorruptible new creation of which this is the central crown jewel, it is absolutely secure, absolutely stable.

12, 14—Gates with Israel's tribal patriarchs' names; foundation stones with the apostles' names.

12—An angel at each gate, insuring that only qualified people enter. The idea is not that there still are any defiled ones who might attempt to sneak in, but rather another assurance that none ever will (reinforced in v. 27).

13—Three gates at each of the four compass points. Why a whole verse telling this? To convey the sense of palpable reality (though, again, this vision is spiritual). It also reflects the style of OT prophets to be complete: Ezek 48:31–34; Num 2:1–31.

15–17—Measurements of walls.

15—Who makes measuring sticks out of gold? The same King who paves the streets with gold. (Reminder: this is a vision of spiritual realities.)

16—Dimensions: ideal (perfect cube), 12,000 linear units (*stadion*) cubed (though he used the word square, *tetragōnas*; etymologically, four-cornered). Prefer to leave the units original (ESV, NIV) rather than modernizing (NAS, NET, NRS, NLT), so as to preserve the number, since this author uses numbers whose symbolic value is more important than physical size.

17—Again, translate 144 cubits (not seventy-two yards or meters), the product of the ideal twelve times twelve.

18–21—Materials: spectacular extravagance! Staggering opulence! Such a waste! The expression "conspicuous consumption" comes to mind. What is so precious in our economy shall become common building materials. Think supply and demand.

As in several previous passages, the exegesis of these verses is a function not of word studies on the various stones, etc., but rather of a slow, deliberate oral reading leading to the general impression of unimaginable opulence.

The idea comes from Isa 54:11–12.

22–27—Glory: all good, no contamination.

22—This is the last of forty-five times the author says, "I saw" (*eidon*). This is the only time it is negative: "I did not see" (*ouk eidon*), here is what I did not see. But this is still part of his prophet's vision.

How can Jerusalem be Jerusalem without a temple? It does have a temple: Father and Son (Lamb). This is how it should be. The old covenant temple kept his people at a distance (cf. Heb 9:8). Here, we do not need priests to mediate; we have free and direct personal access to the Enthroned One (cf. Ps 99:1, plus five more OT references to God as enthroned above the cherubim). Because of our great High Priest, we are now priests. There are no common (profane) defiled ones requiring mediation, only absolutely holy ones, saints (cf. v. 27), all eligible, welcome to approach the Holy One.

23–24—Where once he commanded a dark and shapeless world—"Let there be light"—now he is all the light the city will ever need. Instead of sun and moon, God and Lamb. (Again in Rev 22:5.)

24, 26—Nations and kings bring glory and honor, the best they have to offer, the concept of tribute. Ultimate fulfillment of Isa 2:2–4; Hag 2:7.

25—Gates never close, indicating there is no threat. The nations are cheerfully submissive. (Cf. Neh 7:3, where Nehemiah ordered that the newly completed city walls and gates be securely closed from dusk to midmorning.)

26–27 (24–27)—Gentiles, yes; uncleanness (*koinon* = profane), no.

Chapter 22

Bad chapter break; include Rev 22:1–5 with chapter 21, as this is still new Jerusalem. Epilogue begins at verse 6.

1–2—River from the throne (in heaven; the central feature), in Main Street (Jerusalem), watering the tree of life (certainly referring to Gen 2), healing the nations/gentiles, always producing delicious, nourishing fruit and medicinal leaves—not that any will get sick, but rather indicating the absolute guarantee of health, life. The image of a river of blessing in the city of God is also found in Ps 46:4.

Though this river flows out from the throne of heaven, it flows down Main Street of the new Jerusalem, which is earthly. This speaks to the closeness and perfect harmony between the new heaven and new earth. The earthly scene must be material, while the heavenly must be spiritual. How this river of water begins in heaven, the realm of spirit, and becomes earthly/material must remain a mystery.

1—"Coming out from the throne" recalls the scene in Rev 4:3–6, where all the elements are described by their prepositional relationship to the throne. This time, the throne is shared with the Lamb.

Of this river, we should expect nothing less than absolute purity, never contaminated, perfect visually and hygienically. Fresh water is an essential part of life for us; surely all those benefits are implied in this. (One might then wonder why there is no mention of clean air. If air pollution were not an issue for people of those times, it is likely they were just not nearly as conscious of that necessity as of water.)

3—The curse of Eden will be eradicated—at last, finally!—never to be found in this new creation.

3, 5—God reigns with his saints, in a curse-free, glorious world. Jerusalem is still Jerusalem, still earthly, though closely connected to heaven.

Father and Son co-reign; to worship one is to worship the other (cf. 1 John 2:23).

God's servants are loyally devoted, freely, enthusiastically giving him the adoration he deserves.

His servants, illuminated by God, reign with him. So they are kings, yet they serve (*latreusousin*), indicating their status as vassal kings. As serving kings, all that they do will be at the Supreme King's command. None will ever improve on his ideas. This word for serving is a near synonym to worship (see Luke 4:8). This serving is active worship and characterizes a full and busy life of constant worship (see Luke 2:37; 2 Tim 1:3). We were previously shown saints in God's presence serving him thus (Rev 7:15). This serving is qualitatively different from the service of angels, who are an inferior species, created as a slave class, so to speak (Heb 1:14).

4—"See his face": cf. Exod 33:18–23; Isa 40:5. We must not forget that "God is spirit" (John 4:24), so this seeing is spiritual, which is not make-believe but the highest quality substance. Such seeing must be with eyes of the heart/spirit (cf. Eph 1:18).

His name as their brand: he indelibly and proudly claims them—us—as his own. Collectively, we are, as Paul stated in Eph 1:18, God's richly glorious inheritance.

5—"No night" means we will never grow tired and require sleep, not to mention all the evil connotations night carries (see for instance John 3:19–20; 13:30). All that light means to us—and the priority of light for the world is unmistakably indicated in Gen 1:3 and John 1:4–9—is fully and continuously provided by the light of the world (John 8:12), God himself, Father and Son.

Eternal life is not just about unending existence; it is not just being with God in heaven; it is reigning as kings, ruling over the new earth in ultimate fulfillment of the greatest dimensions conceived in the original commission of man (male and female) in Gen 1:26, 28. We were created to be vice-regents ruling earth as God rules over the higher domain, heaven. Our royal vassal rule is legitimized by being fully submissive under and compliant with his suzerain rule.

6–21—Epilogue

6–7—Review of the main message: Jesus is coming soon
8–9—John's misguided exuberance
10–15—Discrimination between the righteous and unrighteous
16–17—Final invitation
18–19—Warning against tampering with the books
20—Final announcement of the Lamb's soon coming
21—Benediction

6—The truth of these words is absolutely guaranteed. Cf. Dan 2:45, "so the dream is true and its interpretation is trustworthy" (NASB). The speaker is the revealing angel of verse 8.

"Spirits of prophets": cf. 1 John 4:1–6.

"Sent his angel to show his servants what will soon happen" (*ha dei genesthai en tachei*) matches the ending of Rev 1:1 exactly. See comments there and at 6:11.

7—"I am coming." In this epilogue, we hear not once, not twice, but three times the Lord Jesus announcing again, "I am coming" (vv. 7, 12, 20). Each time, he adds, "Quickly."

"Keeps" echoes Rev 1:3. You cannot keep or obey what you have not heard; but hearing without doing is disobedience, and disobedience is defiance. Faithful hearing will certainly be complemented by keeping. Those who faithfully fear this King always take his word seriously. The worst thing in the world is to displease him.

8–9—This is the second time John mistakenly bows to this angel. See comment there (Rev 19:10). Somehow this has to be an important part of the message.

8—"Heard and saw" twice, emphasizing prophethood, which is speaking the message given him by God.

10—"Do not seal" means, get this in the mail as quickly as possible; they need this now. Compare Dan 12:4, 9.

11—"Let [these continue]," because they are going to anyway. This is how God sees, no moral ambiguity.

12–13—The Lord-Judge will call all to account. All must and will answer to him. He is, after all, quite literally the beginning and the end. He (and he alone) was there before there was any there, and he will be there when this creation is brought to its end. Escaping his judgment is not possible.

14–15—Another catalog of the approved and disapproved (cf. Rev 21:7–8, 27; 22:11). All have been served notice. Nothing mysterious or unexpected. Universal salvation is clearly denied.

16—Review of Rev 1:1–2 chain of revelation.

The entire book is to and for the churches—all seven plus all others.

Emphasize again Jesus as King, with special attachment to Israel. He is the greatest, the star that outshines all stars.

17—Invitation to come, this time addressed to whosoever.

Wordplay: the great announcement is Jesus *comes*; the great invitation is for anyone anywhere to *come* to him, before it's too late.

18–19—Warning: as on a stack of Bibles, solemn testimony before the King-Judge, to take these words seriously, more so than any others. Terrifying threats against tampering or altering in any way. These words, no more and no less, are his deadly serious truths that all need to know. "You shall not add to the word which I am commanding you, nor take away from it, that you may keep the commandments of the LORD your God which I command you" (Deut 4:2 NASB).

20—The great declaration, one last time: "I am coming." This is his testimony; he has always been the truthful witness.

21—You cannot ask for a better final wish to readers: may grace be yours. The only alternative is eternal damnation.

BIBLIOGRAPHY

Adler, Mortimer J., and Charles van Doren. *How to Read a Book*. New York: Touchstone, 1972.

Aune, David E. *Revelation*. 3 vols. Word Biblical Commentary 52A–C. Dallas: Word Books, 1997.

Bauckham, Richard. "Revelation." In *The Bible Knowledge Background Commentary: John's Gospel, Hebrews–Revelation*, edited by Craig A. Evans, 341–400. Colorado Springs: Victor, 2005.

Beale, G. K. *The Book of Revelation: A Commentary on the Greek Text*. Grand Rapids: Eerdmans, 1999.

Bullinger, E.W. *The Apocalypse or the Day of the Lord*. London: Eyre and Spottiswood, 1909.

Caird, G. B. *The Revelation of Saint John*. Peabody, MA: Hendrickson, 1966.

Danker, Frederick William, ed. *A Greek-English Lexicon of the New Testament and Other Early Christian Literature*. 3rd ed. Chicago: University of Chicago Press, 2001.

Fanning, Buist M. *Revelation*. Zondervan Exegetical Commentary on the New Testament. Grand Rapids: Zondervan, 2020.

Fee, Gordon D. *Revelation*. New Covenant Commentary. Eugene, OR: Cascade Books, 2010.

Ford, J. Massyngberde. *Revelation: Introduction, Translation, and Commentary*. New York: Doubleday, 1975.

Johnson, Alan F. "Revelation." In *Hebrews through Revelation*, edited by Frank E. Gaebelein, 397–603. Expositor's Bible Commentary 12. Grand Rapids: Zondervan, 1981.

Kistemaker, Simon J. *Exposition of the Book of Revelation*. New Testament Commentary. Grand Rapids: Baker, 2001.

Ladd, George Eldon. *A Commentary on the Revelation of John*. Grand Rapids: Eerdmans, 1972.

Leithart, Peter J. *Revelation 1–11*. New York: Bloomsbury T&T Clark, 2018.

———. *Revelation 12–22*. New York: Bloomsbury T&T Clark, 2018.

MacArthur, John. *Revelation 1–11*. MacArthur New Testament Commentary. Chicago: Moody, 1999.

———. *Revelation 12–22*. MacArthur New Testament Commentary. Chicago: Moody, 2000.

Moffatt, James. "Revelation." In *The Expositor's Greek Testament,* edited by W. Robertson Nicoll, 5:279–494. Grand Rapids: Eerdmans, 1979.

Morris, Leon. *The Revelation of St. John: An Introduction and Commentary*. Grand Rapids: Eerdmans, 1969.

Mounce, Robert H. *The Book of Revelation*. New International Commentary on the New Testament. Grand Rapids: Eerdmans, 1977.

Osborne, Grant R. *Revelation*. Baker Exegetical Commentary on the New Testament. Grand Rapids: Baker Academic, 2002.

Poythress, Vern S. *The Returning King: A Guide to the Book of Revelation*. Phillipsburg, NJ: P&R Publishing. 2000.

Räisänen, Heikki. *Paul and the Law*. Philadelphia: Fortress, 1983.

Rudwick, M. J. S. and E. M. B. Green. "The Laodicean Lukewarmness." *Expository Times* 69 (1958) 176–78.

Ryken, Leland. *How to Read the Bible as Literature*. Grand Rapids: Zondervan, 1985.

Stedman, Ray C. *God's Final Word: Understanding Revelation*. Grand Rapids: Discovery House, 1991.

Swete, H. B. *The Apocalypse of St. John*. 3rd ed. London: Macmillan, 1911.

Tabb, Brian J. *All Things New: Revelation as Canonical Capstone*. Downers Grove, IL: InterVarsity, 2019.

Tenney, Merrill C. *Interpreting Revelation*. Grand Rapids: Eerdmans, 1957.

Thomas, Robert L. *Revelation 1–7: An Exegetical Commentary*. Chicago: Moody, 1992.

———. *Revelation 8–22: An Exegetical Commentary*. Chicago: Moody, 1995.

Wallace, Daniel B. *Greek Grammar Beyond the Basics: An Exegetical Syntax of the New Testament*. Grand Rapids: Zondervan, 1996.

Walvoord, John F. "Revelation." In *The Bible Knowledge Commentary: An Exposition of the Scriptures by Dallas Seminary Faculty (New Testament Edition)*, edited by John F. Walvoord and Roy B. Zuck, 925–91. Colorado Springs: David C. Cook, 1983.

———. *The Revelation of Jesus Christ: A Commentary*. Chicago: Moody, 1966.

White, W. "Number." In *The Zondervan Pictorial Encyclopedia of the Bible*, edited by Merrill C. Tenney, 4:452–61. Grand Rapids: Zondervan, 1975.

Wilson, Mark W. "Revelation." In *Zondervan Illustrated Bible Backgrounds Commentary*, edited by Clinton E. Arnold, 4:244–383. Grand Rapids: Zondervan, 2002.

Printed in the USA
CPSIA information can be obtained
at www.ICGtesting.com
LVHW021132010324
773174LV00001B/4